Fifty Railroads

that Changed the Course of

History

A Firefly Book

Published by Firefly Books Ltd. 2013

Copyright © 2013 Quid Publishing

First printing

Publisher Cataloging-in-Publication Data (U.S.)
A CIP record for this title is available from the Library of Congress

Library and Archives Canada Cataloguing in Publication
Laws, Bill
Fifty railroads that changed the course of history / Bill Laws.
Includes bibliographical references and index.
ISBN 978-1-77085-169-6
1. Railroads—History. I. Title.
II. Title: Fifty railroads that changed the course of history.
HE1021.L38 2013   385.09   C2012-905088-1

Published in the United States by
Firefly Books (U.S.) Inc.
P.O. Box 1338, Ellicott Station
Buffalo, New York 14205

Published in Canada by
Firefly Books Ltd.
50 Staples Avenue, Unit 1
Richmond Hill, Ontario L4B 0A7

Conceived, designed and produced by
Quid Publishing
Level 4, Sheridan House
114 Western Road
Hove BN3 1DD
England

Cover and interior design: Lindsey Johns

Printed in China

Fifty Railroads

that Changed the Course of

History

written by Bill Laws

FIREFLY BOOKS

Contents

Introduction   6

Merthyr Tydfil
Railway   8

Swansea and
Mumbles Railway   14

Stockton and
Darlington Railway   18

Liverpool and
Manchester Railway   22

Baltimore and Ohio
Railroad   28

South Carolina Canal and
Rail Road Company   32

Dublin and Kingstown
Railway   36

Brussels to
Mechelen Railway   40

Nuremberg and
Fürth Railway   42

Paris to Le Pecq
Railway   46

Grand Junction and London
to Birmingham Railways   48

Tsarskoye Selo
Railway   52

Ferrocarril de Camagüey
a Nuevitas   54

York and North Midland
Railway   56

Great Western
Railway   60

Leicester and
Loughborough Railway   66

Sheffield, Ashton under Lyne
and Manchester Railway   72

Paris to Le Havre
Railway   76

Georgetown and
Plaisance Railroad   82

Great Indian
Peninsula Railway   84

Semmering
Railway   90

Panama
Railroad   92

Grand Crimean
Central Railway   94

Chicago to St. Louis
Railroad   100

Hannibal to
St. Joseph Railroad   106

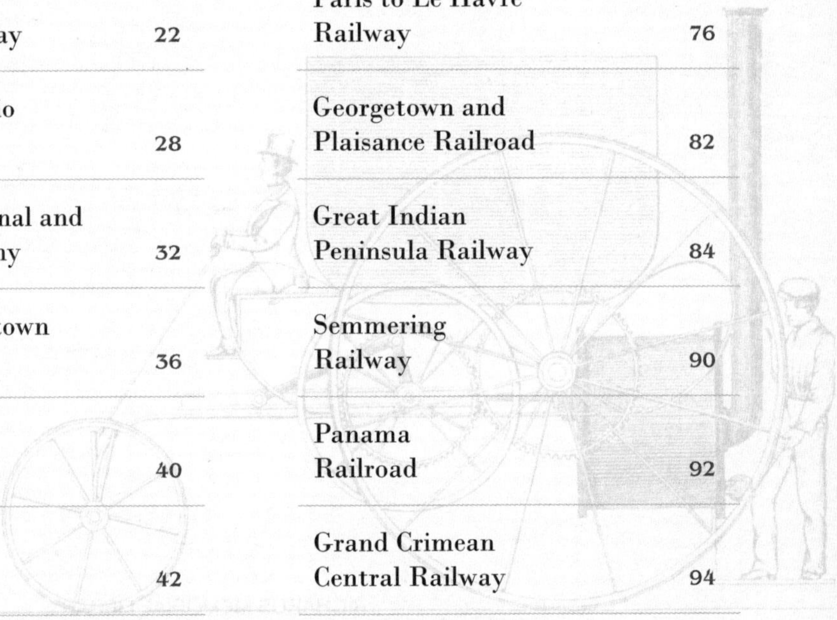

Metropolitan Railway	112
Central Pacific Railroad	118
Port Chalmers Railway	126
Canadian Pacific Railway	128
Jerusalem to Jaffa Railway	136
Highland Railway	138
Valtellina Railroad	144
Cape to Cairo Railway	148
Jingzhang Railway	154
Grand Central Terminal	158
Trans-Siberian Railway	164
Allied Railroad Supply Lines	168
Kalgoorlie to Port Augusta Railway	174
Sydney City Railway	176
Berlin to Hamburg Railway	182
Prague to Liverpool Street Station, London	186
Southern Railway	190
Auschwitz Spur	194
Burma to Siam Railway	196
Dutch Railways	198
Tokaido Railway	202
Bay Area Rapid Transit	204
Talyllyn Railway	210
Paris to Lyon Railway	212
Channel Tunnel	216
Further Reading	218
Index	220
Image Credits	224

Introduction

"When I closed my eyes this sensation of flying was quite delightful, and strange beyond description: yet strange as it was, I had a perfect sense of security, and not the slightest fear."

Actress and writer Fanny Kemble, opening of the Liverpool to Manchester railroad, 1838

Railroads have impacted on the lives of almost everyone on the planet. Since they arrived in the early 1800s, their steely sinews have threaded their way through history, nudging and elbowing it in unexpected directions.

CHANGING LANDSCAPES AND PASSENGER TRAVEL

Railroads modernized the towns they touched and caused the downfall of the ones they left behind: they carried cargo into the most inaccessible places and transformed forever the traditional ways of life there. Trains brought a distinctive cacophony to the urban scene: station bells, bursts of steam, the scream of a whistle, carriage couplings clattering in rail yards, and the ring of the wheel-tapper's hammer checking for cracked steel.

The British monarch Queen Victoria was perfectly satisfied with this progress. On her first railroad journey, 18 miles (29 km) along the GWR or Great Western Railway to Buckingham Palace in 1842, she declared: "We arrived here yesterday morning, having come by the railroad from Windsor, in half an hour, free from dust and crowd and heat, and I am quite charmed with it." The Duke of Wellington, reflecting the sentiments of many of The Queen's citizens, had taken the opposite view. In 1830 he declared he saw "no reason to suppose these machines will ever force themselves into general use." While the railroads increased and multiplied, the anxieties of passengers remained much the same: Have I missed the train? Am I on the right platform? Is my luggage safe?

Railroads undoubtably imposed themselves on the landscape. "There was probably more picturesqueness about the old method of traveling, for a stage coach harmonized better with the landscape than a puffing, smoking steam engine with its train of

STEAM POWER
Developed for use in the coal mines, the steam engine would transform history when it was incorporated into a locomotive.

AN URBAN JOURNEY
Landscapes across the
world felt the impact of
railroad-led infrastruc-
tures. Town and city
populations shot up as
goods traveled farther and
travel times decreased.

practical looking cars," wrote the regretful R. Richardson B.A. in
Cassell's *Family Magazine* of 1875. He nevertheless acknowledged:
"What we have lost in picturesqueness we have undoubtedly gained
in convenience."

MAKING TRACKS ACROSS THE GLOBE

With their speeding locomotives, luxury carriages and romantic boat
trains, the railroads reached a zenith in the early twentieth century
using the latest technology. Although the essential elements—train,
tracks and rolling stock—were standard, idiosyncratic national charac-
teristics were apparent from the start. The dominance of the railroad
was complete, paving the way across the world with its routes and adopt-
ing country-specific structures, while two world wars battled on.

By the mid-twentieth century railroads were exhausted. Polluting,
inefficient, uncomfortable, monopolistic and expensive, they had run
out of favor. Their demise was accompanied, and exacerbated, by the
rush for the road, a development that squandered dwindling natural
resources and left a bill for everyone but the polluter to pay. Then in 1964
a streamlined train slid, like a vision from the future, into Tokyo station.
Within a decade high-speed railroads and rapid transit systems were
racing to change history again, leaving in their wake a charm of pleasant
old lines and railroad memories. As railroad engineer George Stephenson's biographer Samuel Smiles put it in 1868: "Notwithstanding all
the faults and imperfections that are alleged against railroads . . . we
think they must nevertheless be recognized as by far the most
valuable means of communication . . .
that has yet been given to
the world."

INTO THE FUTURE
The arrival of the
high-speed train heralded
a new age for the railroads
in the latter part of the
twentieth century.

1804

Merthyr Tydfil Railway

Country: Wales

Type: Freight

Length: 10 miles (16 km)

+ SOCIAL
+ *COMMERCIAL*
+ POLITICAL
+ ENGINEERING
+ MILITARY

The quick heat of the Industrial Age produced the first steam-powered locomotive in a matter of years, while the evolution of rail from muddy ruts to metal track took five hundred. Merthyr Tydfil is a prime example of the journey of progress from horse-pulled carts to coal-fired machines.

PIONEERS OF THE STEAM AGE

A statue of the steam railroad engineer Richard Trevithick stands proud in his hometown of Camborne, Cornwall. Inventor of the high-pressure steam engine, his experiments at Penydarren Ironworks made their mark in railroad history and put the little principality of Wales on the map. Lest we forget the memorials of other pioneers: James Watt, who enhanced the performance of the steam cylinder, is portrayed with his inventive colleagues Matthew Boulton and William Murdoch in Birmingham (see p.48). At Void-Vacon in France an obelisk celebrates Nicolas-Joseph Cugnot: he developed a *"premier véhicule à vapeur pour tracter des canons,"* the first steam car that could pull artillery. Graceland Cemetery, Chicago possesses a monument marking the grave of George Pullman (see p.100), erected despite his family's fears that disgruntled employees might kidnap the body.

We should also commemorate the Unknown Rail person: the worker who constructed a wooden wheeled wagon and two lengths of timber rail pegged in parallel, and placed end to end. Like many railroad inventions, the epiphany moment ("What we need is a little cart that runs along its own track") probably happened in several places simultaneously.

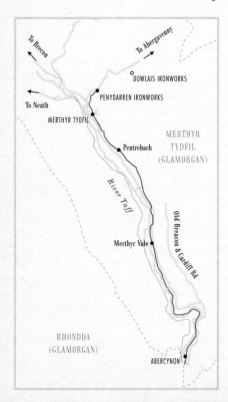

WELSH STEAM
The steam age started in Wales, thanks to Richard Trevithick and an enterprising coal mine owner, Christopher Blackett.

Wagon Rail Beginnings

The concept of converting ruts into rails (see p.37) and running a loaded cart along them started with miners and quarrymen trying to take the weight off their own backs. A German craftsman pictured such a cart in a church window at Freiburg im Breisgau, southern Germany, in 1350. Two centuries later another German, Georg Pawer (1494–1555), illustrated his *De Re Metallica Libri xii* with a picture of ore-bearing carts.

A devout Catholic heralded as the father of mineralogy, Pawer wrote under the name Georgius Agricola and described fossils as mysterious matter that fermented in the earth's heat into animal-like forms. The wagon wheels in his illustration were similarly flawed. His carts ran on tracks formed from wooden planks, but the wheels, lacking a flange, would often slip from the rails. Coal wagons equipped with flanged wooden wheels eventually cropped up in the coal workings in the German Ruhr.

One of the earliest recorded British rail lines was laid for coal workings at Strelley for 2 miles (3.2 km) to Wollaton in the Nottinghamshire coal fields in 1604. The dashingly named Huntingdon Beaumont ran "the passage now laide with rails" and, before he died a debtor in a Nottingham prison, extended rail transport to several mines in northeastern England. The rugged, mineral-rich lands of these northern counties– Northumberland, County Durham, Tyne and Wear, Teesside and North present-day Yorkshire became a testing ground for railroads. They included the Tanfield Waggonway in County Durham, a route built to carry coal from moorland mines down to boats on the River Tyne until the moorland coal gave out in 1739 (see p.177).

Coal, like any freight, wants water. History traditionally heaped riches on cities like Constantinople, Venice, St. Petersburg, London, Liverpool, New York and Auckland, cities that boasted a good, deep harbor. Until the early 1800s the best way to carry cargo to port was to use a navigable river, a canal or a combination of the two. But in the expanding coalfields of northeast England the deep valleys and craggy

Making tracks
The German scholar Georg Pawer illustrated his treatise on the business of mining in the 16th century with detailed drawings of the early railroads.

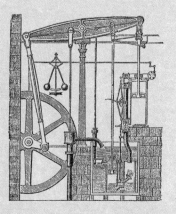

hills militated against canal building: railroads were the only solution and a network of rail was soon spreading its tendrils across the region.

Elsewhere in Britain, rail had been used to cart coal in the Ironbridge Gorge where Abraham Darby of Coalbrookdale had mastered the process of producing cheaper and better iron from local supplies. At nearby Ketley they manufactured cast-iron plates to fasten over, and strengthen, rails made of wood. They were hailed as a great invention and employed in Britain and America, until the moment they fractured. Bare metal tracks tended to spring up like a snake's head, flailing anyone caught standing too close, so an alternative solution—solid iron rails cast in 3–4 foot (0.9–1.2 m) lengths—began to appear in the South Wales coal valleys around Merthyr Tydfil and Blaenavon. Now equipped with stout metal rails and a demand for coal and iron, the industry sought power better than a team of strong horses.

HORSE VERSUS STEAM MACHINE

Richard Trevithick was born and bred at a time when the West Country's mines were among the world's richest. Indeed, the little village of Camborne in Cornwall had been turned into a rough and ready mining town by a boom in tin and copper prices. As excavations plunged deeper underground the miners struggled to keep the mines from flooding, many employing a Boulton and Watt steam engine (see box) to pump them out. Trevithick worked on developing a mine pump of his own in order to avoid paying royalties to Boulton and Watt. (In later years there was constant rivalry between Trevithick and Boulton and Watts: when a Trevithick steam machine exploded at Greenwich, London, killing three men, Boulton and Watt were quick to blame the accident on poor workmanship.)

Above all, the 30-year-old Trevithick wanted to harness the power of steam to drive, not a static machine, but a locomotive. The word, from the Latin *locus,* "a place" and *moveo,* "I move," was still as fresh as the concept.

A minor explosion that happened during Trevithick's testing of a new steam road carriage, the *Puffing Devil*, was the first intimation that horsepower might, one day, be rendered redundant.

The *Puffing Devil* first scaled Camborne Hill on Christmas Eve, 1801. Toasting a successful test run of the *Devil* in a local alehouse, Trevithick had forgotten to shut down the fire beneath the boiler. The steam built up and the boiler blew out. At the same time, the British government started taking an interest in rail, sanctioning a public railroad—the Surrey Iron Railroad—to run from the River Thames at Wandsworth to Croydon. Convinced that the emerging railroads would one day require steam rather than horse power, Trevithick took a stagecoach into the heartland of the iron-making country, Coalbrookdale, to work on a second prototype.

News of his endeavors reached South Wales businessman Samuel Homfray in Merthyr Tydfil. Homfray was not only an iron industry capitalist, he was a betting man. He had won the means to build his Merthyr mansion in a wager and was now prepared to lay a 500-guinea bet that his man

> **"Going up Camborne Hill, coming down**
> **The horses stood still;**
> **The wheels went round.**
> **Going up Camborne Hill, coming down."**
>
> *Traditional folk song, anon*

Trevithick, if he could persuade him, would haul ten tons of iron along a coal railroad from Penydarren to Abercynon in Merthyr. Since a horse and driver could pull, at best, a three-ton wagon of coal at 4 mph (6 kph), Homfray's wager caused a flurry of interest, especially as the line was almost 10 miles (16 km) long.

In 1804, Trevithick's latest locomotive—named the *Penydarren*—hauled not only ten tons of iron in five wagons, but also 70 people. His undertaking stirred international excitement. Pioneering though it was, the *Penydarren* encountered a problem that dogged the early railroad men: the rails kept fracturing.

Trevithick was obliged to use the same type of rails for his next venture four years later, in 1808. He set up a "steam circus" hauling fare-paying passengers around a circular track with a new steam-powered engine, *Catch-Me-Who-Can*. The train raced round at a dizzy 8 mph (13 kph) in fields a short distance from what would one day become a busy London station, Euston. Here Trevithick pitted his iron horse against real horse-flesh during a 24-hour race; the engine won.

Developments on the emerging railroads, however, lay not in the hands of showmen, but mine owners. None had quite the same impact on their development as Christopher Blackett, owner of the Wylam mine in the Northumberland village of the same name, west of Newcastle. By now coal railroads were creeping through the South Wales valleys and the Forest of Dean, while the coal mine tracks in northeast England, dubbed the "Newcastle Roads," ran to a respectable 150 miles (241 km). Blackett, like his neighbors, wanted to shift more coal to the *staithes* (this northern English word for the wharves came from Newcastle's Scandinavian ancestors) of Lemington on the River Tyne. Here the coal could be shipped away in the *keels*, shallow-draft boats that worked the Tyne, and loaded onto barges ready to sail to other British ports. Black-ett approached Trevithick and ordered a similar machine to the *Penydar-ren*, but the Cornishman's efforts were again thwarted by inadequate track and the project was abandoned.

STEAM CIRCUS
In 1808 Trevithick's steam engine performed for the public in north London, close to the site of the future Euston Station.

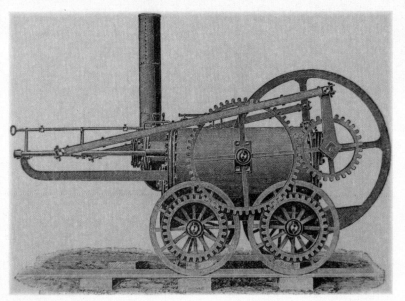

HUFFING INTO HISTORY

Trevithick's son, Francis, went on to become a railroad engineer while Richard's own career languished. He pursued various ill-fated projects in London and South America, on one occasion running into George Stephenson in Colombia: humiliatingly short of funds, the pioneer of steam locomotion was obliged to accept £50 from Stephenson to help him home. Here, where there was little to show for his contribution to railroad history, he died in 1833.

Blackett, meanwhile, turned to his own mining engineer, William Hedley, who, with the mine's foreman, blacksmith Timothy Hackworth, built a big, bull-nosed contraption to replace Trevithick's machine. It was another puffer, the *Puffing Billy*, and in 1814 it huffed into history along with its successor, the *Wylam Dilly*. The *Puffing Billy* kept going until 1862 when it was sold for £200, after much hard bargaining, to the South Kensington Patent Office. Railroad history was gaining momentum.

STEAM ELEPHANT

✦

A painting depicting a tubby-looking, George Stephenson-like locomotive surfaced in 1909. Neither the name of the artist nor the painting's title had survived, and the odd-looking engine was nicknamed the *Steam Elephant*. The *Elephant* was eventually revealed to be the work of Newcastle mining engineer John Buddle (he was credited with introducing the safety lamp into many of the local mines) and Whitby-born engineer William Chapman. On canvas, the *Steam Elephant* appeared to possess the basic attributes of a steam locomotive: boiler, chimney, wheels and pistons. But would it run? The Beamish Museum in County Durham commissioned a replica and tried it on test tracks. The *Steam Elephant* worked.

Swansea and Mumbles Railway

Country: Wales

Type: Passenger, Freight

Length: 5 miles (8 km)

Ｆrom a single, horse-drawn carriage carrying twelve people, to a steam loco-motive pulling 1,800 passengers on a single journey—the Swansea to Mumbles railroad began the business of passenger rail travel.

+ Social
+ **Commercial**
+ Political
+ Engineering
+ Military

TRÊN BACH I'R MWMBWLS

In 2007, two centuries after the world's first railroad service opened in South Wales, Sunday promenaders still stepped aside to make way for a train. This was no full-steam-ahead locomotive, but a mock Wild West-style, rubber-wheeled land train: the historic railroad itself had been hurriedly closed and dismantled in 1960. At the time protesting passengers donned black armbands and carried a coffin, symbolizing the departure of the *trên bach i'r Mwmbwls*, the little train to Mumbles, to its grave.

The line had run from Swansea's Brewery Bank, beside a canal that brought Welsh coal down the valleys to the docks, along the coast to the Mumbles headland and Oystermouth village. Converted into a tramway in later life (see box), the line was ridden, and celebrated, by the local poet Dylan Thomas who was born at Cwmdonkin Drive, Swansea, in 1914. The railroad commanded a panoramic view across Swansea Bay, comparable—according to another poet, the flamboyant Walter Savage

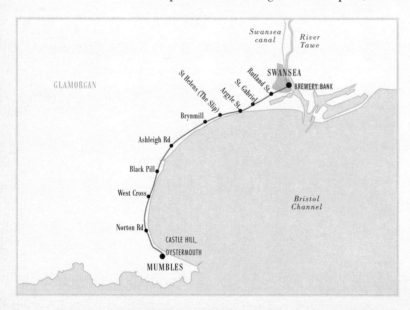

PASSENGER POWER
Railroads were designed to shift coal farther and faster. Yet the little Welsh Mumbles line proved unexpectedly popular with passengers.

Landor—to Italy's Bay of Naples. Swansea's citizens were inclined to agree as they headed off for the traditional Sunday train trip "down the Mumbles," intent on making the most of the scenery, the sea air and a stroll along the beach at Oystermouth.

A PICTURESQUE JOURNEY

The line, founded in 1806 to serve the mines and quarries, carried fare-paying passengers by 1807, including, two years later, a tourist named Elisabeth Isabella Spence. As she explored the "romantic scenery at Oystermouth" she found the railroad a delight: "A carriage of singular construction, this car contains twelve persons and is constructed chiefly of iron, its four wheels run on an iron railroad by the aid of one horse, and the whole carriage is an easy and light vehicle."

HORSE DRIVEN
Early tourists took the "little train to Mumbles" to enjoy the romantic scenery.

Her visit was inspired in part by the eighteenth-century cleric and schoolteacher William Gilpin and his breathlessly titled 1770 work on the picturesque, *Observations on the River Wye, and Several Parts of South Wales, Relative Chiefly to Picturesque Beauty*. Like those of William Wordsworth and Samuel Coleridge, his scholarly observations persuaded many early tourists to take to the coach road, a copy of Wordsworth's and Shelley's *Lyrical Ballads* (1798) clasped in their gloved hands, to study Britain's rural beauties.

The Mumbles scene of sea, sand and tumbling headlands was certainly picturesque on a fine day: aside from the all too regular Welsh rain, Swansea town was scarred by industry. Welsh coal was used to smelt copper brought in by boatload from Cornwall, creating palls of smoke that hung over the city.

The Mumbles train, having shipped its own share of coal and stone, was, in Dylan's day, helping to shift city folk out from the poet's "ugly lovely" city to the seaside. Back in the 1860s the horse-drawn carriage had been obliged to share the single, 5-mile (8 km) line with a rival company, which introduced a steam locomotive, a coke-powered Henry Hughes

TRAM AND TRAIN

✦

A train is a connected line of carriages on a railroad drawn by an engine. A tram is a tramcar, or passenger-carrying vehicle. Originally *tram* was a miner's name for a wheeled barrow or sledge that ran on rails. Like *railroad* and *railroad* (both words were used on early English lines, although *railroad* came to dominate in America), meanings have changed over time. While some tram and train enthusiasts regard the two technologies as quite separate, the railroad world, as the Swansea to Mumbles line showed, embraced whatever suited it best at the time. Many believe the future lies in light rail, a system that uses both tram and train technology.

engine (see box). The steamer made the first journey of the day, allegedly hurling hot coals onto the track behind in an effort to upset the competing horse-drawn carriages following in its wake. The horses apparently suffered fewer accidents than those inveterate victims of the railroads, farm stock. The train regularly ran over wandering sheep.

In the 1880s an inebriated politician who fatefully tried to follow the tracks home after a night out was run over and killed by one of the horses. The accident was distressing for Swansea residents such as Mary Grenfell. Active in the city branch of the British Women's Temperance Society, the wealthy spinster ran a Railroad Mission and tried to lure customers away from their alcoholic follies into the warm embrace of the Golden Griffin Coffee House next door to the Midland Railroad's station. (Swansea possessed at least six different railroad stations, each, inefficiently, unconnected with the other.) In spite of Mary Grenfell's efforts the *Cambrian* newspaper continued to carry regular reports of drunkenness on the last train home from Mumbles.

HENRY HUGHES

✦

Born in 1833 with an abiding interest in engineering, Henry Hughes was in the right place at the right time to pursue his passion for steam locomotion. Inventing and patenting his ideas (they included a clever device for disposing of locomotive smoke), he worked on Brunel's S.S. *Great Britain* and on the Great London Exhibition of 1862. Having founded his Loughborough locomotive and tram works he emigrated to New Zealand where he worked on railroads in the Hutt Valley and Nelson before settling down in Wellington as New Zealand's first patent lawyer.

PASSENGER AND BATTERY BOOM

The horse-drawn service was withdrawn in 1896, seven years after a single company took over the line, which was extended to reach the Swansea Bay Lighthouse and a spanking new symbol of the Victorian era, the Mumbles Pier. The loss of horse power made little difference to the speed of the train. Traveling at a dignified 5 mph (8 kph) the slow train to Mumbles presented a challenge to the conductors extracting fares from passengers, some of whom clung daringly to the outside of the carriage. The snail's pace of the train encouraged local kids to busk, performing cartwheels and somersaults on the trackside.

Passenger numbers rose until the line claimed a world record for carrying the most passengers on a single journey: 1,800. The *trên bach* claimed another world first for the variety of sources of power used to draw the carriages. Aside from horse-, steam- and even sail-power, the company

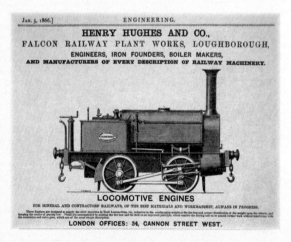

experimented, unsuccessfully, with battery power in 1902. By now the vehicles were more tram than train, and in 1925 they were replaced with eleven shiny, double-decker electric trams from Brush Electrical Engineering in Loughborough, England, each capable of carrying just over 100 passengers (see photograph below). It was a popular move. In 1945 five million people traveled the line, enjoying what Thomas in *The Followers* described as "the sneeze and rattle of bony trams and a ship's hoot like a fog-ditched owl in the bay."

A SAD GOODBYE

The survival of the trams in World War II—they were hidden at different stations along the line—was something of a miracle. The town's docks and oil refinery were targeted by Germany's Luftwaffe, which, in 1941, rained explosives and incendiaries down on the town. Having escaped the bombing, the line celebrated its 150th anniversary, marking the date of 1804, when Parliament first authorized the line. However, the merry bunting masked a serious problem: a bus operator, the South Wales Transport Company, had taken the line over and was said to be sabotaging its own property with piecemeal maintenance. The Company applied to Parliament for closure, claiming the route was suffering unsustainable losses. It was later rumored that the company's problems were due, in part, to charging itself rent on its own line. The government, empowered to rule over rail closures, approved the plan. Contrary to Thomas' poetic maxim "Do not go gentle into that good night," the *trên bach i'r Mwmbwls* departed as quiet as a ghost.

> **"I have never spent an afternoon of more delight."**
>
> *Elisabeth Isabella Spence on traveling the Swansea to Mumbles line in 1809*

<table>
<tr><td>

1825

</td><td>

Stockton and Darlington Railway

</td></tr>
</table>

Country: England

Type: Passenger, Freight

Length: 26 miles (42 km)

T he Stockton and Darlington Railway was only a short rail ride though northern England, but a vital piece of the railroad jigsaw in the emerging age of steam. It was one of the world's first railroads and paved the way for the father of the railroads, George Stephenson.

+ SOCIAL

+ COMMERCIAL

+ POLITICAL

+ *ENGINEERING*

+ MILITARY

BUSINESS MINDS UNITE

Men and women were said to have trembled, or quaked, at the word of the Lord after hearing the English Dissenter George Fox preach from a Cumbrian hillside in 1652. For a period the non-conformist Quakers were rigorously persecuted. Many fled to America, but as times became more tolerant the industrious Friends often proved to be astute business people. There was Quaker Abraham Darby and his Ironbridge iron-making works; the Birmingham banker, Sampson Lloyd; George Cadbury, the Birmingham chocolatier; and the famous shoemakers, Cyrus and James Clark. Several Quakers spotted the business opportunities of the railroads, including Edward Pease and his son Joseph. In the early 1800s they were poised to found the age of steam.

Edward Pease was a wool merchant from Darlington in County Durham, a town visited by the seventeenth-century travel writer Daniel Defoe. Defoe had blessed the quality of its bleached linen and cursed its roads. Pease adhered to the Quaker philosophy of a simple life without

NORTHEAST ENGLAND
The opening of the Stockton to Darlington line paved the way for a railroad boom.

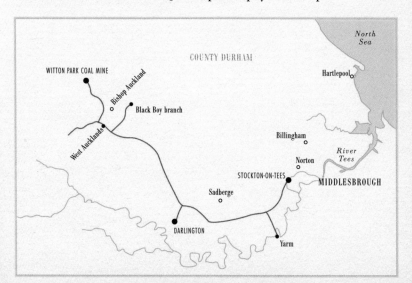

unnecessary adornment, but, like his fellow towns-
man and Quaker, a banker named Jonathan Back-
house, he was a pragmatist. Both men could see the
commercial benefits of improving the carriage road
between their town and the expanding port town of
Stockton, and in the early 1800s Pease proposed a
railroad. He even found an engineer to deliver it:
George Stephenson.

CAREWORN STEPHENSON

A Wylam coal miner's child, Stephenson could neither
read nor write until the age of eighteen. When he joined
Blackett's mine, where his father also worked, he spent
his evenings at night school diligently improving himself. By the time that Pease came looking for an engineer, George Stephenson had met, married and lost a
wife (see box), and shown himself a capable steam man,
managing the steam engines at the nearby Killingworth
coal mine. Samuel Smiles, Stephenson's biographer,
described Pease's first reaction to his engineer: "There
was such an honest, sensible look about him, and he
seemed so modest and unpretending."

"He [Stephenson] certainly turned my head,"
wrote a young celebrity actress, Fanny Kemble, when
she met the railroad men in his middle years. "His
face is fine, though careworn, and bears an expression
of deep thoughtfulness; his mode of explaining his ideas is peculiar and
very original, striking, and forcible; and although his accent indicates
strongly his north country birth, his language has not the slightest touch
of vulgarity or coarseness."

The new line was to be called the Stockton
and Darlington, and Pease raised most of the
capital. He did so again when, in 1824, his
engineer set up the first locomotive factory,
named after his son Robert, at Newcastle
upon Tyne. Once Parliament had sanctioned the
line to carry both goods and passengers "by steam traction," the Stockton and Darlington became the first such
public railroad and a profitable link between the coal mines of
southwest Durham and Stockton, 30 miles (48 km) or so distant. It was
also a useful test bed for George Stephenson and his machines.

RAILROAD WIVES

✦

Much was written about railroad
men Trevithick and Stephenson,
although women, including the
actress Fanny Kemble, often
provided reliable descriptions.
Nothing, however, was heard from
the great railmen's wives. Richard
Trevithick's wife Jane, the daughter
of a foundry worker, outlived her
husband and died aged 96 in 1868,
having remained loyal to him
throughout his financial difficulties
and borne him four children.
George Stephenson was married
three times. His first wife, Fanny,
died along with their daughter in
1806. His second wife (but his first
choice: her father originally refused
to let them marry), Betty, survived
until 1845. When she died, the
gruff Stephenson married his
housekeeper, Ellen Gregory. When
he died, he was buried alongside
Betty, his second wife.

**ENGINEERING
SUPERSTAR**
A bronze of George
Stephenson outside the
station at Chesterfield,
the town where
Stephenson was buried.

Full Steam Ahead

As the first rails were laid for the Stockton and Darlington line in 1822, Stephenson worked on its first steam locomotive: a curious, chunky engine that bore more than a passing resemblance to Trevithick's *Penydarren*. Stephenson had plenty of his own cast-iron rail, but wisely invested in the new wrought-iron rail developed by fellow Northumbrian railroad men John Birkinshaw. Birkinshaw's rail, which would have rescued the fortunes of Trevithick had it been invented in time, proved the breakthrough.

Stephenson, practical man that he was, adopted a solid working title for his steam engine, *Locomotion No. 1*. (He had already built the *My Lord*—it almost begged an exclamation mark—and the *Blücher* at the Killingworth coal mine.) In September 1825, preceded by a man on horseback bearing a superfluous warning flag, the chubby *Locomotion No. 1* successfully heaved coal wagons, empty of coal, but crammed with some 600 passengers, along the line. *No. 1* also drew a passenger carriage crammed with dignitaries: named *The Experiment*, it bore a remarkable resemblance to the stagecoach whose fate was sealed by the railroads.

The line opened only ten years after the English Duke of Wellington had trounced Napoleon at the Battle of Waterloo. Egypt was founding the Sudan city of Khartoum, Simón Bolívar was setting up the Venezuelan state of Bolívar, and British industry, while still profiting from child labor, was recovering from legislation banning the slave trade. It was a momentous historical occasion and Sydney Smith, better known for his doggerel verse on making salad dressing than as a serious nineteenth-century commentator, observed the consequences in his own fashion: "I can now run faster than a fox or a hare and beat a carrier pigeon or an eagle for a hundred miles [161 km]." It was true. For the first time in history, people had overtaken animals. They could even travel faster, farther and for longer periods than their horses. Horses continued to haul passengers until the performance and reliability of locomotives improved.

Miner Lamp Dispute

✦

A formative moment in the career of George Stephenson involved a dispute over a miner's safety lamp. In the latter part of the nineteenth century there were two types in circulation: miners in the northeast swore by their "Stephenson," invented by George. Elsewhere miners used the Davy, invented by Sir Humphry Davy around the same time. Davy accused Stephenson of industrial espionage, and it took a Parliamentary Committee of inquiry to exonerate Stephenson (and settle £1,000 in compensation). Davy never accepted the verdict, while the Geordie (Newcastle man) Stephenson developed a lifelong distrust of any silver-tongued aristocrat.

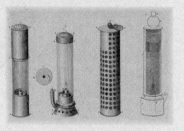

DURHAM COAL IGNITES

Joseph Pease, meanwhile, was proving to be a worldlier fellow than his
father, Edward. Joseph recognized coal as the industrial and domestic
fuel of the future. Coal was more popular in the home than ever,
particularly following the efforts of Count Rumford in making the
nation's fires more efficient. Rumford, born in Massachusetts, had come
to London about 30 years before with a passion for curing coal fires. He
solved the problematic "fire-places for burning Coals . . . in an open
Chimney" (they had a tendency to fill the house with coal smoke) at
several eminent London addresses including those of Lord Palmerston
and Sir Joseph Banks.

Joseph Pease set out to secure new outlets for his Durham coal by
establishing a new port on the end of his railroad line. His choice was a
little farmhouse hamlet on the east coast, Middlesbrough, which, despite
its plain-Jane name was destined to become one of the
busiest ports in northern England with a population of 20,000 people. (It was also to become
the first railroad town.) Joseph Pease
went on to become the first Quaker
Member of Parliament. When he died
in 1872 he was worth a fortune.

BLACK GOLD
The Stockton and Darlington
Railway connected several
inland coal mines with a
seaport. The quest for coal,
the mineral that fueled the
Industrial Revolution,
drove the expansion
of the railroads.

Liverpool and Manchester Railway

Country: England

Type: Passenger, Freight

Length: 35 miles (56 km)

I t was a wonder that the first intercity railroad, designed to carry cotton from Liverpool to the mills of Manchester, was ever built. Political intrigue, professional jealousies and serious geographical obstacles hampered it at every stage. Yet ultimately it made history in more ways than one.

+ **SOCIAL**
+ ***COMMERCIAL***
+ **POLITICAL**
+ **ENGINEERING**
+ **MILITARY**

A FAILED EXPERIMENT

Theater-goers planning an evening with the Royal Shakespeare Company at Stratford-on-Avon often take a pre-theater stroll across the nearby bridge over the River Avon. The brick-built bridge is a little-known testament to the endeavors of William James, claimed by some (mostly his own family) to be the real "father of the railroads."

A surveyor and engineer, James spent too much of his own money on ambitious railroad ideas. He was convinced that people would one day race from city to city on railroads powered by steam engines. He even evolved a plan for a line through the center of England, from Stratford-upon-Avon to London. The plan was pared down to a mere 16 miles (24 km) out of Stratford to a canal head at Moreton. John Rastrick, who helped build Trevithick's *Catch-Me-Who-Can* and became one of the early English locomotive builders, successfully argued that horses would best work the line. Was it Rastrick's or James' fault that the railroad, opened in 1826, languished and eventually died? It did not matter much to James. Having surveyed the route in 1820, and still running England's largest surveying business, he was already working on another proposed railroad line, between Liverpool and Manchester.

THE L&MR
The opening of the Liverpool to Manchester Railroad paved the way for a railroad boom. The line was extended later to Warrington and Bolton.

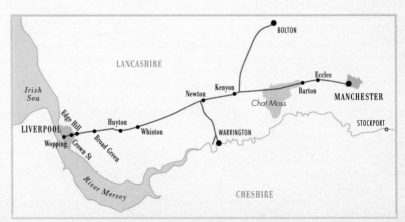

CANAL CROSSING
Freight was shipped by river
and canal before the railroad
arrived. George Stephenson
had to build his viaduct
high over the Sankey Canal
to clear the masts of the
cargo-carrying Mersey
barges or "flats."

TRAFALGAR TRIANGLE

The idea of running a railroad with cars pulled by horse, sail or even steam locomotives from Liverpool to Manchester was deeply attractive to those cities' business communities. Liverpool was a slave city, its fortunes resting on the "Trafalgar Triangle," a three-way trade that shipped cloth, guns and other non-essentials to the West African slave ports. There the ships' holds were unloaded and the cargo replaced with African slaves who headed out on the Middle Passage to plantations in the West Indies. (In a curious railroad parallel it was said that the slaves occupied a space equivalent to a tenth of that taken up by a standard-fare seat on a modern train.) The final stage of the journey saw ships returned to ports such as Liverpool, bringing rum and sugar for Britain's fashionable tea-drinking set.

The townsfolk of Manchester, meanwhile, were turning a pound or two in the cotton trade, transforming the raw material into cloth at its water- and steam-powered mills. Shipping the cotton from Liverpool, or sending the finished goods back from Manchester, involved loading them onto the barges that bustled along two key canals, the Mersey and Irwell, and the Bridgewater. Both made the most of the duopoly, charging rates that businessmen like John Kennedy and a Quaker corn merchant, Joseph Sandars, considered outrageous. Manchester businessman John

> "The golden age is past, and it is to be feared that the iron age has succeeded."
>
> *Henry Booth, director of the Liverpool and Manchester Railway (1830)*

Kennedy's yarn spinning mills generated such generous profits that he could afford to build one of the city's biggest mills using the hot new technology of cast-iron framing, the same material that helped the British railroads forge ahead.

Seeing how the Stockton and Darlington Railway (see p.18) had reduced the price of coal, Kennedy and Sandars promoted the line between Liverpool and Manchester, although it was Sandars who initially met with William James. "Mr James brought a letter of introduction to Mr Sandars a gentleman who having had practical experience of the insufficiency of the existing modes of conveyance from Liverpool to Manchester, was prepared to give all due consideration to any plan which promised a remedy for a tried grievance," explained director Henry Booth in *An Account of the Liverpool and Manchester Railway* (1830).

Overcoming Obstacles

Many were deeply suspicious of the railroads, and Sandars encouraged William James to be discreet as he started surveying the proposed route in 1821. The rural communities rose up in opposition the moment he and his chainmen set out with compass, theodolite and maps. "The farmers stationed men at the field-gates with pitchforks, and sometimes with guns, to drive them back," reported Samuel Smiles in *The Life of George Stephenson and his son Robert Stephenson*. He added that men, women and children ran after the surveyors wherever they made their appearance, "bawling nicknames and throwing stones at them."

A bodyguard—"a noted bruiser"—was hired after one chainman was run through with a pitchfork. His task was to defend that symbol of the surveyor, the theodolite. The country people promptly hired their own man, "a St. Helen's coal miner, cock of the walk in his neighborhood," wrote Smiles, to challenge him. "A battle took place, the coal miner was soundly pummeled, but the natives poured in volleys of stones upon the surveyors and their instruments, and the theodolite was smashed to pieces."

The problems James encountered on his survey, however, were nothing compared to the physical obstacles confronting the railroad

builders. There was the 10 square miles (26 sq km) of Chat Moss, a boggy moor just outside Manchester with a reputation for swallowing straying cattle whole. (In the 1950s it would yield up the severed head of some poor Celt, murdered during the Roman occupation of Britain.) The overweight William James almost became a victim of the moor himself. At one point he started sinking into the quagmire and "threw himself down, and rolled over and over until he reached firm ground again, in a mess," reported Samuel Smiles.

If the line was to be kept level it would have to cross the Sankey Brook valley, which would need to be bridged, while the sandstone pile of the biblical-sounding Olive Mount would have to be sliced in two with a deep cutting. Then there was Liverpool itself. In 1760 just over 2,500 vessels had paid dock duties. Now the figure was closer to 10,000, and the tonnage had doubled in a decade. As a result, the city had sprawled out of the docks and spread into neighboring hamlets and villages. Although canal men had built plenty of tunnels before, no one had yet burrowed beneath a whole city.

When James finished the survey, he and his assistant reported back to Newcastle. His assistant was Robert Stephenson. Robert's father, George, now began the laborious business of applying to Parliament for the new line. William James, however, could no longer assist. His passion for railroads had caused him to ignore the profitable side of his business, which was now on the rocks. As Samuel Smiles explained in his biography of the Stephensons: "Mr. James" financial embarrassments reached their climax and out of illness and debt he was no longer in a position to fulfil his promise to the committee." The great railroad advocate slipped away into obscurity, settling to support his family by working for temporary-help agencies in Cornwall (where, ironically, the business of locomotive steam power had first started).

George Stephenson now considered the project: a 35-mile (56 km) line requiring the world's first under-city tunnel, a 2-mile (3.2 km) long cutting through Olive Mount, 60 or so bridges, and a viaduct over the Sankey Brook that would need at least nine arches. Stone quarried from Olive Mount could be used to build up the bridges and lay down the embankments, but what of the daunting 4 miles (6.4 km) or so of track across the peaty wastes of Chat Moss? With his son Robert now working

CHAT MOSS MOOR

+

George Stephenson took his railroad line across the moor by sinking a floating foundation of wood, heather and stones into the bog and running the line over the top. He was apparently inspired by a historian turned farmer, William Roscoe. Roscoe (1753–1831), the son of a Liverpool market gardener, had set himself the task of taming the moor, cultivating the ground with plow horses wearing wooden shoes or pattens. When the actress Fanny Kemble crossed the moor by train in Stephenson's company she remarked: "We passed over at the rate of five and twenty miles an hour (40 kph), and saw the stagnant swamp water trembling on the surface ... on either side of us."

on railroad projects in South America, George Stephenson submitted his own plans for the line to Parliament. One of the project's arch-opponents, Robert Bradshaw, condemned the "dupes of these schemes" and helped to have it thrown out. (Bradshaw was the agent for the Duke of Bridgewater's canal and was said to "revel in the profits" of the waterway.) The railroad promised to reduce the 36-hour canal journey between the two cities to five or six hours. Bradshaw was offered shares in the scheme, but refused the offer, convinced the whole idea of railroads was a "chimera."

Ditching Stephenson, the railroad promoters tried again, this time with Charles Vignoles and two brothers, the surveyor-engineers George and John Rennie. Their father, also John, was already famous for bridging the River Thames in London twice, once at Southwark and again with the Waterloo Bridge. The brothers successfully re-presented the scheme, the railroad's sponsors reappointed George Stephenson, and the Rennie brothers, who apparently despised the self-made railroad man, walked off the job. Bradshaw, the great opponent to the scheme, was persuaded to change sides and act in support. Work could at last begin.

BREAKING NEW GROUND

The Liverpool and Manchester line ultimately took around five years to construct (despite that fact that William James had originally estimated eighteen months). It made Stephenson's reputation. It also cost the lives of many workers. The *Liverpool Mercury*, for example, reported on May 1, 1830 how a team of construction workers was pitched into the River Irwell when the boat carrying them to breakfast capsized. "Twelve at least, were drowned, having sunk before the strenuous exertions which were being made for their rescue could be available," the newspaper reported, adding: "the Railroad Company have taken upon themselves the funeral expenses."

The year before, in 1829, speed trials had been held at Rainhill to find a suitable engine, and in September 1830 the *Rocket* and the *Planet*, both Stephenson engines, made the maiden journey between Manchester and Liverpool, along with six others including *Northumbrian*, *Phoenix* and

PIONEERING PASSAGE
Wapping Tunnel was bored beneath Liverpool to link the railroad with the city docks. Artist Thomas Bury exaggerated the perspective of the gas-lit tunnel to make it appear larger than life.

North Star. The Liverpool and Manchester Railway would set several new railroad records, but the day of its opening heralded an unwelcome precedent: the first death of a railroad passenger.

Samuel Smiles described what happened: "At Parkside, about 17 miles [27 km] from Liverpool, the engines stopped to take in water. The *Northumbrian* engine, with the carriage containing the Duke of Wellington, was drawn up on one line, in order that the whole of the trains on the other line might pass in review before him and his party. Mr. Huskisson (the member of parliament for Liverpool) had alighted from the carriage, and was standing on the opposite road, along which the *Rocket* was observed rapidly coming up. At this moment the Duke of Wellington, between whom and Mr. Huskisson some coolness had existed, made a sign of recognition, and held out his hand. A hurried but friendly grasp was given; and before it was loosened there was a general cry from the bystanders of "Get in, get in!" Flurried and confused, Mr. Huskisson endeavored to get round the open door of the carriage, which projected over the opposite rail; but in so doing he was struck down by the *Rocket*, and falling with his leg doubled across the rail, the limb was instantly crushed. His first words, on being raised, were, "I have met my death," which unhappily proved true, for he expired that same evening in the parsonage of Eccles."

It was not all bad news, as Smiles went on: "It was cited at the time as a remarkable fact, that the *Northumbrian* engine, driven by George Stephenson himself, conveyed the wounded body of the unfortunate gentleman a distance of about 15 miles [24 km] in 25 minutes, or at the rate of 36 miles an hour [58 kph]. This incredible speed burst upon the world with the effect of a new and unlooked-for phenomenon."

WITHOUT EQUAL?
Novelty, Sans Pareil and *Rocket,* all competed in 1829 to run on the new line. Neither *Novelty* nor *Sans Pareil* ("Without Equal") could match the performance of *Rocket.*

RECORD BREAKER

✦

The Liverpool and Manchester line continued to knock down records like pins in a bowling alley. The company responded to an approach from a freight company, Pickfords, to carry what were effectively the first freight containers; they agreed to a novel idea of conveying letters and parcels between the two cities; and, seeing a curious increase in passengers wanting to travel aboard the train, began to ferry more and more people. Stephenson's double line of rail track allowed trains to pass both ways, the trains traveling on the left, a convention that would be adopted in most parts of the world. The not infrequent accidents, caused when one train ran into the back of another, prompted the railroad to adopt a basic warning system of signaling, with red for stop, green for danger and white for all systems go, which was also adopted worldwide.

Baltimore and Ohio Railroad

Country: U.S.A.

Type: Passenger

Length: 380 miles (611 km)

A ny judge of horseflesh would have put their money on the stagecoach owners beating the steam locomotive *Tom Thumb* at Baltimore in 1830. Their gallant gray did indeed win the race, but not the day: the Baltimore and Ohio Railroad would make history with America's first regular passenger steam service.

+ **SOCIAL**

+ ***COMMERCIAL***

+ **POLITICAL**

+ **ENGINEERING**

+ **MILITARY**

Tom Thumb, invented and driven by Peter Cooper, was carrying a car full of passengers to Ellicott's Mills in Maryland in August 1830. According to railroad lawyer John H.B. Latrobe, relating the story in 1868, "the trip was most interesting. The curves were passed without difficulty at a speed of fifteen miles an hour [24 kph]; the grades were ascended with comparative ease; the day was fine, the company in highest spirits."

Tom Thumb happened to pull up alongside a horse-drawn car on the adjacent track at Relay House on the return journey. Harnessed to "a gallant gray of great beauty and power," the horse-drawn car was driven by the "great stage proprietors of the day," Stockton & Stokes. An impromptu race home followed, with the gray accelerating into an early lead. Gradually *Tom Thumb* gained ground and overtook the horse, only to be halted when a band slipped from the drive wheel. Cooper maneuvered the hot band back, lacerating his hands, and worked up steam again, reaching home behind the horse.

FROM HORSE TO LOCO

The back story of the horse that beat the locomotive was, of course, a little more complicated. The locomotive's designer, builder and engineer, Peter Cooper, was an inveterate inventor from New York who had already made good with a slaughterhouse business. Hearing of plans for a

THE B&O
After its initial 12-mile (19.3 km) run to Ellicott's Mills, the Baltimore and Ohio Railroad was extended to Washington in 1835, Wheeling in 1853 and Parkersburg in 1857.

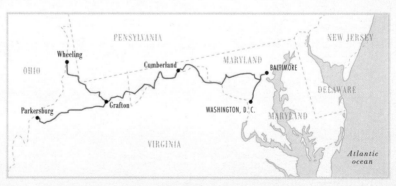

railroad between Baltimore, Maryland, and the Ohio River at Wheeling, West Virginia, Cooper borrowed on his profits and bought a plot of Maryland real estate, fully expecting the railroad line to pass through it. As he cleared the land, he stumbled on deposits of the raw material railroads consume: iron ore. He set about founding an ironworks in Baltimore to build rails for the railroad company.

The Baltimore and Ohio Railroad directors were initially dubious about the merits of steam power and favored the preferred source of power used on the South Carolina: the horse. This prompted Cooper to cobble together *Tom Thumb*. Although the Baltimore and Ohio line used horses for a spell, *Tom Thumb*'s performance persuaded the railroad's owners that the future lay in steam-powered engines.

One historical footnote relates how two years later the unfortunate stagecoach owner, William B. Stokes, was to be found defending himself in a Maryland court. The stagecoach, from Baltimore to Wheeler, had overturned and injured a lady passenger whose family sued the company. Since his partner Richard Stockton had died, Stokes was left to defend the company against the charge that the driver had been drunk. The company lost.

Meanwhile, the railroad company had thrived. It had been launched by a Quaker, Philip E. Thomas. He and a fellow businessman, George Brown, had originally taken ship to England to see the Stockton and Darlington line (see p.18). Like their counterparts in Charleston, both men were concerned about the loss of potential business to the emerging markets of the West. Baltimore had a big port,

"I consider this among the most important acts of my life, second only to my signing the Declaration of Independence, if even it be second to that."

Charles Carroll, ceremonially breaking ground on the railroad (1828)

HOLDING THE LINE
By the 1860s the railroad
ran American locomotives
like the Baltimore-built
Thatcher Perkins with its
characteristic spark-
arresting smokestack, cow
catcher and innovative
truck, which gave a better
grip on the track. The
truck was first tested
back in the 1830s.

but its rivals, New York, Philadelphia and Washington, were busy forging links with the West where, in places like the Ohio Valley, the principal export was grain. Unless the farmer turned his produce into the more profitable form of whiskey, he faced the problem of transporting a product that was low in price and high in volume. If he could send it direct to a port he was assured of better profits. In the early 1800s the most promising method of doing so was along the Erie Canal linking Lake Erie with the Hudson River and New York.

The Erie Canal was inspired by the British Duke of Bridgewater's lucrative canal (whose dominance was upset by the Liverpool and Manchester Railway) and dubbed "Clinton's Big Ditch" after Governor Dewitt Clinton who promoted the project. In 1825 Clinton ceremonially emptied two casks of water from Lake Erie into New York Harbor after sailing down the canal. The waterway was soon awash with barges filled with up to 30 tons of freight heading for the port.

Thomas and Brown planned to rival the Erie with an ambitious 380 miles (611 km) of railroad, laid as a double track to facilitate two-way traffic. To maintain a gentle gradient the line was designed to follow the meandering river's course, but over such a distance steeper inclines were inevitable, leaving the directors assuming that horsepower would dominate. The first ground was turned in 1828 by 90-year-old Charles Carroll, one of the signatories to the 1776 Declaration of Independence. Two years later the first 12 miles (19.3 km) of track were laid and the first section, from Baltimore West to Ellicott's Mills, opened. At first horses hauled the trains, but gradually steam locomotives took over.

A Transport Trailblazer

The early engines were strange "grasshopper" locomotives, so named because the arrangement of their mechanics gave them the long-legged, stalker's stance of a grasshopper. It was not long before the first conventional locomotive, the *Lafayette*, arrived. Named after the French soldier who had distinguished himself on the American side during the Revolutionary War, the *Lafayette*, with its stovepipe chimney at the front, broad, horizontal barrel of a boiler in the middle, and engineer's platform at the back, looked like a real locomotive. It was also equipped with a truck, a recent invention that gave it a better grip on the tracks than its predecessors.

Lafayette had been built by William Norris, who, having started out as draper, switched to building locomotives in Philadelphia in 1831. He would become a major locomotive builder, even selling locomotives back to the British. In 1836 he delivered the *Washington County Farmer* to the Philadelphia and Columbia Railroad company. The locomotive featured a four-wheeled truck, which looked like an independent pivoted chassey, at the front. The truck had been trialled on a locomotive, the *Brother Jonathon* ("Brother Jonathon" was an early nickname for the all-American guy), built by John B. Jervis at the New York West Point Foundry. The four-wheeled truck ensured that the *Farmer* and subsequently the *Lafayette* (and almost all passenger locomotives of the future) held the rails even on a curve. The Baltimore and Ohio managers were sold on the idea: they placed an order for eight engines.

It would take until 1842 for the railroad to finally reach the Ohio River, by which time a web of new railroads had spread out along the Eastern Seaboard. (The Camden and Amboy, and the Mohawk and Hudson Railroads came hot on the heels of the Baltimore and Ohio.) Nevertheless, the railroad continued to set national records: it was the first to publish a timetable, to use electric engines, and, in 1930, to introduce fully air-conditioned trains.

Latrobe's Folly

✦

The name of the Baltimore and Ohio's promoter, Philip Thomas, was enshrined in a ground-breaking piece of engineering: the Thomas Viaduct. The railroad had been granted a charter to extend from Baltimore to Washington in 1831, and this section opened in 1835 after the viaduct had been built. The eight-span structure, America's longest when it was first built, was also the first masonry bridge on the continent to be built on a curve, the only way it could cross the Patapsco River and Valley. Many were convinced that "Latrobe's Folly" (after its designer Benjamin Henry Latrobe II, the brother of John H. B. Latrobe) would never stand up. In fact it survived two of the worst floods in the valley's history in 1868 and 1972.

South Carolina Canal and Rail Road Company

Country: U.S.A.

Type: Passenger, Freight

Length: 136 miles (219 km)

+ **SOCIAL**
+ **COMMERCIAL**
+ **POLITICAL**
+ **ENGINEERING**
+ **MILITARY**

LOOKING AHEAD
Oliver Evans foresaw the potential of steam to power locomotives and transport people over hundreds of miles.

The 1920s dance craze that put Charleston on the map originated in the city's industrial docklands. A century earlier, the same city was making history as it founded one of America's first public railroads.

FAST AS BIRDS FLY

Being able to breakfast in Baltimore and eat supper in New York on the same day was an absurd claim to be making in 1813. But the author was a man of vision. Within fifty years the *Monthly Chronicle* was reporting: "The distance between Baltimore and New York may be easily traveled [by train] in a day."

Oliver Evans, born in 1755, was apprenticed to a wheelwright. The village wheelwright's shop, like the blacksmith's forge, was a favorite evening gathering place with its warmth, light and, if the wright was fixing a wheel, action. To fit a wheel the iron tire was fired until red hot and then, fully expanded, eased over the wooden rim. The wright's boy would douse it with cold water to make it contract around the wheel, enveloping everything in a cloud of steam. This, and a party trick of the blacksmith's boy, impressed Evans. The lad would heat a rifle barrel, filled with water and packed with wadding, over the smith's fire until the steam produced an explosion, which shook the crows from their roosts.

For Evans the object lesson was the power of steam. Heated in a boiler, water expands as it turns to steam. Evans knew that steam could drive a piston: he had examined the Boulton and Watt low-pressure steam engines and recognized their limitations. Like Richard Trevithick, refining plans for the *Penydarren*, Evans conceived a steam-driven vehicle that could run along rails. He even imagined a time "when people will travel in stages moved by steam engines from one city to another almost as fast as birds fly—15–20 miles (24–32 km) per hour. Passing through the air with such velocity—changing the scenes in such rapid succession—will be the most exhilarating, delightful exercise."

> **"A carriage will set out from Washington in the morning, and the passengers will breakfast in Baltimore, dine in Philadelphia, and sup in New York the same day."**
> *Oliver Evans, railroad visionary, 1813*

As far back as 1789 Evans patented plans for an amphibious steam engine. America in the early nineteenth century, however, had plenty of new ventures, but little free capital, and he ran into difficulties either securing an income from his patents or funding new projects. A friend traveled to England to attempt to secure capital there. The friend died before finding Evans a backer, but there has been speculation that Richard Trevithick might have chanced upon Oliver Evans' steam locomotive plans. Did the *Penydarren* owe anything to the American inventor?

Evans died in 1819 following a fire at his engineering company, possibly started by a disgruntled employee. A year later his dream of people "traveling in stages moved by steam engines" started down the tracks as Charleston, South Carolina, set out to build one of America's early railroads.

LAND AND WATER
Oliver Evans patented
plans for a steam-powered
amphibious vehicle in
the 1780s.

CHARLESTON'S HARD AT IT

The jazz musician Jimmy Johnson immortalized the city of Charleston with his dance hit in the mid-1920s—music, he said, inspired by Charleston's African American dockworkers. The city originally took its name from the English King Charles II (with some resentment after it was attacked by the British during the Revolutionary War) and its aspiration, to become a "great port towne," from one of the early English settlers. Blood money from a booming slave trade, and a fashion for buckskin breeches, a significant trading item in the 1700s, placed the city among America's top ten. But in the 1820s its fortunes were uncertain.

CELEBRATORY RIDE
The *Best Friend of Charleston* drew the first train out of Charleston on Christmas Day, 1830.

Not only were its white citizens recovering from rumors of a slave revolt (thirty-five people, including the supposed ringleader Denmark Vesey, were hastily hanged), but the city's trading position was also being challenged by economic expansion in the West. Members of the South Carolina Canal and Rail Road Company, formed in 1827, set out to boost the local economy by connecting Charleston and the inland markets with a railroad.

It opened on Christmas Day 1830. According to the *Charleston Courier* "the one hundred and forty-one persons flew on the wings of wind at the speed of fifteen to twenty-five miles [25–40 km] per hour" returning "in quick and double quick time." Drawing the five cars whipping along the 6-mile (10 km) line was the first full-size steam locomotive on the American continent. Built in New York at the West Point Foundry and shipped in parts to Charleston, it was named the *Best Friend of Charleston*.

STEAM'S BEST FRIEND

The *Best Friend* looked unlike any of its steam-driven predecessors. The driver perched behind his safety rail at the front of the engine with a boiler, erect as a rocket, behind him. With its vertical boiler and its water tank, it was a solid piece of engineering capable of hauling five cars filled with more that fifty passengers along at a steady 20 mph (32 kph). It had one annoying feature, a safety valve on the boiler that whined under pressure. One fireman solved the problem by tying it down, with inevitable consequences. In 1831 the boiler exploded, killing the unfortunate fireman and wreaking havoc on the locomotive. The engine was rebuilt and rebranded as the *Phoenix*, the mythical bird that rose from its own ashes. Boiler safety valves were eventually made tamper-proof.

The man behind the locomotive was local businessman Ezra L. Miller. He shared the optimism of the railroad men (he may have been among the crowds, along with Charleston's chief engineer, Horatio Allen, at the Rainhill speed trial in England) and was quick to join the railroad's board of directors. When his business colleagues baulked at the idea of commissioning a locomotive, he put up the cash ($4,000) and came up with the design. He teamed up with Matthias Baldwin, founding the Baldwin Locomotive Works and building the *E.L. Miller*, which was sold to the South Carolina Canal and Rail Road Company, and the famous locomotive *Old Ironsides*.

INVESTING IN TRACKS

Miller's locomotive, *Best Friend*, was not the first on the American mainland. As in the U.K. and Europe, it was American miners and quarrymen who built the early railroads for wagons hauled by man or beast. The Delaware and Hudson Canal Company imported a steam locomotive, the *Stourbridge Lion*, from the Stourbridge, England workshop of Foster, Rastrick and Company. (It was the first locomotive to operate outside of the U.K.). Horatio Allen was the Delaware and Hudson's engineer at the time and he ordered four engines: the *Lion* and two others from Rastrick, and a fourth from George Stephenson. Stephenson's was completed and shipped first, but it was Rastrick's *Stourbridge Lion* that made the maiden run.) A year later the diminutive *Tom Thumb* rolled down the line in Baltimore.

On the face of it the little line out of Charleston was a small, cranky affair. But it was an opening salvo in the battle to build railroads. Railroad development in America was going to be very different from that in England where distances were short, traffic relatively high and, once George Stephenson had persuaded the bankers to part with their money, capital was in plentiful supply. America during the early 1800s had neither the cash nor the traffic, but land was cheap and the success of the Charleston line encouraged businessmen and politicians to invest in tracks. Within ten years there would be around 3,000 miles (4,828 km) of railroad: that figure promised to triple over the next twenty years.

FIRST AMERICAN ENGINEER

✦

South Carolina rail employees turned out in force for the funeral of Nicholas W. Darrell in 1869, according to newspaper reports. The man was, in their eyes, the first locomotive engineer in America. One John Degnon from New York subsequently claimed to have taught Darrell everything he knew, but it seems that Darrell did have prior claim to have run not only *Best Friend*, but a second engine, *West Point* (named after the New York foundry). Eventually a third engine, the *South Carolina*, the first eight-wheeler to be brought into service, joined the route.

1834

Dublin and Kingstown Railway

Country: Ireland

Type: Passenger

Length: 6 miles (10 km)

+ **SOCIAL**

+ **COMMERCIAL**

+ **POLITICAL**

+ **ENGINEERING**

+ **MILITARY**

Ireland's railroads might have had a smoother ride if the determining track width used throughout the country had been the same as that William Dargan laid for the Dublin to Kingstown line. Instead, the adoption of a different gauge in Ireland prevented such success, and its problems even reached as far afield as Australia.

A MULE'S BACKSIDE?

Irishman William Dargan, a farmer's boy educated at the village school, was pleased with his accounts in the 1820s: they showed £300 in profit, the result of working with Scottish engineer Thomas Telford. Telford's reputation had improved after predicting that part of St. Chadd's Church in Shrewsbury, Shropshire, would fall down. It did, three days later.

Telford took Dargan on during his road-building work in North Wales and Dublin. In the railroad rush that came on the heels of the Stockton and Darlington Railway, Dargan became embroiled in plans for Ireland's first passenger railroad, a 6-mile (10 km) line from Dublin to Kingstown. Although it was a relatively easy route to lay, there were local

COAST LINE
William Dargan laid down his railroad between Dublin and Kingstown on the same gauge that George Stephenson used.

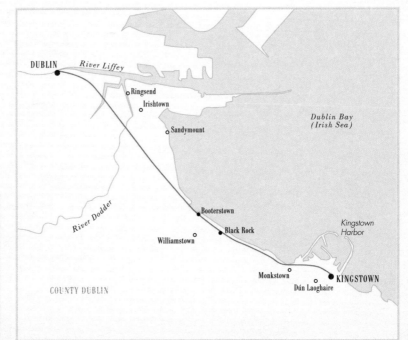

difficulties. The seaside line threatened
the privacy of a squire who took a daily
constitutional swim in the Irish Sea.
The railroad company obliged him with
a bridge and bathing temple.

Dargan was exacting about the
distance between the rails, the gauge. He prescribed a precise 56.5 inches
(1.435 m) or "Stephenson's Gauge" as adopted on the
Stockton and Darlington. Stephenson used this width
because that was the traditional width of the *chaldron*,
or coal wagon, and he wanted his line to link with the
coal mine tracks.

> **"I admire commercial enterprise . . .
> as wherever it goes . . . all that we
> call civilisation goes with it."**
> *Thomas Telford*

The wagon gauge dated back centuries. A paved road
at Diolkos near Corinth, Greece, still bore the score marks of a rutted
track, the ruts, or rails, set at about 60 inches (1.5 m) apart. Some historians claimed this was an ancient Greek railroad, the width reflecting the
simple fact that, save for slave power, the traditional beast of burden
was the horse, ox or mule and rails had to be far enough apart to accommodate a team, or pair, of beasts. On this theory, Stephenson's Gauge
could have been dictated by the width of a mule's backside.

Stephenson might have adopted
a broader gauge, which would have
delivered a broader carriage and a
more comfortable ride, when he
engineered the Liverpool and Manchester line. But by then he was
already building locomotives and
designing railroads. It made sense
to stick to what he knew.

CRITICAL GAUGE
The gauge, the distance between a
pair of rails, was set down by George
Stephenson on the Stockton and
Darlington Railway and owed its
origins to the width of a wheeled cart.

Switching to the Irish Gauge

The first Irish railroad opened in 1834 and proved a popular commuter line. Other Irish railroads appeared: the Ulster in 1839 and the Dublin and Drogheda in 1844. Unfortunately, different engineers took an Irish approach to the matter of gauge: Ulster adopted the broadly comfortable 74 inches (1.880 m), while the Dublin and Drogheda went for a narrower 62 inches (1.575 m). Foreseeing problems ahead, a commission investigated the matter and recommended an entirely new gauge: 63 inches (1.600 m), which became the Irish standard gauge. The old Dublin line had to tear up its tracks and convert.

Around this time the governor of New South Wales, Australia, having sought advice on track gauge, opted for Stephenson's. South Australia and Victoria followed suit when a former Dublin and Kingstown man, Francis Shields, began New South Wales' first railroad between Sydney and Parramata. Shields later resigned, but not before altering his track to the Irish gauge. Other lines were in planning— the Victorian Railroad, built in 1854, and the South Australian Railroad in 1856. To keep in step, Victoria and South Australia switched to Irish gauge.

First Class
Bradshaw's Monthly Railroad Guide for 1843 listed fare prices on the Dublin to Kingstown Railroad as "First Class 1s, second class 8d, third class 6d."

Scottish engineer James Wallace replaced Shields. He reverted to the
Stephenson Gauge and, bizarrely, governor William Denison gave his
consent. Sydney's railroad opened in 1855 with a different gauge from
the rest of the country. Australia would wrestle,
expensively, with the problem ever since.

Other gauges evolved as the railroads expanded.
Sixty percent of the world's railroads eventually
opted for Stephenson's or "Standard" Gauge. Just
under a quarter of the railroads, including those of
Russia, Iberia, and parts of India, Pakistan and Ireland, adopted a wider gauge. The rest, including
South America, and south and central Africa, used a
narrow gauge. Passengers' journeys were inevitably
delayed where two gauges met: one solution was
to build dual-gauge railroads that could be used by
different trains.

Curiously, the problem was nothing new. Neolithic
farmers appear to have had little agreement over the
gauge of their carts, which varied from 51 inches
(1.30 m) to 71 inches (1.75 m). It took the Bronze Age
cart maker to come up with a standard size that was
not so very different from Stephenson's Gauge of
between 55 inches (1.4 m) and 57 inches (1.45 m).

LISTOWEL TO BALLYBUNION

✦

In 1888 another Irish railroad
line broke with convention when
its designer, Frenchman Charles
Lartigue, proposed a radical solution
to the issue of railroad gauge:
a single rail. The one-line railroad
was supported on a trestle of
ironwork that snaked across country
from Listowel to Ballybunion by the
sea in County Kerry. Apart from
requiring special locomotives with
twin boilers that straddled the track,
passengers and freight had to be
evenly balanced on either side of
the rolling stock. After being
damaged during the Irish Civil War it
closed in 1924. A section of the
line was reconstructed in 2003.

1835

Brussels to Mechelen Railway

Country: Belgium

Type: Freight, Passenger

Length: 12.4 miles (20 km)

✦ SOCIAL

✦ **COMMERCIAL**

✦ POLITICAL

✦ ENGINEERING

✦ MILITARY

It was after railroad history began in Britain that Belgium broke ranks with the rest of Europe and went on to build the first railroad on the continent. This little nation eventually developed a more intensive rail network than anywhere else in the world.

KING LEOPOLD'S LINE

The new country of Belgium emerged from the Netherlands in 1830 like a butterfly from its chrysalis. The nation-state, which had been absorbed by its neighbor after the defeat of Napoleon in 1815, was formed after a revolt in 1830. Although it became a country in its own right under its king, Leopold I, minor skirmishing continued along its borders. Plans were ordered for a series of strategic rail routes to cover the country from east to west and north to south, with Brussels at the center.

By 1834 the framework for this state railroad network lay on the king's desk awaiting his majesty's approval. It was a grand plan and Leopold signed off the first leg, a railroad from Brussels to Mechelen (Malines). It was to be the first passenger railroad in continental Europe.

Leopold, meanwhile, was making arrangements for the marriage of two royal first cousins, his niece Victoria and his nephew Prince Albert of Saxe-Coburg and Gotha. Victoria was destined to inherit the English throne (the royal family would abandon their Germanic names and adopt the more English-sounding Windsor to placate anti-German sentiments during the First World War) and to oversee an empire that was founded on its railroads.

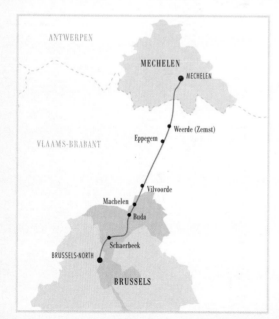

BELGIUM
The Belgian King
Leopold I promoted
the building of
the first railroad on
the European mainland.

Leopold's railroad, meanwhile, was progressing. As the lines were laid, locomotives were ordered from across the English Channel, the ponderous sounding *L'Elephant* coming from Charles Tayleur's Merseyside foundry (originally set up to supply the Liverpool and Manchester Railroad) while Stephenson provided *La Flèche* (the Arrow) and the *Stephenson*. On the inaugural run in May 1835, when all three locomotives drew the train of 30 carriages filled with some 1,000 passengers, George Stephenson himself, supposedly traveling incognito, was on board. On the return journey, *L'Elephant* alone hauled the train.

A Flying Start

Belgium's troublesome Dutch neighbors had yet to make a start. There was talk of a rail route from the major port of Amsterdam through to the Rhinelands, but an early plan, conceived by a former Liverpool and Manchester man, William Bake, to run a line from Amsterdam to the German city of Cologne, foundered. In the end it fell to one of Blake's men, W.C. Brade, to plan a trial line from Amsterdam to Haarlem, initially for passenger traffic. The line duly opened as the first railroad in the Netherlands in 1839 although, curiously, it was built on the "wrong" gauge of 76 inches (1.945 m) which had to be hastily changed. Again, two British-built locomotives, *Arend* (Eagle) and *De Snelheid* (Speed), hauled the first train. It was a small beginning for the Dutch Railways.

INAUGURAL RUN
George Stephenson traveled incognito onboard the train from Brussels to Mechelen.

Back in Belgium the line to Mechelen had, a year later in 1836, been extended to Antwerp and within eight years the railroad extended to Ghent and Ostend and as far as the German and French borders. During the Belgian Revolution of 1830 the town of Sittard had sided with the revolutionaries. As part of the treaty between Belgium and the Netherlands, Belgium had been allowed to build a road or canal over Dutch territory to the Prussian border. Belgium decided to make their Iron Rhine, as it became known, a railroad, running it from Sittard in 1868. After its flying start, Belgium went on to develop the greatest extent of rail track per square mile in the world.

Nuremberg and Fürth Railway

Country: Bavaria

Type: Freight, Passenger

Length: 3.8 miles (6.4 km)

The first railroad in any country marks a significant step forward in that nation's history. Bavaria's Ludwigsbahn not only presaged a railroad rush in central Europe, it also helped to create a unified Germany.

✦ SOCIAL

✦ *COMMERCIAL*

✦ POLITICAL

✦ ENGINEERING

✦ MILITARY

ENGLISH LESSONS FOR BAVARIA

When Bavaria's Ludwigsbahn opened in December 1835 the crowds were there, but the monarch after whom it was named was absent. In Prussia, Prince William, brother to the King of Prussia, had managed, four years earlier, to turn up for the opening of the railroad that would be named after him, the royal party making the maiden voyage in empty, carpet-covered coal wagons.

King Ludwig I of Bavaria, however, had lost interest in the exciting new venture to which he had lent his title. He was distracted by plans for a canal to link the Danube and Main rivers (he was a canal enthusiast). He may also have been smarting at the loss of the extravagantly attractive English aristocrat Lady Jane Digby, who had recently ceased to oblige him as his mistress. Initially King Ludwig had been enthused by the idea of linking Nuremberg and Fürth with a metal railroad. The proposition that wagons could be pulled by horses or even one of the strange locomotives under construction at George Stephenson's English workshops filled everyone with delight. Europe had watched with interest as England's railroads developed.

GERMANY
It was King Ludwig I who initially encouraged the construction of the first railroad in Bavaria.

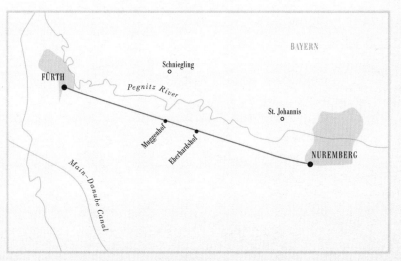

In France there was a contemplative pause partly triggered by that nation's exhaustion after the Napoleonic Wars. The Belgians and the Dutch had not remained on the sidelines for long. But Bavaria was unsure which way to turn. Initially the king dispatched his man, Joseph von Baader, to England to study the railroads there (he would go on to become one of Bavaria's railroad pioneers), and the issue of railroads was discussed in the Bavarian parliament. There were even plans to build a steam circus at Munich's Schloss Nymphenburg, although they came to nothing.

It was left to local business to make the first move, and in 1833 the Gesellschaft zur Errichtung einer Eisenbahn mit Dampffahrt zwischen Nürnberg und Fürth was founded. The key figures behind it were more briefly described: George Platner and Johannes Scharrer. Somewhat to everyone's surprise, Platner and Scharrer raised the necessary capital, 132,000 guldens, without difficulty and an engineer was appointed. The fact that it was French-born Paul Camille Denis did raise eyebrows. Bavaria, having supported Napoleon during the invasion of Austria, had subsequently backed down and was now part of a loose Germanic alliance along with Austria and Prussia. In the ensuing political turmoil Monsieur Denis had made his own political affiliations public. He was censured for doing so and, piqued, he had marched off to England, like Joseph von Baader, to study the emerging railroads.

PASSENGER TRAFFIC
Although it was expected to ferry more freight than people, the railroad was soon carrying up to 9,000 passengers a week.

ADLER

+

In 1935 a replica of the *Adler*
was built to celebrate the centenary
of the Ludwigsbahn line. The
locomotive even had a roll-on part
in the 1935 film *Das Stahltier* (the
Steel Beast), about the opening of
the railroad line. The founder of the
Gestapo, Hermann Göring, who
considered it bad taste to portray
an English-made engine on a
German railroad, banned the film.
The *Adler*, exhibited at the
Nuremberg Railroad Shed, was
partly destroyed by fire in 2005,
and rebuilt two years later.

Despite reservations over his politics, Scharrer and Platner were confident of their man and his appointment turned out to be fortunate: Denis saw to it that the line would be laid, like the Liverpool and Manchester, on Stephenson (or Standard) Gauge, ensuring that much of Europe, with some exceptions, would follow suit. (The Prince William Railroad, built on a narrow gauge, had to be relaid sixteen years after it opened.)

With the money, the line and the land in place, Platner and Scharrer looked for an engine. Although horses were expected to do the bulk of the work, as they did on the Prince William Railroad, the success of Stephenson's locomotives had not escaped their attention. Scharrer wondered what Stephenson would charge to supply one of his English locomotives. Too much, it seemed, for Scharrer was soon commissioning two Bavarian engine makers to build and supply a locomotive for just £560. As the line neared completion Scharrer checked on its progress and was horrified to discover that not only had the contractors moved (to Austria), they also wanted double the money to finish the job. Scharrer hurried back to Stephenson's Newcastle works, agreed a price of £1,750 and, just in time, took delivery of a 14.5-ton engine proudly plated with the name *Adler* (Eagle).

For its inaugural journey the English engine was manned by an English driver, William Wilson. Having worked on the Liverpool and Manchester line he now proudly rode the *Adler*, which, according to paintings of the occasion, drew a train of pretty yellow carriages in pleasant contrast to its own green and red livery.

A NATIONAL NERVE SYSTEM

Wilson took a liking to Bavaria and settled to live there, although he would not be permitted to stay overnight in Nuremberg. A curious bylaw forbade "laborers and foreigners" to remain after their day's work, legislation that contributed to an unexpected bonus for the Ludwigsbahn directors: passenger traffic. The Ludwigsbahn was primarily designed to shift beer and newspapers, but it was soon ferrying up to 9,000 passengers a week and generating healthy dividends for its investors.

When the line opened Germany was still a hodgepodge of disparate and competitive states just emerging from their agricultural roots. The pastoral joys of village life where peasant families lived and worked in harmony with the seasons had their drawbacks: isolation, petty squabbles and bitter blood feuds. The German economist Friedrich List considered it an unhealthy state of affairs and one that promoted philistinism, vanity and provincial prejudice. What the German states needed, he insisted, was a national nerve system composed of iron rails.

Hindsight is a wonderful thing, but foresight is better. Friedrich List knew a lot about railroads, having worked in America on what was, at

"I could not watch the astonishing effects of railroads in England and North America without wishing that my German fatherland would partake of the same benefits."
Friedrich List in a pamphlet, 1833

the time, the country's longest iron-capped railroad, a 21-mile (32 km) mining line through the Blue Mountains at Little Schuylkill. Even before the building of Bavaria's Nuremberg line he had sketched out in a pamphlet in 1833 the implications for a unified Germany of a railroad system with Berlin at its center. He even proposed a pioneering railroad to be powered not by horses, but steam: the Leipzig to Dresden railroad. The Saxon authorities were persuaded to provide the £210,000 capital and a Scottish engineer, James Walker, a former Liverpool and Manchester man, surveyed the route. He handed his plans over to another English railroad man, John Hawkshaw (he would go on to work on an early and ill-conceived idea for a tunnel between England and France—see p.216), and four years after the Nuremberg to Fürth line opened, so did the Leipzig–Dresden line. It was 1839.

Friedrich List was celebrated in the 1980s, his portrait printed on stamps celebrating 150 years of the Leipzig and Dresden line. Ernest in his intentions and sincere in his beliefs, List, however, did not live to see his predictions come true. Disappointed by his lack of recognition or the little acknowledgment (or remuneration) he received from the line, he shot himself while on holiday in the Tyrolean Alps.

Steam prophet
Friedrich List foresaw a future Germany united by the railroads.

The thirty–nine German states were eventually unified in 1871, thirty-two years after the Nuremburg line opened, but by then the rail companies had already agreed on open border policies and were running cross-border trains. The railroads were making Germany long before Germany made itself.

<table>
<tr><td>

1837

</td><td>

Paris to Le Pecq
Railway

</td></tr>
</table>

Country: France

Type: Passenger

Length: 12 miles (19 km)

+ **SOCIAL**
+ **COMMERCIAL**
+ **POLITICAL**
+ **ENGINEERING**
+ **MILITARY**

The effects of republican schools, conscription and the railroads are said to have dragged France into the nineteenth century. But an early railroad accident in the country's capital threatened to stop railroad history in its tracks.

LES CHEMINS DE FER

In 1830 Eugène Delacroix's stirring depiction of the Revolution, *Liberty Leading the People*, was unveiled to the public. His painting portrayed Liberty bearing the tricolor over the barricades toward the new values of liberty, equality and fraternity. Yet for all its modern ways (silk workers in Lyon were about to hold one of the world's early workers' revolts) France in the 1830s was reluctant to embark on "the iron road," *les chemins de fer*.

When it came to laying down 82 miles (132 km) of railroad between Paris and Rouen, the French set aside their traditional hostility and hired the English. With Joseph Locke as engineer and the indefatigable Thomas Brassey and William Mackenzie as contractors, the line cut north across the old Seine floodplain, driven by around 5,000 British laborers. Onlookers were amazed by how hard they worked.

The line was successfully in operation by 1843 despite the opposition of a group of Rouen businessmen who argued that the iron horse would destroy the Gallic way of life and disrupt canal and river trade. (France's canal network was the pride of the nation.) Their view was colored by events on France's first real railroad line, which had been laid between Paris and the little township of Le Pecq, which straddled the Seine 12 miles (19 km) west of the city. The locomotive-powered Paris–Le Pecq was part financed by the banking family of Rothschild and aimed at passenger traffic.

PARISIAN PLEASURES
The Republic was slow to embrace the railroad age, especially following a fatal accident on the Paris to Le Pecq line.

Sponsored by Émile Péreire and his *Compagnie du Chemin de fer de Paris à Saint-Germain* (Paris–Saint-Germain Railroad Company), it was judged a success when it was opened by King Louis-Philippe's wife, Maria Amalia, in August 1837. After more than a million passengers had reportedly enjoyed the journey in their open cars and closed, four-door *berlines fermées*, a second line of track was added. Later the 30-minute journey was extended to take in that palatial symbol of the old regime, Versailles.

Optimism about the railroads seemed to be gathering strength at last, prompting minister Louis Legrand to propose a national network with lines emanating like the rays of the sun out of Paris. But there was a cloud on the horizon.

REMEMBER MEUDON

Everything went wrong one day in May 1842 as passengers were returning from Versailles. An axle on the leading locomotive sheared, a common occurrence in these early days, and the locomotive pitched off the tracks and burst into flames. (Scottish engineer William Rankine later concluded that the axle had suffered metal fatigue.) Charles Adams took up the story in his 1879 *Notes on Railroad Accidents*: "Three carriages crowded with passengers were . . . piled on top of the burning mass. The doors of the cars were locked . . . and it so chanced that they had all been newly painted. They blazed like pine kindlings." The fifty-five dead included the well-known French explorer Jules Dumont d'Urville. In an early example of the forensic sciences, a phrenologist who had recently taken a cast of his head identified him.

The accident came to be known as *Le catastrophe ferroviaire de Meudon* (the crash occurred near Meudon) and for years afterward, French railroad promoters could be instantly silenced by the words: "*N'oubliez pas Meudon!*" Remember Meudon!

TRAGIC DAY
Fifty-five people returning from Versailles were killed when the Paris train crashed and burst into flames.

Grand Junction and London to Birmingham Railways

Country: England

Type: Freight, Passenger

Length: 82 miles (132 km) and 112 miles (180 km)

+ SOCIAL
+ **COMMERCIAL**
+ POLITICAL
+ ENGINEERING
+ MILITARY

The London to Birmingham and the Grand Junction were branded as two separate lines, yet they formed the world's first real intercity railroad. Objectors feared the destruction of all they held dear; the proponents, railroad men one and all, promised social change. They were to be proved right.

THE BENEFITS OF A RAILROAD

James Watt was the father of mechanical engineering. His son, also named James, was not. He was, in fact, implacably opposed to it—or at least to the idea of steam engines crossing his land.

Thanks to his father's fortune, James junior could afford to live in the grand surroundings of a Jacobean country house just outside Birmingham, Aston Hall. When the route for the London to Birmingham line was being surveyed, much of it under the cover of darkness in an effort to prevent the confrontations that had ensued when William James surveyed the Liverpool to Manchester line, Aston Hall lay in its path. James Watt blocked its passage and the London to Birmingham had to make an expensive detour to Curzon Street, Birmingham in order to connect with the Grand Junction Railway.

CENTRAL ENGLAND
The first intercity railroad line was laid from Warrington on the Liverpool and Manchester line to Birmingham and, a year later, from Birmingham to London.

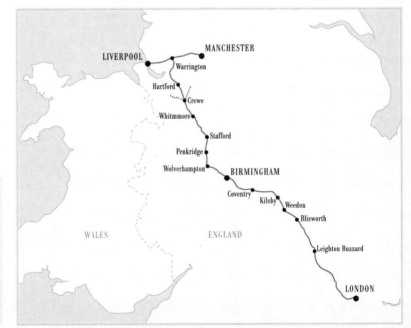

Watt was not the only objector. One clergyman refused to allow the surveyors over his land unless he was busy preaching from the church pulpit. Another, knighted for his services as surgeon to the king, remonstrated with Robert Stephenson for threatening the very social fabric of society: "Your scheme is preposterous in the extreme. You are proposing to cut up our estates in all directions for the purpose of making an unnecessary road." It prompted one disgruntled negotiator to remark quietly: "It is really provoking to find one who has been made a 'Sir' for cutting that wen out of George the Fourth's neck charging us with destroying the noblesse because we proposed to confer on him and his neighborhood the benefits of a railroad."

There were others who foresaw the advantages of a railroad. The boards of directors of the two new lines noted the generous dividends paid on shares of the Liverpool and Manchester. They noted too the curious fact that people seemed to enjoy traveling on trains. One early railroad author, Francis Coghlan, suggested that rail travel was anything but pleasant: "Always sit with your back towards the engine, against the boarded part of the waggon; by this plan you will avoid being chilled by the current of cold air which passes through these open waggons and also save you from being blinded by the small cinders which escape from the funnel." Despite all the discomforts passenger numbers on the Liverpool and Manchester line continued to climb. Then there was the question of freight.

The Liverpool and Manchester line, which had cut the price of coal and forced freight rates down on the canals, not only carried more coal than ever, it was fast becoming the farmer's friend, shifting live animals direct to market.

The two lines, almost six times the length of the Liverpool and Manchester line and designed to join up with it at a little town named Warrington, were to be the London to Birmingham and the Grand Junction, from Birmingham to

LEAPFROG RAILROAD

◆

A "stunningly ambitious" plan to provide London with a public railroad the same year as the London to Birmingham line opened was also stunningly expensive. Costing the same as the 35-mile (56 km) Liverpool and Manchester while crossing only 3.5 miles (5.6 km) of the city, the London to Greenwich Railroad had to cross swathes of city streets, leapfrogging them on more than 870 big brick arches. The project took five years to complete and used so many bricks it triggered a national shortage. Yet the railroad directors were uncertain whether the line would appeal to rail travelers. Having set the trains to run on the right (one of only four lines in the U.K. to do so), they built a boulevard alongside the track for paying pedestrians. Almost from the day it was opened the line was swamped with passenger traffic and the boulevard abandoned.

STEAM PIONEERS
A statue of Matthew Boulton, James Watt and William Murdoch in Birmingham.

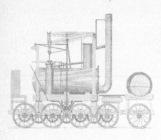

Warrington. (They would be amalgamated into one, the London and North Western, in 1846.) George Stephenson was appointed chief engineer on the Grand Junction (he later passed the work on to his successor Joseph Locke) and son Robert on the London to Birmingham line.

Robert, who was said to have walked the entire length of the line more than twenty times, designed it so that it ran almost level for all 112 miles (180.2 km). The one exception was a short, but steep incline out of Euston, the London station. This was to be overcome with the use of a stout rope and a stationary engine that could haul trains up the slope.

"CIVILIZATION AND IMPROVEMENT"

The builders of the 78-mile (125.5 km) Grand Junction line had obstacles of their own to overcome. Aside from a deep, 2-mile (3.2 km) long cutting at Preston Brook, there were four major viaducts to construct, the most troublesome of which, across the River Weaver at Dutton, took 700 men and two years to build. Yet the Grand Junction was completed in 1837 and the Birmingham to London in 1838, allowing a passenger to board a train at what became the gateway to the north, Euston Station, and travel all the way to Liverpool.

It was, according to Peter Lecount, an assistant engineer on the London to Birmingham line, almost a miracle. Writing in his *Practical Treatise on Railroads* (1835), Lecount described its building as more ambitious than the construction of the pyramids and gave detailed calculations to explain just how. Lecount also provided a wealth of minute detail on the workings of the railroad. These, for example, were the "duties of the engine man": "He should be very attentive of his water-gauge and test it whenever he thinks it recommended by his gauge-cock. He should never use his pumps without turning his pet-cock, and ascertaining by them that every thing is working properly."

However it was the Victorian novelist Charles Dickens who, in *Dombey and Sons*, fleshed out the social scene as a railroad (almost certainly the London to Birmingham) drove its path through the city. "A bran-new Tavern, redolent of fresh mortar and size, and fronting nothing at all, had taken for its sign The Railroad Arms. The Excavators' House of Call had sprung up from a beer shop; and the old established Ham and Beef Shop had become the Railroad Eating House, with a roast leg of pork daily." At the "yet unopened Railroad" there were "frowsy fields, and cow-houses, and dunghills, and dust-heaps, and ditches, and gardens, and summer houses, and carpet-beating grounds, at the very door of the Railroad. Posts, and rails, and old cautions to trespassers, and backs of mean houses and patches of wretched vegetation, stared it out of countenance." And where the finished line began, "from the very core of all this dire disorder, [the line] tailed smoothly away, upon its mighty course of civilisation and improvement."

The promise of "civilisation and improvement," of social change, was not a hollow one. The headmaster of Rugby School, Dr. Thomas Arnold, was reported to have mounted one of Stephenson's bridges crossing the newly opened London to Birmingham line in order to watch the trains. According to the author of *The Life of George Stephenson* (1857), Samuel Smiles, Arnold declared as the trains swept by: "I rejoice to see it, and to think that feudality is gone forever: it is so great a blessing to think that any one evil is really extinct." Clearly "civilisation and improvement" was on track.

BERKHAMSTED STATION
The railroads promised to bring "civilisation and improvement" to the country. They also threatened to ruin the canal trade.

1837

Tsarskoye Selo Railway

Country: Russia

Type: Passenger

Length: 16 miles (25.7 km)

+ **SOCIAL**
+ **COMMERCIAL**
+ **POLITICAL**
+ **ENGINEERING**
+ **MILITARY**

Russia's first railroad was but a brief affair in the late 1830s and it would take almost another fifteen years before a railroad was laid to connect St. Petersburg and Moscow. Yet the little line out of St. Petersburg marked a significant step forward in Tsarist history.

A RICH MAN'S PLAYTHING

There were those in the 1830s who believed the railroad age would bring nothing but trouble. Some were convinced that passing steam engines would blacken the fleeces of grazing sheep. Others thought the speed of the trains would cause irreparable damage to the human organs. Still others expected the average Russian winter to simply freeze the steam age in its tracks.

Two men, an Austrian and a Russian, believed the opposite. They were Franz Anton von Gerstner and Pavel Petrovich Melnikov, engineer and one-time Russian transport minister. What convinced these two men of the viability of rail was their time abroad: both had seen the American railroads in action.

Russia was a difficult country. Like its Baltic neighbors, Finland, Sweden and Norway, long-distance travel involved crossing huge wastes of empty countryside where the rivers froze in winter or dried up in summer. Shifting goods from some outpost on the Caspian Sea to the imperial capital, St. Petersburg, could take up to two years.

Von Gerstner persuaded a dubious Tsar Nicholas I that a 400-mile (643.7 km) railroad from St. Petersburg to Moscow had

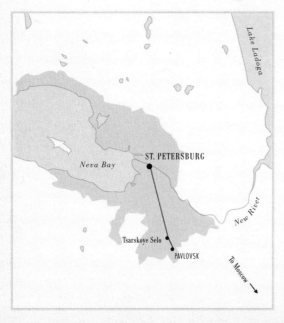

TESTING CONDITIONS
Russia's first foray into the railroad age was accompanied by doubts that any locomotive could operate through the St. Petersburg winter.

potential. As he pointed out, when Ireland turned troublesome the English dealt with the problem by rapidly deploying the troops, sending them by rail to the port of Liverpool. Having suppressed a revolution of his own in 1825, the tsar's interest was aroused. In 1837 he ordered the new line.

One Russian journalist, Nikolai Gretsch, related how the route was built dead straight, but for one sharp bend. It had been summarily drawn across the map by the tsar who accidentally ran the pen over his finger. The engineers were too nervous to point out the error.

Overseen by Melnikov, the line opened in 1851 after a trial railroad between St. Petersburg and Tsarskoye Selo, the imperial palace at Pavlovsk. Work started here in May 1836 with a bevy of English engineers, laborers and Russian soldiers. The line was ready in a year, too early for the steam locomotive that Gerstner had ordered, which was still under construction. The horse, that railroad beast of burden, was left to haul trains through the winter snows until the locomotive arrived. Doubts about steam locomotives operating through the Russian winter were dispelled more quickly than the tsar's qualms about allowing any but the nobility near his railroad. For the rest of the tsar's reign the Tsarskoye Selo Railway remained a rich man's plaything, conveying wealthy Russians to the grand concerts at Pavlovsk to admire artists such as the Viennese composer Johann Strauss II performing his risqué new dance, the waltz.

Gradually the rest of northern Europe began to make tracks of their own. Denmark founded its first railroad in 1847. Norway opened a line from Oslo (then Christiania) to Eidsvoll in 1854, Sweden its 260 miles (418 km) from Stockholm to Gothenburg in 1862 (Sweden eventually built more track per citizen than anywhere else in the world) and Finland from Helsinki to St. Petersburg in 1870. Yet the reactionary Tsar Nicholas I, who boasted of bringing the railroad to the Russians, still presided over a mere 500 miles (805 km) of track in 1855. The little Russian line was, nevertheless, a first step forward in what was to become the world's longest railroad, the Trans-Siberian (see p.164).

STATUS SYMBOL
The railroad line to the imperial palace at Pavlovsk was the exclusive preserve of the rich and famous.

Nicholas I, the follower of Peter I, introduced railroads to Russia.

Commemorative medal struck at the opening of Russia's first railroad

1837

Ferrocarril de Camagüey a Nuevitas

Country: Cuba

Type: Freight

Length: 17 miles (27.5 km)

✦ SOCIAL
✦ **COMMERCIAL**
✦ POLITICAL
✦ ENGINEERING
✦ MILITARY

Spain, suspicious of neighboring France, built its early railroads on a different gauge to prevent any Gallic rail invasion. It resulted, instead, in prolonged economic isolation. Spain's first railroad, however, was in Cuba. It was also the first in Latin America.

AGING IN ISOLATION

After three centuries as a colonial superpower the Spanish empire, by the 1800s, was beginning to look its age. Bids for independence were breaking out across the Spanish fiefdoms, in Mexico, Venezuela, Chile and Peru. The nation's hold on its Latin American colonies was turning into a fistful of dry sand: the tighter she gripped, the faster the sand leaked away.

England, the United States, France, Bavaria, Austria and even Russia had made a start on their railroads. Italy was working on a short, 5-mile (8 km) stretch in Naples and planning a longer route from Milan to Venice. Spain held back and it would not be until 1848 that a 20-mile (32 km) line opened between Barcelona and the little port of Mataró. Since a hardworking Catalan, Miquel Biada, rather than a Castilian, planned the railroad, the line hardly counted as a national victory. When imperial Spain finally did take the railroad plunge it adopted a wider gauge than the rest of Europe in order to prevent trainloads of invading French troops rushing its borders.

The decision to physically isolate their railroads from the rest of the continent (Portugal followed Spain's lead on gauge) would, as it did in

LATIN AMERICA
Cuba was the first South American country to build a railroad. It was designed to serve the sugarcane fields.

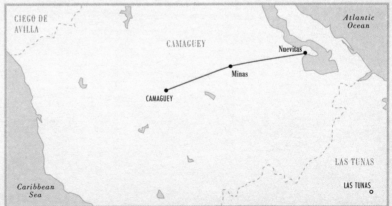

Australia, cause endless problems down the line. (Worse still, many of the connecting lines across the 200,000 square miles (518,000 sq km) of the country were built on an incompatible narrow gauge.) Spain had another reason not to rush into railroads. Crisscrossed by the *sierra* (the word for a mountain range is the same as that for the teeth of a saw), it was the most mountainous country this side of Switzerland. Railroads were going to be a challenge.

SUGAR TRAIN
By 1837 steam locomotives had taken over from horse-drawn freight cars on Cuba's Ferrocarril de Camagüey a Nuevitas.

A CUBAN START

The Spanish Regent, the improbably named Maria Christina of the Two Sicilies, did give her consent to a Spanish railroad in 1834—though it was not one she was likely to travel on, since it lay 4,500 miles (7,242 km) away in Cuba.

Cuba was a slave island. Settled by the Spanish in 1492, its original inhabitants were rapidly wiped out and the island resettled with African slaves. The island had, by now, become one of the world's tobacco and sugar factories, supplying a third of the world's sugar. Elsewhere the early railroads were built to serve mines and quarries: the horse-drawn *Ferrocarril de Camagüey a Nuevitas* was one of the first built to serve agriculture.

Farther west, steam engines were operating a 16-mile (26 km) route from Havana to Bejucal by 1837. By 1843 this line had crossed the island from north to south, reaching the seventeenth-century port of Batabanó.

Railroads represented the first form of rapid mass communication in Latin America. They would become one of the most significant inventions on the continent, opening up Panama in 1855 (the site of the first transcontinental railroad; see p.92), Costa Rica in the 1870s, and El Salvador and Guatemala in the 1880s. The short Ferrocarril de Camagüey a Nuevitas was the sign of things to come.

BLESSED TRAIN
♦
One of those who visited the Ferrocarril de Camagüey a Nuevitas was Miquel Biada. Biada fled to the Americas after the French attacked his hometown, Mataró. Inspired by the Cuban railroad, he returned to his native Catalonia in northeast Spain, with plans of the railroad. Although he raised some capital in London, his railroad was constantly underfunded and regularly sabotaged by hostile villagers. Nevertheless the fourty-four bridges and a tunnel beneath the town of Montgat were built and the line opened with a blessing from the priests and a maiden journey by a train pulled by the locomotive *Mataró*. Biada missed the fun: he had succumbed to pneumonia and died months earlier.

York and North Midland Railway

Country: England

Type: Passenger, Freight

Length: 38 miles (61 km)

Every booming economy attracts its share of saints and sinners. George Hudson, who fell into the latter category, was one of the first to make and lose a railroad fortune.

+ SOCIAL
+ **COMMERCIAL**
+ POLITICAL
+ ENGINEERING
+ MILITARY

THE RAILROAD KING

George Hudson was a familiar figure in London during the 1840s. Since he controlled more than a quarter of the country's railroads, and since the British railroad boom was reaching its zenith, he had plenty of business to attend to. People whispered behind their hands as he passed by: "It's Hudson, the Railroad King."

The Railroad King was an honorable member of the British parliament and a lord mayor. He had been presented to Queen Victoria. But the one-time draper's assistant was also a swindler. In the 1840s he was busy brokering deals. Then, as now, new business involved raising capital (in this case subscriptions), lobbying influential people, especially politicians, and generating plenty of positive publicity. If necessary it also involved paying generous inducements, bribes by any other name, when all else was about to fail.

The son of a Yorkshire yeoman farmer, Hudson was working for a draper in the city of York by the age of fifteen. He was also making eyes at the boss' daughter, and in 1821 he married her and became a partner

NORTH MIDLANDS
The businessmen of York saw commercial advantages in having a railroad that was linked to the Leeds and Selby line and on to London.

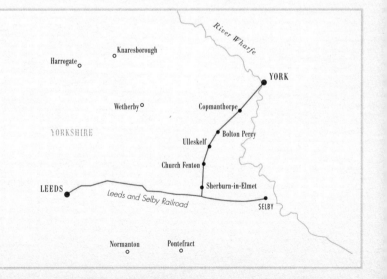

in the firm. Nothing more might have been heard of him, but for the fortuitous death of a great uncle whose bedside he diligently attended and whose £30,000 fortune, and fine house in York he duly inherited.

OFF THE RAILS
George Hudson was a convincing rogue whose railroad empire eventually collapsed. The crash had a serious impact on the economy.

YORKSHIRE PLANS APPROVED

The city of York's wealth had been founded on its medieval wool business, but it was about to profit from the nation's sweet tooth and the ambitious business plans of two York-based Victorian confectioners, Rowntree and Terry. Hudson's ambition was to see York at the center of the regional railroad network. The railroads had already taken his fancy—he had been made treasurer of a local horse-drawn railroad in 1833—when he bumped into George Stephenson at Whitby. Stephenson had come to advise the townspeople of Whitby, an east coast seaport that depended on the whaling trade and that was now endeavoring to keep up with the times. The steep toll road that struggled out of the town and over the Yorkshire moors was inadequate for transporting the whale oil out of the town, and the townspeople planned to replace it with a railroad to nearby Pickering (it would open as Yorkshire's first in 1836), hoping to extend it later to York.

The city fathers in York, meanwhile, realizing the disadvantages of being left behind in the railroad race and the advantages of linking their city with neighboring Leeds, welcomed Hudson on board as an investor. When Hudson delivered George Stephenson as the engineer for their new railroad, the one-time draper's assistant was made chairman of what was to become the York and North Midland Railway Company.

WAITING IN WHITBY
The North Yorkshire town expected its new railroad to improve the local economy.

Its plans were approved in 1837. Apart from the building of thirty or so bridges and having to punch a hole in York's medieval walls for the line, the railroad presented no major construction difficulties Once it opened in 1839, it became the busy route between York and London. Hudson himself became a regular ticket holder, traveling to the capital in a quarter of the time taken by the old stagecoaches.

MIDDLE-CLASS INVESTMENT

Hudson began acquiring shares in other lines, each generating generous dividends. Word went round the City: "Hudson the Railroad King is a good bet." More and more lines were being proposed to Parliament and the flood of investors showed no sign of abating. Queen Victoria had come to the throne in 1837 but nearly lost it, and the child she was expecting, when a gunman tried to assassinate her outside Buckingham Palace in 1840. Now she presided over a nation growing in confidence. Her citizens were keen to invest in the country's economy and the railroads were eager to take their money. Investors, according to Stephenson's biographer Samuel Smiles, were drawn from beyond her lords and landowners and included "merchants and manufacturers, gentry and shopkeepers, clerks in public offices and loungers at the clubs." Even "quiet men" were reproached for "doing injustice to their families by declining to invest." The rising middle class was earning money, and the expectation of making a few more shillings on the side from railroad stocks was irresistible. Like tulip mania in the 1630s, the South Sea scandal of the 1720s and the subprime mortgage crisis of 2005, the railroad bubble grew and grew until a combination of too few financial checks and a rapacious demand for more, caused the bubble to burst. As Samuel Smiles put it, "Folly and knavery were completely in the ascendant."

FIRST TICKET

✦

When his frauds were found out George Hudson fled to Paris, returning to England in 1871 to die. Yet Hudson was responsible for several railroad improvements. In the early days of rail travel, a passenger planning to cross England using several different railroad companies had to buy a different ticket (often from a different station) for each leg of the journey. Hudson helped establish the Railroad Clearing House in 1842 to deal with the problem. The Clearing House also adopted standard Greenwich Mean Time in September 1847. Prior to this, while every station had its own public clock, each gave a marginally different time depending on its distance from Greenwich.

"Amongst the many ill effects of the [railroad] mania, one of the worst was that it introduced a low tone of morality into railroad transactions."
Samuel Smiles, 1859

RAIL STOCKS CRASH

All this time Hudson had expanded his railroad empire or acquired new lines on the basis of his reputation: the flagging Eastern Counties Railroad, struggling to make money in the near-saturated market, drew up a rescue plan that relied on recruiting Hudson to the board. It was a poor choice. By now Hudson was using money from new investors to pay existing shareholders, selling his stock at inflated

RAILROAD STOCKS
The railroad builders relied on share issues to fund their enterprises. The Hudson scandal caused a temporary loss of confidence.

prices to companies he already owned, and ladling the cream of the funds into his personal accounts. It was unsustainable. When investors took a closer look at the account books it was clear the books were cooked. Hudson was revealed as less of a railroad king than a railroad rogue.

The York and North Midland Railway survived the crash while their previous chairman entered the annals of history as a railroad fraudster. He was neither the first nor the last. In 1856 Irish financier John Sadleir shot himself on London's Hampstead Heath after defrauding investors with his "Swedish Railroad Company." In the 1870s, during the building of the first American transcontinental railroad, U.S. congressman Oakes Ames was caught distributing shares of stock in Crédit Mobilier, the French banking company, together with some generous bribes to other congressmen. In 1873, a scandal involving Canada's transcontinental forced Canadian prime minister John A. Macdonald to resign. For Sadleir, Oakes Ames and Hudson, the anonymous *Spiritual Railroad*, published in Scotland in the 1850s, would serve as an apt epitaph:

The line to Heaven by Christ was made,
With heavenly truth the rails are laid,
From Earth to Heaven it doth extend,
And eternal is the end.
Come then, poor sinner, now's the time,
At any station on the line,
If you repent, and turn from sin,
The train will stop and take you in.

DOWNFALL
In the end Hudson could not even afford to travel third class (below) on the York and North Midland.

Great Western Railway

Country: England

Type: Passenger, Freight

Length: 152 miles (245 km) in 1841

Isambard Kingdom Brunel masterminded England's Great Western Railway, designed Bristol's iconic Clifton Suspension Bridge and was the brains behind three ocean-going steamships including the S.S. *Great Britain*. He was an engineering genius who had a profound effect on rail history. But even a genius can make mistakes.

+ **SOCIAL**

+ **COMMERCIAL**

+ **POLITICAL**

+ **ENGINEERING**

+ **MILITARY**

NOT THE CHEAPEST, BUT THE BEST

"The time is not far off when we shall be able to take our coffee and write whilst going noiselessly and smoothly at 45 mph [72 kph]," wrote Isambard Kingdom Brunel in his diary. One hundred and fifty years later travelers did indeed sip their coffees and handwrite their business reports (the ubiquitous laptop had yet to appear) on his railroad. Speeds, however, were well in excess of 45 mph (72 kph).

Like his Western Railroad, Isambard Kingdom Brunel was often described as "great." A familiar photograph of the engineer pictured him beside the launching chains of his steamship S.S. *Great Eastern*, stovepipe hat clamped on his head, cigar clamped between his teeth and hands thrust in his pockets. He exuded a steely greatness and yet there

BRISTOL BOUND
Since England's western seaport was the shipping link to America, a London railroad link was considered essential.

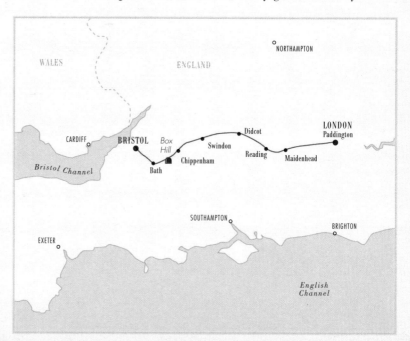

were those who took the Lord's name in vain and cursed the famous Brunel for his choice of gauge as they were thrown into the turmoil of changing for the Birmingham train at Gloucester Station in the 1840s.

The engineer who masterminded the London to Bristol railroad, authorized by Parliament in the mid-1830s, was determined to provide a railroad that was "not the cheapest, but the best." Before he began construction he rode to Manchester to see Ellen Hulme, a young woman who was, according to his diary, his "oldest and most constant" love. (Too poor to marry, Brunel concentrated instead on his career: "My profession is after all my only fit wife.") The journey to Manchester gave him the opportunity to travel along Stephenson's Liverpool and Manchester line and, although he had the greatest respect for his rival Robert Stephenson, he was unimpressed. As the train rattled along he took out his notebook and attempted, unsuccessfully, to scribe a circle freehand. "One day," he thought: "Coffee, writing, speed …"

A WIDER GAUGE

The Great Western Railway was to run from London to the nation's biggest and best port, Bristol. Ships from America sailed up the Avon Gorge to the docks—Brunel had already designed the suspension bridge that would cross the Gorge. As Bristol's dealings with America were being challenged by the Port of Liverpool and the new Liverpool and Manchester railroad, Brunel was given the job of engineering the Great Western line into Bristol.

EXPRESS LOCOMOTIVE
The eight-wheeled *Great Western* was designed as an express engine for Brunel's railroad. The early locomotives were less successful than the railroad itself.

That he survived into his twenties was a matter of luck. The son of a successful French engineer, Sir Marc Isambard Brunel (Marc married Sophia Kingdom, hence his son's unusual second name), Isambard joined his father on a difficult project to tunnel beneath the River Thames in London. The roof of the tunnel was highly unstable. Eventually Joseph Aspdin, a manufacturer of Portland cement, would persuade Brunel to use his cement, twice the price of the ordinary "Roman" cement, to repair the tunnel. According to Aspdin's advertisements "This cement has been proved for upwards of twenty years in the Thames Tunnel to resist the action of water." But in January 1828 a partial collapse flooded the tunnel, drowning six men and almost killing young Brunel.

> **"Your railroad mounds, vaster than the walls of Babylon; your railroad stations, vaster than the temple of Ephesus, and innumerable."**
>
> *John Ruskin*, Traffic, *1866*

When he moved to the Great Western Railway, Brunel decided immediately to have the rails set as far apart as was practicable. A wide gauge would produce a more comfortable ride, broader carriages and an altogether superior public railroad. Arbitrarily he chose 7 feet (2.13 m), almost 50 percent wider than the Stephenson Gauge. It was a mistake.

TUNNELS COME AT A COST

The estimated cost of the Great Western was £2.5m. A considerable part of that was allocated to pay off bickering landowners whose estates lay in its path. One of the more vociferous, John Keate, was headmaster of England's premier private school, Eton. Keate, an enthusiast for the practice of birching the boys (beating them across their backsides with a

LUCKY ESCAPE
Brunel's father, Sir Marc Brunel, engineered the Thames Tunnel in which his son almost died in 1828. Trains started running through the tunnel in 1865.

bundle of twigs), was concerned, mysteriously, that the railroad would "interfere with the discipline of the school." He even appealed to former pupil and future prime minister William Gladstone to intercede. (Gladstone, however, favored rail. In 1844 he even introduced a system of cheap rail services, dubbed the Parliamentary Trains.)

The line went ahead. Brunel himself surveyed the line, sometimes with his solicitor, Jeremiah Osborne. When it came to dealing with the major obstacle of Box Hill near Bath, Brunel, drawing on his experience with the Thames Tunnel, pitched in with his 4,000 laborers. He earned their respect, and the nick-name Little Giant, as they ground their way through the oolite stone with pick, shovel and a hundred tons of the "black powder" (gunpowder) a week. When Brunel was shown the names of all the workers treated for their injuries at nearby Bath hospital he remarked: "I think it is a very small list considering the heavy works and the immense amount of powder used."

The tunneling teams met finally beneath Box Hill. The margin of error between the two tunnels measured no more than the top joint of Brunel's thumb. He was said to have slipped the ring from his finger and ceremonially presented it to the foreman. Rumors circulated that the tunnel, completed in 1841, had been so designed that on April 9, Brunel's birthday, it was possible to sight the rising sun right through the 1.8-mile (2,937 m) tunnel. The theory has never been proven.

When the final construction bills came in, the Great Western Railway had cost three times the original estimate—partly because Brunel insisted on serious architectural designs for the most utilitarian items, from tunnel heads to bridges, and partly because his engineering abilities created a line that ran so straight and true (it was dubbed "Brunel's billiard table") that it was still in good service well over a century later.

Brunel went on to experiment with, and lose money on, an "atmospheric" railroad (the train was propelled by a stationary engine and air pressure rather than a locomotive) in Devon. The early trials were not successful. However, the Great Western acquired the track, pressing ahead until it reached Penzance in Cornwall. For a while it was the longest

FLYING DUTCHMAN

For many years the fastest train in the world, the *Flying Dutchman*, was drawn along the Great Western Railway by one of Daniel Gooch's *Iron Duke* class locomotives. The *Iron Duke* took its name from the Duke of Wellington while the *Flying Dutchman* was named, not after the legendary ship that restlessly sailed the oceans, but Britain's most famous nineteenth-century thoroughbred racehorse. The train itself trailed a plume of steam through the countryside between Paddington Station in London and Exeter, over 190 miles (306 km) away in the West Country train at an average speed of 53 mph (85 kph) in 1851.

PADDINGTON STATION
Like the rest of the station, the wrought-iron and glass roof was designed by Brunel. The London terminus has served the West Country for over 175 years.

railroad route in Britain. Promoted somewhat fancifully as the Cornish Riviera, it was imbued with all the romance of sea, sun, sand and steam.

In its formative years the directors of the Great Western had questioned Brunel about how their broad-gauge trains would transfer to lines on the Stephenson Gauge. He declared it to be a trifling matter and left the details of these seamless transitions vague. In the event they were almost unworkable. One broad-gauge spur met the Birmingham train at Gloucester, and magazine illustrators were soon portraying distressed mothers clutching their offspring as their menfolk, fighting to hold on to the luggage, were swept along in a storm of porters and panic toward the connecting train.

The problem prompted a parliamentary commission and, in 1892, the universal adoption of the Stephenson Gauge. On May 21 that year, over 4,000 gangers and platelayers, the men who maintained the line, gathered to replace the rail. Two days later they had successfully, but expensively, relaid 177 miles (285 km) of line in time for the Paddington to Plymouth night mail train to make its scheduled run.

RAIN, STEAM AND DREAMS

The painter J.M.W. Turner was already an established artist when in 1844 he depicted Brunel's work in *Rain, Steam and Speed—The Great Western Railway*. It showed an early locomotive, its blazing firebox open, advancing across the recently completed three-arch viaduct that Brunel had designed and built across the River Thames at Maidenhead. In the foreground a barely discernible hare races away before the locomotive. This and Turner's swirling, fiery colors suggested an artist coming to terms with a new age of steam power, and the impressionistic painting proved to be one of the most significant of all railroad paintings.

The last days of broad gauge on the Great Western line, like the final decades of the steam age, saw railroad sidings jammed with redundant locomotives and rolling stock, among them the old *Iron Duke* class express locomotives (see box on p.63). They were the work of a Northumbrian engineer, Daniel Gooch, a friend of George Stephenson and eventually the chairman of the Great Western. Gooch was only twenty-one when he wrote to Brunel asking to become his locomotive assistant. Gooch stayed loyal to the Brunel's railroad throughout his working life, and he was a genius when it came to designing successful and speedy locomotives. Brunel's engineering capabilities seemed to fall short when it came to choosing good, strong locomotives. Many bore promising names—*Premier, Thunderer, Vulcan, Hurricane*—but their performance was often lackluster. Gooch designed several locomotives and helped turn the little Wiltshire hamlet of Swindon into a major railroad town. The year 1864 saw Gooch on board the Brunel-designed S.S. *Great Eastern* with Thomas Brassey and one William Barber, laying the first transatlantic cable between Britain and America. Brunel did not live to see it. He died in his early fifties, it was said of overwork, in 1859.

Despite his occasional misjudgments, Brunel was a visionary. He saw his palatial Paddington Station in London (it cost an additional £1m) as the first stop in a steam-driven journey from London to New York. He foresaw the day when passengers could disembark at Exeter or Bristol and travel on across the Atlantic aboard one of his steamships (he built the S.S. *Great Britain*, the S.S. *Great Western* and S.S. *Great Eastern*). As he predicted, by 1840 passengers would travel the 200 miles (320 km) from London to Exeter at over 40 mph (65 kph).

MAIDENHEAD BRIDGE
J.M.W. Turner painted this Great Western train coming away from London.

<table>
<tr><td>

1841

</td><td>

Leicester and Loughborough Railway

</td></tr>
</table>

Country: England

Type: Passenger

Length: 12 miles (19 km)

The railroad age offered everyone the opportunity to broaden their horizons and travel, often for the first time in their lives, away from home. It was Thomas Cook from Leicester who was the first to exploit its potential.

SAFE AND SOBER

In the 1850s, as a new railroad was making its way through her estate in Monmouthshire, Wales, the lady of the manor, Augusta Hall, shocked her tenants by closing all the pubs. Augusta, like many in the mid-1800s, was a staunch supporter of the temperance movement. Australia, New Zealand, America and Britain were all seeing a rise in the consumption of booze. In Britain the biggest increase in alcohol consumption coincided with the rapid expansion of the railroads from 1850 to 1876. It had an inevitable impact on railroad safety. "Among the most frequent minor accidents of railroad travelling," wrote a correspondent for *Cassell's Family Magazine*, "are those arising from leaving the train while the carriages are in motion, and those due to the thoughtless habit of throwing open the doors even before the platform is reached." Among the culprits were "nervous, hysterical women" who "attempt to leap from the carriages" and careless drunks.

+ **SOCIAL**
+ **COMMERCIAL**
+ **POLITICAL**
+ **ENGINEERING**
+ **MILITARY**

NORTHEAST
The short stretch of line between Leicester and Loughborough played a pioneering role in the history of mass tourism thanks to Thomas Cook.

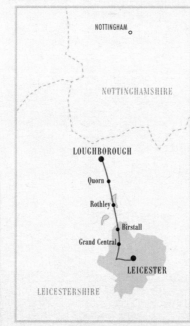

No such danger attended the 500 or so individuals who traveled on the first public railroad excursion (it could be described as the first package tour) between Leicester and Loughborough in July 1841. All were members of the local temperance movement and each had paid a shilling to a Leicester Baptist who had privately chartered the train.

He was Thomas Cook, a cabinetmaker turned preacher, who had himself taken a pledge of abstinence in 1833. Born in the Derbyshire village of Melbourne (the

Australian city was named after another of its famous residents, Viscount Melbourne), Cook had come up with the idea of bringing trains and the temperance movement together as he walked the 15 miles (24 km) from his home in Market Harborough to his future home, Leicester, the hosiery capital of England.

Railroads, Cook realized, widened the human horizon. Who would not prefer to travel to new places aboard a modern train than stay at home drowning their sorrows in gin and strong beer? Cook was not alone in associating temperance and train travel. Quakers such as Edward Pease attributed the exemplary safety record of the Stockton and Darlington Railroad to the management's refusal to sell intoxicating liquor at their stations.

So Cook chartered his train from Leicester's Campbell Street Station to the pretty environs of Loughborough and provided his sober families with a visit to a stately home, a cricket match, bouts of archery and musical entertainment from what were described as "powerful brass bands." He did so again the following year and the year after, reaching a special agreement with the railroad company to run yet more temperance society and Sunday-school group outings further afield to Liverpool and Scotland. His business acumen let him down at one point and Cook was forced to declare bankruptcy, but, by the time of London's Great Exhibition in 1851, he had recovered his composure and presumably his credit and was chartering Exhibition Excursion trains from Leicester.

WIDENING HORIZONS
Thomas Cook took full advantage of the expanding rail network to promote his business interests, chartering trains at home and abroad.

TOURS AND TRAVELERS' CHECKS

Cook was a cautious man. However, the rapid expansion of the railroads allowed him to risk a few foreign tours with trips to Paris and, in the 1860s, several "grand circle" tours of Switzerland, Italy, Egypt and even America. When his son, John, reached an age when they could call their company Thomas Cook & Son, the two men opened shop in London. In 1874 the shop not only sold railroad tour tickets, but guidebooks, travel clothing, hotel coupons and "circular notes," which could be redeemed for cash while abroad. American Express launched their own version of circular notes, traveler's checks, in 1891.

Thomas and John were very different in character. While Thomas maintained his temperance links (he ran a small temperance hotel above the London shop), John was launching a new venture: railroad tours of the American Civil War battlefields. War tourism was not unheard of—Mark Twain would lead a party around the ragged battlements of Sevastopol in the Crimea (see p.94) some years later—but it was a departure for the company. Thomas decided to take a back seat and reluctantly stepped down from the company, retiring to Melbourne. (He was refused the tenancy of Melbourne Hall, former home of Viscount Melbourne, on the grounds that he was nouveau riche.)

John Cook and his own sons took the travel business into overdrive, arranging tours of the Middle East and opening overseas offices in Australia and New Zealand. John died of dysentery in 1899 and the company was eventually sold to the Wagons-Lits Company (see p.103). Later, when Wagons-Lits was seized by the Germans during World War II, Thomas Cook & Son was nationalized by the British government and became part of British Railways. What had started life as a day out for non-drinkers had turned into a worldwide, railroad-based business.

BRIGHTON BOUND
In Charles Rossiter's
To Brighton and Back
for Three and Sixpence
(1859) passengers were
pictured escaping to the
seaside by train.

DAY TRIPPERS

Thomas Cook's customers were not the only ones enjoying an occasional day out on the railroads. Since travel was still the prerogative of the rich, few working people expected to take a vacation day in the 1850s. But the railroads were sweeping in with social change. Rail companies across Europe started operating special services to seaside towns, and the towns responded by reorganizing themselves to make the most of the new business.

When the railroads reached the French Riviera in 1864, places such as Nice blossomed; when it reached Monte Carlo in 1870 the population of the principality of Monaco doubled. The story was the same in northern France at seaside resorts such as Deauville and Trouville, while the line to Quimper in Brittany in 1862 attracted so many painters, their palates jaded by city life, that an artists'

SEASIDE DELIGHTS
Blackpool owed its origins as a resort to the arrival of the railroads.

colony was established around nearby Pont-Aven. There was such a stirring of painters from Paris, America, Canada and England that it drove away the one who proved to be the most famous, Paul Gauguin. He left the artistic crowd for the little hamlet of Le Pouldu before heading off to Tahiti.

In 1844 the British prime minister William Gladstone introduced a standard, low minimum fare. It opened rail travel not only to the village squire, but also to his gamekeeper and housekeeper. In England the

"In England and Wales since 1857–61, drunkenness has increased 36 percent."
Joseph Rowntree, "a great authority on temperance," Harmsworth Magazine, *1899*

railroads founded the fortunes of seaside towns such as Blackpool, Southport, Eastbourne, Torquay, Weston-Super-Mare, Barry in Wales and the biggest beneficiary of them all, Brighton, the south coast seaside town and former playground of George, Prince of Wales. The train traffic was not always welcome. One provincial newspaper, the *Bury and Sutton Post*, reported in 1867 that when a train stopped at Ipswich, carrying 600 "of the lowest class and bettering men," passengers removed everything from the counter including a six-pound cheese, buns and biscuits with "no coin . . . paid by the hungry pleasure seekers."

Some seaside towns, such as Saltburn and Hunstanton, were the creation of the railroads themselves. The entrepreneur Henry Le Strange persuaded a group of investors to sink their spare cash into a new line from Kings Lynn, Norfolk, to the East Anglian seaside village of Hunstanton. The Lynn and Hunstanton Railroad reaped profits for its shareholders from the moment it, and Le Strange's commodious New Inn, opened in 1862. (It helped that Queen Victoria had purchased the nearby Sandringham estate a year earlier.)

FROM SEAS TO SPAS

The railroads did not confine their day trips to the booming bathing resorts. As in France and Germany, no spa town could match the competition unless it boasted a railroad station. There was Cheltenham and Bath Spas in the 1840s, Woodhall Spa in Lincolnshire in the 1850s and Matlock Bath in the 1870s. Even the little Welsh hamlet of Llandrindod Wells was propelled into the excursion age by the arrival of the Central Wales Railroad in 1865. When the railroad line from Worcester reached the spa town of Malvern in 1859, the number of day trippers soared to a barely manageable 5,000. Among the more distinguished visitors were Alfred, Lord Tennyson, Charles and Kate Dickens and Florence Nightingale. They were drawn by the curative powers of the "great douche," "the direct descendent of Niagara," which, according to John Leech from *Punch* magazine, was "capable of launching down upon the body in a straight unbroken column of water one hogshead per minute, and with such force . . . it knocked me clean over like a ninepin." The brainchild of two physicians, James Wilson and James Gully, it continued to pour down therapeutically on the portly and over-indulgent until Gully was involved in a murder scandal involving his lover, Florence Ricardo, and the poisoning of her husband. The murder remained unsolved and, despite its rail route, the spa's reputation took a battering.

WATER WORKS
Spa towns across Europe benefited from the arrival of the railroads and those with no station faced an uncertain future.

INTO THE HILLS

The interwar years saw another breed of vacationer taking to the trains: the outdoor enthusiast. The post-World War I craze for camping, cycling and hill walking saw the railroads parking special camping cars on scenic sidings and vying with one another to be the most bicycle-friendly.

In the 1920s thousands would set off from Manchester's London Road Station to take the train to Hayfield and hike the hills around Kinder Scout. In April 1932 policemen on the lookout for radical rambler Benny Rothman swelled the crowds heading for the Pennine peaks. News of a planned public trespass over the private grouse moor on Kinder Scout had been chalked on the pavements of Manchester and Leeds, and Benny was regarded as one of the ringleaders. He eluded the police and with a crowd of ramblers made it up Kinder Scout after a few scuffles with the gamekeepers. A police squad later grabbed him and five others as they tried to reach Hayfield station and the train home. Benny Rothman was given a four-month jail sentence, but the point of public access for all had been very publicly made. It seemed that the railroads would transform every level of society. The railroads opened up the countryside to everyone. The philanthropist John Ruskin had predicted such a state of affairs back in the 1870s when he foresaw the railroads tipping tourists into the Lake District like "coals from a sack," causing a rash of "taverns and skittle grounds" and "a beach of broken ginger beer bottles." The visitors' minds were "no more improved by contemplating the scenery of such a lake than of Blackpool," declared Ruskin. Doubtless he turned in his grave when the 1930s saw yet another new attraction appear at the end of the railroad line: the holiday camp. In the postwar era, and before the advent of mass car ownership, the railroads carried thousands away from the cities to sample the delights of Hayling Island, Skegness, and Douglas on the Isle of Man. It was over a century since Thomas Cook's first railroad excursion and railroad tourism was proving to be as unstoppable as the tides.

ROUND THE WORLD

✦

In 1865 Thomas Cook set up railroad tours in North America covering 4,000 miles (6,437 km) of rail. Seven years later, after the opening of America's transcontinental railroad and the Suez Canal, he led a small party on a round-the-world trip. They crossed the Atlantic by steamship and America by rail before sailing to Japan, China, Singapore, Ceylon and India. Thomas carried on through Egypt and Palestine before returning to England through Turkey, Greece, Italy and France. The trip, which became an annual event, took 222 days.

Sheffield, Ashton under Lyne and Manchester Railway

Country: England

Type: Tunnel

Length: 3 miles (4.8 km)

In the rough and ready world of railroad building, the welfare of the workers received short shrift. But the deaths of the men struggling to build a railroad tunnel through the rugged British Pennines exposed one company's shocking disregard for the safety of its workers.

+ SOCIAL

+ COMMERCIAL

+ POLITICAL

+ ENGINEERING

+ MILITARY

RUNNING RISKS WITH WOODHEAD TUNNEL

When the early transport ships bearing British miscreants to New South Wales landed in Australia, hundreds had perished during the voyage. The prisoners, including a few of those disreputable railroad laborers, notorious for their hard drinking and fighting, were so crammed into the ships' holds that they died.

The British government ordered that, in future, the charterers be held responsible for the convicts' well-being. It produced immediate results. The transporters, paid a bonus for every prisoner safely landed, now took care of their cargo. Yet the principle that contractors should be responsible for the safety of their workers received short shrift in Victorian boardrooms. What use had a mill owner for some eight-year-old girl who, through her own carelessness, lost her hand in a machine? Why should a rail company be responsible for a worker's family when the man died, dead drunk, in a tunnel collapse? And why should the shareholder, risking his capital on such a brave enterprise as

PENNINE WAY
The Woodhead Tunnel lay on the Sheffield, Ashton-under-Lyne and Manchester Railway built between 1841 and 1845 across the challenging terrain of the Pennines.

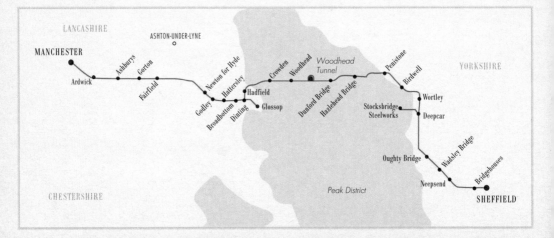

the Sheffield, Ashton under Lyne and Manchester Railway Company's plan to tunnel under the Pennines, have to coddle workers who were being paid to do their job?

As Wellington Purdon, assistant engineer on the tunnel, told a government inquiry when asked if it was not wiser to use safety fuses while blasting rock: "Perhaps it is: but it is attended with such a loss of time, and the difference is so very small, I would not recommend the loss of time for the sake of all the extra lives it would save." His comments revealed how little the railroads valued their laborers. It should have changed the course of industrial history. Instead, Parliament shelved the committee's report.

In 1845 the first train through the completed Woodhead Tunnel was met by a celebration of dignitaries and the few railroad laborers left behind after the rest had tramped off to work on the next railroad. The social reformer Edwin Chadwick did not celebrate. According to his calculations, the attrition rate at Woodhead was "nearly equal to the proportionate casualties of . . . a severe battle." With 32 killed and 140 injured, the casualty rate was higher than in the Battles of Waterloo.

The beaming and bearded Chadwick, his thinning hair plastered over his balding crown, was a Victorian campaigner who counted men such as socialist John Stuart Mill among his friends. He was also friendly with several doctors. Crucially they included a Manchester surgeon, John Roberton, who in his turn was friendly with the surgeon Henry Pomfret. The workers on the Woodhead Tunnel paid to keep their own doctor on hand. Pomfret was their man.

> **"I would not recommend the loss of time for the sake of all the extra lives it would save."**
> *Engineer Wellington Purdon to a Commons Select Committee, 1846*

UNDERGROUND
Brunel's Box Tunnel
at Bath was the longest
in Britain until the
Woodhead Tunnel
was blasted through
the Pennine hills.

The treeless hamlet of Woodhead lay in one of the wilder Peak District dales on the Pennines, the stony spine separating northeast England from the northwest. The cotton industry had seen the population of these gritstone villages expand as weavers set up business. In 1839 the cobbled streets rang with the tramp of boots, heralding the arrival of the Scots, Irish, Lancashire and Yorkshire railroad navvies, come to blast their way through the Woodhead Hill. The tunnel, at 3 miles (5 km), was going to be Britain's longest, relegating Isambard Kingdom Brunel's Box Tunnel at Bath to second place.

The chief engineer and Willington Purdon't superior was Charles B. Vignoles who was also a shareholder in the railroad company. When the contract ran over time and over budget, the job bankrupted him. The pioneering engineer Joseph Locke took over as more than a thousand laborers hewed away at the muck and mud from seven different shafts, one at each end and five vertical shafts from above, with pick, shovel and explosives. It was obvious to Locke that the only way to complete the project was to drive the men like animals and, if questioned, lie.

A bevy of anonymous slate headstones still stands like an unwelcome congregation at one end of the little chapel graveyard in Woodhead. They mark the graves of some of the people whom Dr. Pomfret failed to save. The job had taken six years. When it came to an end Dr. Pomfret talked to Dr. Roberton.

THE NAVVY

✦

In U.S. parlance the "navvy" was a steam-driven shovel, the mechanical machine that laid out much of the early railroad routes. In Europe the navvies, originally the canal builders or "navigators," were the seasoned laborers who gathered in their thousands to build the railroads. Farm laborers and office clerks, tinkers and Gypsies, they came from every walk of life. From the cold hills of County Clare in Ireland, where the potato famine was destroying whole communities, to the Scottish Highlands, where the land clearances had driven men away to tramp for work on the railroads, the best recruiting agency by far was poverty.

Dr. Roberton talked to Edwin Chadwick and, in January 1846 Chadwick delivered a paper to the Manchester Statistical Society: *The Demoralization and Injuries Occasioned by Want of Proper Regulations of Labourers Engaged in the Construction and Works of Railways.* Despite the exhausting title, the contents were as volatile as navvies' explosives. They revealed how injured men were forced to fend for themselves, how most workers lived in homemade hovels (occasioning an outbreak of cholera) through the worst of the Pennine winters. Chadwick exposed the practice of not paying wages for several weeks and then paying them in public bars. The pubs encouraged the navvies to drink their wages, while delayed payments forced them onto the *truck* system, a version of the company store principle that kept the men and their families in

BACK TO BASICS
A pick, a shovel and a powerful pair of forearms were the navvy's natural tools.

debted to the railroad company. (The truck system was already outlawed in Britain, but the statute, laid down before the railroad rush, had not specified railroad workers.) Chadwick showed how the reputation of the average worker as a feckless, reckless drunk was a direct result of the industry plying him with booze instead of providing him with proper food and housing.

The rail company and the engineers denied the charges against them. Nevertheless, the government committee of inquiry in July 1846 recommended extending the Truck Act to the railroads, making the companies responsible for the health, welfare and accommodation of their navvies and, most important of all, putting the liability for deaths or injuries on the company. The Members of Parliament also insisted that men should be paid weekly, and in cash, not in tokens for the truck. The report was never even debated.

Chadwick's friend John Stuart Mill declared in his *Dissertations and Discussion*, 1859: "When society requires to be rebuilt, there is no use in attempting to rebuild it on the old plan." The railroads promised to meet the old ways head on, and to bring about a new age and social change. However, although no railroad man was censured over the Woodhead Tunnel scandal, Chadwick's efforts were not in vain. His correlation between losses on the battlefield and those on the railroads caught the public imagination and in future, when navvies were killed, the press was quick to take up the story. The same could not be said of railroad builders in India.

Paris to Le Havre Railway

Country: France

Type: Passenger, Freight

Length: 142 miles (228 km)

+ **SOCIAL**
+ **COMMERCIAL**
+ **POLITICAL**
+ **ENGINEERING**
+ **MILITARY**

Writers took a while to adjust to the era of the train, but once Leo Tolstoy had thrown his heroine Anna Karenina under a locomotive, authors and filmmakers made the most of this dynamic new vehicle for adventure. The Paris to Le Havre line is a prime example of railroad's influence in the artistic consciousness.

GARE SAINT-LAZARE

"From the depths of this lake of darkness there emerged sounds—giant gasps of breath like someone dying of a fever, sudden sharp whistles like the screams of women being violated, the dismal wailing of horns and the rumble of traffic in nearby streets." (Zola, *La Bête Humaine*.)

Penny dreadfuls and dime novels, with their tales of romance, derring-do and macabre goings-on, traditionally found shelf space on station bookshop shelves. However, in the Victorian age one of the most popular sources of fiction was magazines such as *La Vie Populaire*. Charles Dickens and Arthur Conan Doyle (whose characters, Sherlock Holmes and Doctor Watson often relied on railroad miscellanea, especially timetables, to solve their cases) both had their work serialized in magazines.

Passengers who settled in their carriage seats with a copy of *La Vie* in November 1889 were looking forward to a sensational new serialization set on the Paris to Le Havre railroad line. It was *La Bête Humaine*

TERROR TRAIN
Émile Zola's story of murder and mayhem on the Paris to Le Havre express, *La Bête Humaine*, captured the French public's imagination.

(The Beast Within) by celebrity novelist Émile Zola. The author had researched his material with care. Technical information included his locomotive, *La Lison*, named, like many French engines, after the towns in the districts served by that railroad; the salaries of rail staff; the coupé compartments (end carriage compartments with seating on one side only); and, an important detail for a discreet murder to occur, the absence of corridors on the trains. While railroad historians glean useful material from *La Bête Humaine*,

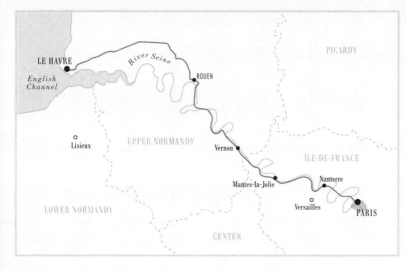

Zola's readers in 1890 relished a ripping yarn and some impressionistic prose: "A mist had gathered. Everything was still wet from the rain; here and there a red light pierced the night like a splash of blood..."

Zola's story of sexual abuse, adultery, murder and suicide on the trains was set between 1869 and 1870, when the Compagnie des Chemins de Fer de l'Ouest operated trains out of the Gare Saint-Lazare in Paris (which, curiously, Zola avoided naming) to northern Brittany and Normandy. Zola drew on contemporary events: a series of unsolved murders in Victorian London, committed against prostitutes by Jack the Ripper; and another murder, this time of a Département prefect on the Cherbourg to Paris train in 1886. He was also inspired by the work of his friends in the Impressionist movement who had recently taken a particular interest in the trains traveling north from the Gare Saint–Lazare.

The station stood with designer Adolphe Jullien's huge iron structure, the Pont de l'Europe, bridging its tracks. In 1877 Claude Monet strode purposefully into the station and placed his easel upon the platform. His friend, the painter Gustave Caillebotte, who had an apartment nearby and who had himself painted a portrait of the Pont de l'Europe, planned to fund a new exhibition for the artists who had taken to calling themselves Impressionists. The exhibitors would include Camille Pissarro, who frequently returned to the theme of railroads, Édouard Manet (who had also

ANNA KARENINA

✦

Leo Tolstoy strove to portray contemporary Russia in his novels. When it came to his 1878 *Anna Karenina* he made the railroads of the day central to his story, even down to the heroine's suicide: "She descended the steps that led from the water tank to the rails, and stopped close to the passing train. And exactly at the moment when the space between the wheels drew level with her . . . dropped on her hands under the truck." Ironically Tolstoy himself died beside the railroad. He was suffering from pneumonia when he collapsed and died at Astapovo Railroad Station in 1910. The station was later renamed Leo Tolstoy.

painted the Gare), Edgar Degas, Pierre-Auguste Renoir and Monet, all exponents of the *plein-air* (outdoor) movement. Monet needed more material and he bustled into the Gare Saint Lazare, ordering bemused staff to move a locomotive so that he might better capture the plume of steam framed by the canopy, or to reposition a train for the sake of his composition. No one knew who he was until seven of his eleven station paintings opened at the Impressionist exhibition later that year. Afterward station staff could proudly tell their passengers: "Yes, Madame, we assisted Monsieur Monet with his work."

Honoré Daumier captured a more intimate railroad scene with *The Third-Class Carriage*: a grandmother resigned to the journey, her wicker basket in her lap, sat with a slumped, sleeping lad on one side and her daughter cradling a slumbering toddler on the other. The woman behind, people-watching as rail travelers will, steals a furtive glance. Daumier produced his painting in the 1860s, around the time that William Frith executed one of the most commercially successful railroad paintings of all time. It was also one of the most expensive. Frith unveiled his portrait of Paddington, *The Railway Station*, in London in 1862. He had faithfully rendered life at the racetrack in his *Derby Day* in 1858, and *The Railway Station* was its much-anticipated successor. Now, with the aid of dozens of models, photographs and a draftsman paid to paint the tedious structural details, Frith had, according to *The Times*, produced a masterpiece. "The subject is typical of our age of iron and steam," remarked their correspondent, adding, "The price of Mr Frith's picture . . . is only possible in a period of bold speculation . . . bringing that public and their shillings to a focus." It did so, too:

ECONOMY CLASS
Honoré Daumier pictured a scene of weary resignation in his painting *The Third-Class Carriage* (1862–1864). The artist took pleasure in portraying railroad travel.

more than 21,000 people paid their twelve pence to see the portrait, to marvel at the panorama—the gamekeeper marshaling his dogs, the gentleman arguing over the cabbie's fare, the wedding party preparing for departure and two London policemen arresting a criminal. Frith's business partner, Louis Victor Flatlow, was pictured as an early train fan deep in conversation with the driver of the locomotive, the *Iron Duke* class *Sultan*. All human life, as it was on the railroads, was here.

As nineteenth-century printmakers such as New York's Nathaniel Currier and James Ives added the railroads to their list of subjects (each print was hand-colored on the assembly-line principle, one girl to each color), railroad companies, as mindful of their image as any twenty-first-century multinational, started to pay artists to improve their brand. Twentieth-century artists included the English Terence Cuneo (his statue would be erected outside London's Waterloo Station) and the Russian-born Adolphe Mouron, who signed his Bauhaus-influenced posters such as the *Chemin de Fer du Nord* ("*Vitesse—luxe—confort*": Speed—Luxury—Comfort) as Cassandre. Frank Pick, head of London Transport, commissioned artists such as Man Ray, Graham Sutherland (who started his working life as an unhappy apprentice engineer on the Midland Railroad at Derby) and Paul Nash.

Cartoonists such as Rowland Emett, Fougasse and the contraption illustrator W. Heath Robinson (England's Rube Goldberg) all produced railroad-related work. After the demise of the steam locomotive,

RAILROAD TIMETABLES

✦

"Look up the trains in Bradshaw," the fictional detective, Sherlock Holmes, tells his assistant Dr. Watson in *The Copper Beeches Case*. The Lancashire printer George Bradshaw started printing railroad timetables in 1838 when there were few railroads around. His *Monthly Railway Guide* continued in print into the early 1960s. Based on information taken from the advance printers' proofs of railroad company timetables, the *Guide* became a market leader despite its disclaimer, the ultimate cop-out clause for any timetable: "The proprietors do not hold themselves responsible in any way for inaccuracies."

bread-and-butter artists managed a decent living from their railroad pictures. (In the 1950s passengers were fed up with slow steam trains: twenty years later they were wistfully nostalgic for the bygone age.) No image, however, had quite the popular appeal of the skipping sailor of John Hassall's *Skeggy*. In 1908 the Great Northern Railroad paid the graphic artist 12 guineas for his "Skegness is so bracing" poster to advertise a seaside resort.

TRAINS HIT THE BIG SCREEN

If the nineteenth century was the age of the blockbuster portrait, the twentieth century was the age of the railroad movie. After the documentary style of Auguste and Louis Lumière (see p.212), filmmakers looked, like Zola, for a strong storyline. Railroad travel, with its romance, intrigue and adventure, was packed with possibilities. In the early 1900s Edwin Porter's twelve-minute *The Great Train Robbery* attracted large audiences to the new nickelodeons, the small, five-cent storefront theaters with cheap wooden seats and disreputable reputations. His railroad chase was followed by a spate of silent movies featuring pretty, terrified ladies being chained to the tracks as the oncoming train bore down upon them.

Porter turned the familiar Western into a celluloid drama and set a trend for films such as Cecil B. de Mille's *Union Pacific*, John Ford's silent 1924 *The Iron Horse* (about the first American transcontinental railroad) and his epic 1962 *The Way The West Was Won*. (One subplot centered on the double-crossing of Arapaho Indians by the railroad companies.)

Ford, a pioneer of location filming, also made the 1962 *The Man Who Shot Liberty Valance.* In the early scenes James Stewart reflects on how the western town of Shinbone has changed: "You only know it since the railroad came through. It was a lot different then, a lot different."

European and Asian filmmakers also focused on the railroads, from Polish director Jerzy Kawalerowicz's sinister *Ludzie z pociągu* (*Night Train,* 1959) to Czech director Jiří Menzel's coming of age film *Ostře sledované vlaky* (*Closely Watched Trains,* 1966). In Bent Hamer's 2007 *O'Horten* a Norwegian train conductor of the same name considers retirement, while in Yoshinari Nishikori's 2010 *Railroads* Hajime resigns from his office job to work as a train driver. Inevitably a filmmaker was going to return to Zola's story *La Bête Humaine.* It fell to Jean Renoir, the son of Zola's artist friend Auguste, to make the film in 1939. "The train," he said, "itself constituted one of the film's main characters."

The railroad station in Paris had not yet finished with art history. In 1932 the then little-known photographer Henri Cartier-Bresson took a black and white photograph at the rear of the station. When he photographed "Derrière La Gare Saint-Lazare" (*Behind Saint Lazare Station*), the 24-year-old photographer had decided to quit painting and concentrate on his photo-documentary work. According to *Time Magazine* Cartier-Bresson's portrait of a blurred, silhouetted figure leaping over a puddle, was the photograph of the twentieth century.

"What brought you to Hollywood?" journalist Jean-Luc Goddard asked the film director Henry Ford. "A train," replied Ford.

Les Cahiers du Cinéma

END OF THE LINE
The Gare d'Etainhus–Saint-Romain on the Paris–Le Havre line, early 1900s. It was not the first railroad to inspire artists. Neither would it be the last.

Georgetown and Plaisance Railroad

Country: Guyana

Type: Freight

Length: 5 miles (8 km)

+ SOCIAL
+ **COMMERCIAL**
+ POLITICAL
+ ENGINEERING
+ MILITARY

GUYANA
South America's second railroad heralded a rapid rail expansion across the continent. When foreign investors pulled out, however, many railroads struggled to survive.

A small sugarcane line in Guyana was part of the profitable expansion of South American railroads. The railroads, especially those in economically advanced Argentina, earned generous dividends for foreign investors, but only as long as the West could profit by their riches.

THE SUGAR LINE

In the nineteenth century British and French investors kept their valuable South American railroad stocks safe in the bureau. By the 1930s the now worthless stock certificates were abandoned: when Western economies caught a cold, the South American railroads developed a fever.

South America had become the land of opportunity in the late 1800s after the North Americans had gone their own, independent way. Colonized by the Spanish and Portuguese conquistadores, South America, and Argentina especially, lay ready for exploitation. European and North American entrepreneurs needed only to lay railroads from the interior to the ports to start siphoning off everything from beef and bauxite to grain and wine.

Two of the continent's early railroad men were John Lloyd Stephens and Frederick Catherwood. They had astonished the world when they published descriptions of the Mayan ruins they visited in the late 1830s. Stephens, a New Jersey merchant's son, went to work on the world's first transcontinental line, the Panama Railroad (see p.92), as Catherwood, in 1848, opened a modest little sugarcane railroad in Guyana (then British Guiana) between Georgetown and Plaisance. Catherwood's sugar line was only the second railroad in South America, Cuba having founded the first (see p.54). Although both were designed to ship sugar, they marked the start of the expansion of South America's railroad. It was evident in South America's second-largest country, Argentina where, by 1914, a wealthy rancher could cross much

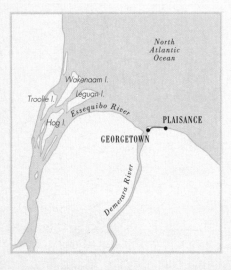

North Atlantic Ocean

Wakenaam I.
Troolie I.
Leguan I.
Hog I.
Essequibo River
PLAISANCE
GEORGETOWN
Demerara River

of his country by rail and even travel the capital, Buenos Aires, on South America's first metropolitan transit system.

Aside from collecting smoking ephemera, Birmingham engineer William Bragge started Argentina's first railroad, the Ferrocarril Oeste de Buenos Aires, in 1857. Samuel Peto's Great Southern Railway followed in 1865 and a third British-built line, between Rosario and Córdoba, in 1870. By the start of the First World War Argentina possessed the tenth-largest railroad network in the world. This was a country making its mark: as the tango went sashaying out of the Buenos Aires suburbs into Europe (even London's prestigious Waldorf Hotel was hosting Tango Teas by the early 1900s), Argentina's railroads were shipping out its biggest export, corned beef. When Europe's armies gathered to confront each other in one of the worst wars ever, the armies fought on a diet of "bully beef"—tinned meat from Argentina.

However, the over-reliance on foreign markets would prove fatal to Argentina's railroads. In 1948 there were national celebrations in Buenos Aires when president Juan Perón announced his decision to nationalize the seven British- and three French-owned railroads. But investment failed to meet expectations, and when the railroads were privatized in the 1990s there was still too little investment. Despite an increasing demand for freight, the nation's rail networks, and much of those across South America, lagged behind those in other countries.

In 1992 the railroad axe threatened to fell an obscure little freight line running through the Andean foothills from Esquel to Ingeniero Jacobacci. The Ferrocarilles Patagónicos (see box) were nicknamed *La Trochita*, the Little Narrow Gauge Railroad, because they had been built from redundant, small-gauge stock left over from the trenches in the First World War (see p.168). After a protest campaign the Argentine authorities had a change of heart: instead of closing the whole line, they declared part of *La Trochita* a national monument.

LA TROCHITA

✦

In *The Old Patagonian Express* (1975) the writer Paul Theroux described his rail journey from a freezing Boston subway to the arid plateau of Argentina's most southerly regions. During the journey he rolled up on board *La Trochita*, the little freight train that ran for 250 miles (402 km) through Patagonia in Argentina. So light it could be blown from the tracks in a severe crosswind, *La Trochita* was to become the last and longest 100-percent steam-operated railroad in South America. Theroux's travels made it one of the world's most famous trains.

"All this epical turmoil was conducted by gentlemen in frockcoats, and with a view to nothing more extraordinary than a fortune and a subsequent visit to Paris."

R.L. Stevenson, The Amateur Emigrant, *1895*

Great Indian Peninsula Railway

Country: India

Type: Passenger, Freight

Length: 21 miles (34 km)

+ SOCIAL
+ *COMMERCIAL*
+ *POLITICAL*
+ ENGINEERING
+ MILITARY

Building India's railroads promised to be the biggest public engineering works since the construction of the pyramids. The British-built system brought a nation together and then, during Partition, helped to divide it with the largest mass movement of people of all time.

RAJ RAILROADS

A popular myth ranks India's railroads as the second-biggest employer in the world, after the Chinese army and before the British health service. In 2012 the railroad, employing around 1.4 million people and carrying 11 million passengers a day, actually placed eighth, after the U.S. Department of Defense, Walmart and McDonald's. Yet a century and a half earlier, people were asking: "If you build railroads for Indians, who could ever afford to use them?"

India's railroads began when the country was a colony under British rule. It would continue to be ruled by the British until 1947 when Partition divided the country along religious lines, Sikhs and Hindus gravitating toward India and Muslims to the new nation, Pakistan.

A century earlier, as the British considered how best to consolidate their prize possession, the Indian governor general, Lord Dalhousie,

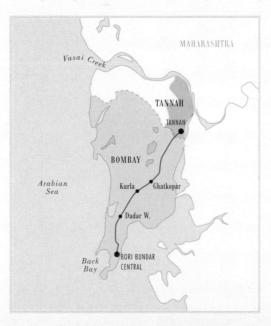

COLONIAL EXPANSION
India's first railroad,
a 21-mile (34 km) route
from Bombay to Tannah.
As they crossed the
continent, the railway
builders faced some of
the most challenging
terrain yet encountered.

advocated "this great instrument of improvement," the railroad. He was not the first to propose an Indian railroad system, but he was one of its most influential voices. And, having earlier chaired a parliamentary commission on the rapidly expanding railroads in Britain, he understood the power of rail. There were two good reasons to bring rail to India: cotton and arms. The failure of the American cotton crop in 1846 unnerved the English weaving industrialists who lobbied for a secure source. Cotton-rich India was the best alternative, if the means of transporting the crop to the Bombay (Mumbai) port could be improved.

Then there was the business of troop transport. Beyond India's northwest frontier, Afghanistan continued to threaten British interests: as recently as 1842 a 4,500-strong army together with 12,000 civilians had been annihilated after abandoning Kabul, a single bloodstained officer being left to bring the news back across the frontier. Railroads were strategically important: the military argued that an Indian national railroad would strengthen the borders.

Dalhousie's plan for a structured "railroadization" of the Indian subcontinent was to be nothing like Britain's or America's haphazard, market-driven free-for-all. Although privately funded, India's railroads would be planned by the colonial powers and engineered by the best available railroad brains. Two trial lines were proposed: a 21-mile (34 km) route from Bombay (now Mumbai) to Tannah (now Thane) in the east, to be engineered by Robert Stephenson, and a 121-mile (195 km) line in Bengal from Howrah to Raniganj, an insignificant outpost until coal was discovered there by the East India Company (see box) in the 1770s.

Instead of Stephenson, the Bombay to Tannah line fell to his assistant, James Berkley. He discovered a marsh and a hill that would require a deep cutting—nothing more challenging than had been encountered

LORD DALHOUSIE
One of the most vociferous advocates for India's railroads, Dalhousie had witnessed the railroads at work in Britain.

EAST INDIA COMPANY

✦

Like its French and Dutch equivalents, the British East India Company was a buccaneering trading business with close political and economic ties to the British government. The Company secured and helped develop trading ports in Madras, Bombay and Calcutta and wrested control of the rich northeastern provinces of India from their Bengali leaders. Having expanded and profited from the lucrative opium trade between Bengal and China, the Company was eventually deprived of its monopoly on the eve of the railroad era.

COMPANY CONTROL
The East India Company lost its grip on India as the railroads expanded.

on the Liverpool to Manchester line (see p.22) and, as he pointed out in a paper delivered to the Bombay Mechanics Institute in 1850, "the prevailing price of labor [is] at a minimum." This was not Edge Hill or Old Trafford, however, but mysterious, exotic India, a country with a complex caste system, strict religious observances and a killing climate. Berkley would shortly lose two of his "most skilful, experienced, and upright contractors" (including Solomon Tredwell: see box) and pass into an early grave himself.

Nevertheless his line was built and opened by the Great Indian Peninsula Railway Company in April 1853. A vast crowd (which included observers from east Africa, the Persian Gulf and even Afghanistan), gathered to watch a train of fourteen carriages filled with dignitaries draw out of Bombay at a belting 20 mph (32 kph). The first railroad in southern Asia was going to be a success, even if it did not please everyone. "What India wants is water carriage," argued the architect of an irrigation system on the Kaveri and Godavari rivers, Sir Arthur Cotton. "[Railroads] cannot carry at the price required, they cannot carry the quantities, and they cost the country three million rupees a year to support." As it turned out, the three million rupees would be well spent.

Work was soon started on the Bengal line by the East Indian Railroad. (It was a British company: as Berkley pointed out, "The whole Railroad system of India [is] being executed almost entirely with British capital.") Completed in February 1855 by its engineer George Turnbull, it was not without setbacks. H.M.S. *Goodwin*, carrying the carriages from England, sank, and two Calcutta firms, Stewart and Seton, had to build the replacements. Then the ship bringing the locomotive from England was, due to clerical error, sent to Australia instead of Calcutta. Finally, the route was found to have trespassed on French territory at Chandernagore (now Chandannagar), necessitating long negotiations to resolve the issue.

CROSS OVER
James Berkley engineered the Bombay to Tannah (Mumbai to Thane) line, which opened in 1853.

James Berkley now began work on the expansion of the line west from Bombay through the Western Ghats, a mountain range on the west coast. As he explained in 1850, "the passage of the Ghauts [*sic*] has always been a costly and serious obstruction in the trade of India." He could have no idea of the eventual cost in human terms.

TEXTILE TRADE SECURED

The dramatically beautiful Western Ghats rose 2,500 feet (762 m) above the plain. On two major ascents the rock face either cracked in the heat or was sluiced down by the monsoon rains that halted work for four months of the year. Berkley started with "more than 30,000 including 10,822 drillers and 2,659 masons," but the "visitations of cholera" meant another 12,000 being recruited as he tackled the ascents with a series of ingenious reversing sections for the locomotives. (His system would be employed later on the Brazilian and Andean railroads.) The line required twenty-five tunnels and eight major viaducts, which pushed costs up to £70,000 per 1 mile (1.5 km). (Turnbull's East Indian line had been estimated at £15,000 per 1.5 km.) The human costs, however, were far higher: an estimated 25,000 died, or more than 1,000 lives per kilometer. Berkley, in "failing health," returned exhausted to England and died in 1862 before the line was completed.

"The commercial benefits that are likely to arise from railroads [in India] are unquestionable and almost incalculable."

Rowland MacDonald Stephenson

The loss of life was forgotten almost as soon as the line opened and by 1870 it was possible, for the first time, to cross India from Bombay to Calcutta, as one of James Berkley's obituary writers put it, for "a total length of 1,237 miles [1,990 km], forming a grand trunk communication." It was an extraordinary railroad achievement and one which inspired 45-year-old author, Jules Verne, to pen his novel about Phileas Fogg's attempt to circumnavigate the globe, *Around the World in 80 Days*. Equally important, the line to "Nagpore, passing through some of the most extensive cotton districts of Western India" had now been created to the satisfaction of the British cotton mill owners. The textile trade was safe.

FRONTIER MAIL

From here on, wherever two major cities stood apart, a railroad was built to link them. India began building locomotives at Ajmer in Rajasthan in the 1890s and in the same decade was dispatching its engineers overseas to build a railroad in Uganda. Like the men who ran the railroads, most were Anglo-Indians, usually people with British blood on the paternal side and Indian on the maternal. In theory the recruitment policy ensured their loyalty to British rule. During Partition it would place them in jeopardy from all sides.

The Indian government took over the Great Indian Peninsula Railway lines in 1900 and began to run classic trains such as the *Frontier Mail*, which, in 1928, started to trade between the steamship dock at Bombay and Peshawar, close to the North-West Frontier Province between India and Afghanistan. The *Mail* brought the wives, families and letters of British officers serving with the Indian Army. The daughter of an English officer in the 19th Hyderabad Regiment, Peggy Leech, recalled traveling aboard the *Mail*: "The carriages were separated into closed compartments each equipped with a tiny lavatory, which opened directly onto the rail, and a little brass wash basin. There were shutters and fly screens over the windows and a case of ice, set on the carriage floor." Travel arrangements were made by her father's bearer, a tall, dignified Hindu named Ram Kissen who "did everything from securing your ayah [Indian nurse] to arranging the officers' dinner parties."

Japan's advance through Southeast Asia in 1941 brought "tiffin" (lunch) and dinner parties to an abrupt end. Now the railroads were devoted to sending troops and supplies to the Burmese border. (Burma Railroads had opened a line from Rangoon to the River Irrawaddy in the 1880s and Allied forces and Japan fought to control it.) At least one ill-fated train delivered troop reinforcements from Bombay to Singapore. They arrived as it fell to the Japanese and many of the combatants would die on the Burma to Siam Railway (see p.196).

The war ended in 1945 and British rule in 1947. Partition, as it was known, divided the Indian Hindus, Sikhs and Christians from the predominantly Muslim community in the new country, Pakistan. The British withdrawal saw over 10 million people leave their homes, the biggest mass movement of a population in history. At first, crowds set off for their new homelands by train, accompanied by honor guards and military bands. Peggy Leech and her baby took the train to Bombay and the ship home to England, sharing her carriage with five Anglo-Indian railroad men. Nervous of sectarian attacks, they too were fleeing India. Despite the efforts of Mahatma Gandhi (he had traveled the railroads spreading his message of independence and non-aggression, and was murdered in 1948 by a Hindu nationalist) or of political leaders like India's Jawaharlal Nehru and Pakistan's Muhammad Ali Jinnah, extremists from both sides attacked the trains. Thousands of passengers were slaughtered on the trackside. By the end of 1947 a million had died, including the bearer Ram Kissen, who had boarded the Bombay train for home, but was never seen again.

HERITAGE HEIGHTS

✦

The British built a number of small mountain railroads in India during the colonial era. They included the Nilgiri Mountain Railroad in the Western Ghats, the Darjeeling Himalayan Railroad (completed in 1881) and the Kalka to Shimla Railroad (opened in 1898) in the rugged north of the country. The hill station of Shimla, or Simla as it was, had been the summer capital of the British in India. The eccentric charm of these mountain railroads placed them on India's tourist trails and several became registered World Heritage Sites.

Semmering Railway

Country: Austria

Type: Passenger, Freight

Length: 25 miles (41 km)

In the mid-nineteenth century there was a fashionable frenzy among daring young men and women to be the first to conquer the Alpine heights. The railroads were never far behind.

+ **SOCIAL**
+ **COMMERCIAL**
+ **POLITICAL**
+ **ENGINEERING**
+ **MILITARY**

MOUNTAIN RAILROADS

The 1850s proved to be a golden age for the alpinist. The intrepid young mountaineers who progressively conquered one Alpine ascent after another regarded the 1854 ascent of the Wetterhorn as their opening gambit. The climber was an English lawyer, Alfred Willis. (He later chaired a commission into Britain's railroads and canals.) Yet even as Willis struggled up the frozen rockface with his rudimentary hemp ropes and polished pitons, railroads too were heading for the summits.

The first transalpine to use standard gauge, the Semmering, opened in the year of Willis' Wetterhorn triumph (although Willis turned out to have been beaten to the summit by one Stanhope Speer ten years earlier).

An Italian engineer, Carl von Ghega, had meticulously surveyed the railroad, designed to forge the missing link between Gloggnitz and Mürzzuschlag in Austria. At the time he was one of the few who believed transalpine rail was even feasible. Although it took over 20,000 men and six years to build the necessary bridges, viaducts and tunnels, Ghega's railroad succeeded. Finding a locomotive that could cope with the climb was a different problem and the special Engerth locomotive, designed by Austrian engineer Wilhelm von Engerth, was introduced. In 1998 the Semmering became a UNESCO World Heritage Site.

WORLD'S FIRST
Austria was the site of a groundbreaking transalpine railroad that proved to be one of the first mountain railroads.

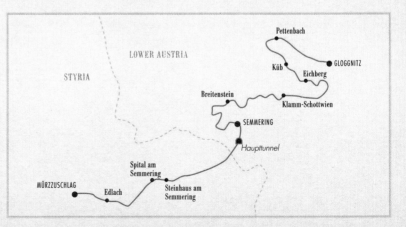

Ten years after the Semmering, Alpinist Lucy Walker scaled the 12,133 feet (3,698 m) Balmhorn in the Swiss Alps. Railroad engineers, meanwhile, were studying another, equally troublesome ascent near Mont Cenis in the Rhône Alps. The old packhorse pass, built by Napoleon's men in the early 1800s, was a source of irritation to the British. When the Indian mail was rushed out of England to the Mediterranean ports and transshipment to India, there were long delays at Cenis. The mail had to be portered over the pass by packhorse. The British were eager to see a railroad tunnel at Mont. Cenis that would link Modane in France and Bardonecchia in Italy and open up a direct route through the Alps.

The 8-mile (13 km) tunnel, commissioned by the Italian king Victor Emmanuel II, was expected to take twenty-five years. While the tunnelers were blasting their way through the mountain, a temporary railroad system put the packhorses out of business. Designed by Cumbrian John Barraclough Fell, the special three-rail line and its steam engine were constructed by a Lancashire man, James Brogden. It ran for only four years, since the Mont Cenis tunnelers broke through the mountain in record time. Their work had taken only fourteen years because of that curse of the modern street scene, the recently invented pneumatic drill, and Alfred Nobel's dynamite. With the Savoyard engineer, Germain Sommeiller in charge, the tunnel opened for business in September 1871.

John Barraclough Fell's technology was exported to Brazil, the Isle of Man (proposed by Barraclough Fell's son George, this opened in 1895) and, with James Brogden himself, to New Zealand. Brogden—also involved in shipping migrants, dubbed "Brogdenites," to the new country—installed the railroad over the Rimutaka Range on the Wellington to Masterton line. But it was the Semmering that inspired railroad engineers to ascend mountains like alpinists. Mount Washington (scene of the world's first mountain cog railroad) was conquered in 1869. Colorado's Manitou and Pike's Peak Railroad was built by the owner of Simmons Beautyrest Mattress company in 1891 and Mount Snowdon in Wales acquired a railroad in 1896.

STOPPING POWER
◆

George Westinghouse, born in 1846, lived through the heyday of the early railroads, patenting his ideas on engineering at the rate of eighteen a year. He was following in the footsteps of his father who had devised an early threshing machine. Inspired by the concept of the compressed air that drove the pneumatic drills used on the Mont. Cenis tunnel, Westinghouse, working in Pittsburgh, developed the compressed-air brake used between each coach on a train.

**"Mountains interpos'd
Make enemies of nations."**
William Cowper, The Task, 1785

ALPINE CONQUESTS
The success of the Semmering railroad encouraged the construction of the Mont. Cenis Summit Railroad.

<table>
<tr><td>

1855

</td><td>

Panama Railroad

</td></tr>
</table>

Country: Panama

Type: Passenger, Freight

Length: 47 miles (76 km)

✦ SOCIAL

✦ **COMMERCIAL**

✦ POLITICAL

✦ **ENGINEERING**

✦ MILITARY

CROSSING CONTINENT
The business of linking
the Atlantic Ocean to
the Pacific Ocean with
a canal started
with a railroad,
the Panama Railroad.

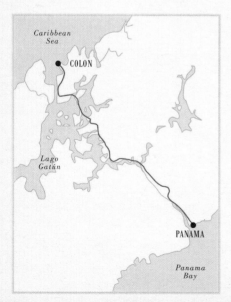

The railroads killed the canals as surely as they finished off the horse-drawn stagecoach. In the case of the Panama Railroad, however, the canal came after the trains and the famous California gold rush.

BUILDING THE CANAL LINE

The California gold rush of 1849 created a new race of workers, the "forty-niners" or "Argonauts." They came from as far afield as Germany, Poland and Russia, many of them landing in New York and then taking ship around South America by Cape Horn. The journey could last over 140 days. There was another route: sailing to the Caribbean and crossing Panama by dugout canoe and pack mule, then catching a boat in the Pacific Ocean to California. It was a journey through hell. The Argonauts risked being robbed by guides, eaten by wild animals or dying from disease.

Around a thousand forty-niners were considering the prospects when their two paddle-steamers, S.S. *Georgia* and S.S. *Philadelphia*, landed them at Aspinwall (now Colón) in 1851. Word went round that the township was named after one William Aspinwall who had already built a railroad extending 8 miles (13 km) along the trail. Despite the exorbitant rate of 50 cents per mile, the argonauts piled aboard. It was not a pleasant journey. Aside from rudimentary graves beside the track, there were stories of wooden barrels filled with the pickled corpses of workers, and distressed railroad laborers paying local natives for the swift death of decapitation by machete. The rumors were true. Staff at the railroad hospital raised funds by selling bodies to medical schools. Meanwhile many of the 800 Chinese laborers, deprived of their opium, had been killed themselves.

The line was started, not to meet the Argonauts' needs, but those of the U.S. Postal Service. Before the Pony Express or the American Transcontinental Railroad (see p.106 & 118), the U.S. Mail traveled from one side of the country to the other by sea, the postal service having opened shipping ports along the east and west coasts. William Aspinwall ran the shipping contract between Panama and Oregon and realized the potential of a railroad through Panama. Colonel George Hughes, who surveyed the line, estimated a cost of $1 million and a timescale of twelve months. It was a näive estimate. The Panama took five years, cost over $7 million and killed so many people that, until the arrival of the S.S. *Georgia* and S.S. *Philadelphia*, there was a possibility of the railroad being abandoned.

The gold diggers saved the day. Their cash injection stimulated investment from New York and in 1855 the Panama Railroad opened for business. It was brisk. Investors realized a fat 24 percent in dividends and for a while the railroad carried more freight than any other in the world. As Aspinwall predicted, the U.S. Mail was delivered in a fraction of the former time. The line became rich enough to fund a church and library for the workers. Then, to spoil it all, the Panama Canal arrived.

When Ferdinand de Lesseps started work on the Panama Canal, having built the Suez Canal, he began by buying out the railroad. It was already on the wane. By 1881 the American transcontinental railroad had opened (see p.118) and the gold rush had gone. But conditions in Panama defeated even de Lesseps and in 1904 the United States bought up the Panama Railroad. An American engineer, John Stevens, took over the project and, although he resigned before its completion (he went to work on the Trans-Siberian), the Canal opened for shipping in 1914. The railroad survived.

OCEAN TO OCEAN

✦

Panama was the world's first transcontinental railroad. In the nineteenth century the transcontinental was the holy grail of railroad builders. Some nations saw a transcontinental railroad as the needle and thread needed to stitch their countries together. Others, like imperial Russia, regarded them as a status symbol, while old colonial powers much as Britain, France and Germany saw them as efficient means of increasing economic activity while consolidating military control in their colonial territories. By the late twentieth century the transcontinentals had become places of pilgrimage for railroad enthusiasts.

ATTRITION RATE
Conditions on the Panama Railroad were horrendous and drove some workers to suicide. No one knows how many died.

"There are three diseases in Panama. They are yellow fever, malaria, and cold feet; and the greatest of these is cold feet."

John Stevens, engineer of the Panama Canal

Grand Crimean Central Railway

Country: Ukraine

Type: Military

Length: 29 miles (47 km)

+ **SOCIAL**
+ **COMMERCIAL**
+ **POLITICAL**
+ **ENGINEERING**
+ **MILITARY**

Every time technology took a step forward, the armaments industry was there to make the most of it. The railroads were no exception as, the Crimean War, the American Civil War and the Boer War demonstrated.

MILITARY DEADLOCK

It was 1854, Brazil and Norway were building their first railroads and Australia was inaugurating a steamship line between Melbourne and Hobsons Bay. But on the Crimean peninsula on the Black Sea's northern coast, Russian soldiers were head to head with British, French and Turkish troops. Following the Battle of Balaclava, the scene of the successful but misguided Charge of the Light Brigade, when over 600 British dragoons drove their steeds into the mouths of the Russian cannon, the Russians had retreated to the armed fort of Sevastopol. It was so well-built that it steadfastly resisted the resulting siege.

The London *Times* used the new telegraph line to provide graphic reports on conditions, and the coverage weighed heavily on public opinion. As 34-year-old Florence Nightingale set up her revolutionary new nursing station to minister to the wounded and dying, the military deadlock was considered by three railroad men, Samuel Morton Peto

CRIMEAN PENINSULA, UKRAINE
The narrow-gauge railroad that was built on the much fought-over Crimea was to change the fortunes of the war.

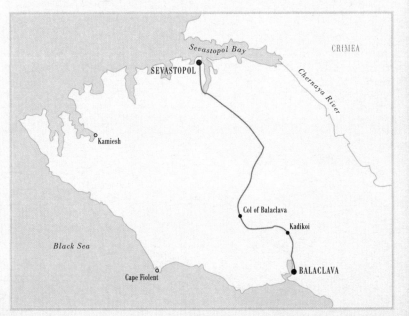

(see box on p.99), Peto's partner Edward Betts, and Thomas Brassey. They came up with a simple solution to the impasse: a siege-busting railroad between the port of Balaclava and the fortress of Sevastopol. They even offered to build it at cost.

The British government accepted and in November 1854 an army of platelayers, navvies, smiths, bricklayers, gangers, roughmasons, carpenters, timekeepers, engineers, clerks and clergymen assembled at the port of Liverpool. Together with all the necessary materials (including a case of Deane and Adam revolvers) they were taken in twenty-three ships to Crimea. "If ever these men come to hand-to-hand fighting with the enemy, they will fell them like ninepins," predicted a jingoistic *Illustrated London News* in 1885. "There cannot be a doubt that, when it [the railroad] has reached its terminus, those engaged upon it may safely adopt the motto of their honored chief, Sir Morton Peto—Ad Finem Fidelis (Faithful to the End)," trumpeted the *News*.

SIEGE BUSTERS
The navvies saved the day for the British forces in Crimea when they laid down a railroad between the port of Balaclava and the fort at Sevastopol.

Peto was the epitome of the successful Victorian businessman. At fourteen he had been a contracter-builder in his uncle's firm. By his mid-thirties, he had established a construction company that employed the world's largest workforce. Having worked on Nelson's Column and the Houses of Parliament, Peto branched out into the railroads, building both the 539-mile (867 km) Canadian Grand Trunk Railroad from Quebec to Lake Huron and the little domestic line linking the fishing port of Lowestoft, close to his East Anglian country estate, with the rest of the rail network.

Conditions in Crimea were not going to defeat Peto. The Crimean railroad was laid, with 1,800 tons of rail and 6,000 ties, from the Balaclava quay to the siege head, together with several branch lines, in record time. The moment it was finished, the siege army was provided with food, forage, shot and shell. The injured were carried back to Balaclava on what was one of the world's first hospital trains, and in September 1855 Sevastopol fell. The railroad had won the Crimean War.

PETO'S GIFT
The railroad magnate offered to build the Crimean railroad at cost.

RAILROADS WIDEN THE SCALE OF WAR

It was six years later that the Civil War plunged the American North,
the Union, against the American South, the Confederacy. The issue was
slavery and the railroads played a significant role in the conflict from
the outset.

In 1859 an unlucky railroad porter named Heyward Shepherd was
killed when he went out to meet the Baltimore and Ohio express train
at Harper's Ferry, Virginia. An African American, Shepherd had the
misfortune to run into a party of raiders and stopped a bullet. The
raiding party was led by abolitionist John Brown (his party included
several African Americans). He planned to seize the local arsenal and
arm rebellious slaves. Instead, the alarm was raised, the Colonel
Robert E. Lee moved eighty-six U.S. marines in
by rail and Brown was captured and hanged.

Nothing happens until something moves.

U.S. Army Transport Corp motto

Throughout the Civil War from 1861 to 1865
the Baltimore and Ohio Railroad, in particular,
was caught in the line of fire between South and North, the Union
trying to defend it, the Confederates to destroy it. The Southerners
were at a disadvantage, possessing only around 9,000 miles (14,484 km)
of track compared to the North's 22,000 miles (35,406 km), using a
mixture of gauges that necessitated time-wasting transfers from one

train to another. Yet the Southerners were quick to use the railroads to ferry their troops into battle. In July 1861, as the Union general Irvin McDowell dispatched 35,000 troops toward Manassas, Virginia, to capture the railroad, the Confederate General Pierre G.T. Beauregard met them with a force of only 23,000.

The tables were turned in the Confederates' favor when 10,000 extra troops were brought in by rail as reinforcements for Beauregard. Recognizing the strategic value of both locomotives and stations, the Confederate General "Stonewall" Jackson destroyed more than forty locomotives at the Baltimore and Ohio's yard in Martinsburg, Virginia (now West Virginia) in May 1861. The Confederate "Jeb" Stuart, meanwhile, targeted stations and their telegraph offices, often sending misleading messages down the line before torching the buildings. Both sides used special train-mounted artillery during the conflict, and in the final push for Georgia and Virginia the Union generals Grant and Sherman made the most of the railroads. At the outset of the war it took a day to move an army 20 miles (32 km): now it took an hour. Railroads were widening the scale of war.

SECURING THE RAILROADS

✦

When the American Civil War broke out President Lincoln responded by putting the railroads and telegraph under government control. D.C. Callum, general superintendent of the Erie Railroad was made a brigadier general in charge of the railroads (in 1862) while the Philadelphia Railroad's chief engineer Herman Haupt was charged with maintenance and repair. Many observers later attributed the success of the North to its mastering the railroads and the lessons were learned by military men in the twentieth century. Wherever war broke out governments promptly took control of the railroads.

STRATEGIC CROSSING
U.S. railroads like this one in Tennessee widened the scale of the conflict during the Civil War.

MAFEKING RELIEVED

Railroads played a significant role in the Franco-Prussian War of 1870, with Prussia's early victories assisted by their railroad troops, or *Eisenbahntruppen*. Railroads again had a pivotal role to play, both in providing arms and supplies and mounting direct attacks, during the Boer Wars. In the 1880s British forces were battling in the Transvaal and the Orange Free State. The British had seized Cape Colony on the southern tip of Africa in 1806 while the Afrikaners or Boers, descendants of Dutch, German and French colonists, settled the northern territories of the Transvaal and Orange Free State. When diamonds were discovered in the region in 1867 the British were eager to lay their hands on a share of the booty. When gold, too, was discovered, the British war machine went into action.

The conflict had been sparked by the British annexation of the Transvaal in 1877. The Boers expected the British prime minister William Gladstone to grant independence or at least self-government. When he failed to do so the Boers successfully fought for it. Peace, and the foundations of what would become the apartheid state of South Africa, followed.

Meanwhile, in 1899, another siege situation was developing as 80,000 Boers surrounded the garrisons of Ladysmith, Kimberley and Mafeking. Robert Stephenson Smyth Baden-Powell, the garrison commander, had chosen the town of Mafeking for its strategic position on the railroad between Bulawayo and Kimberley. He planned to draw the Boers' troops

WAR ON WHEELS
Troop and hospital trains were in action again during the Franco-Prussian War of 1870 when the Prussian military commandeered the railroads.

away from the coast where British reinforcements were expected to land. Powell, better known as Robert Baden-Powell, would go on to found the Boy Scout movement after meeting the American Scout Frederick Russell Burnham. As befitted the future Scout leader (and, as it happened, the grandson of the railroad engineer Robert Stephenson), Baden-Powell used the local railroads to maximum effect. A howitzer was built in Mafeking's railroad workshop and at one point Baden-Powell had an armored locomotive run right into the midst of the enemy camp. The attack succeeded (even if its commander, Colonel Holdsworth, died in the process), according to the account given by Arthur Conan Doyle in *The Great Boer War* (1900). "The train appears to have had better luck than has usually attended these ill-fated contrivances," wrote the author more usually concerned with the fate of Dr. Watson and Mr. Holmes.

Mafeking was relieved in May 1900 (Baden-Powell's brother was among the relief force) after some prodigious train journeys. The London and South Western Railroad successfully moved 528,000 troops together with their horses and equipment to Portsmouth docks. From here on, reported Conan Doyle, "these contingents had been assembled by long rail journeys, conveyed across thousands of miles of ocean . . . to Beira, transferred by a narrow gauge to Bamboo Creek, changed to a broad gauge to Marandellas, sent in coaches for hundreds of miles to Bulawayo, transferred to trains for another four or five hundred miles to Ootsi; and finally a forced march of a hundred miles."

The sun was setting on the century that had seen the start of the railroads. The British monarch, Victoria, was in her final days and her grandson Kaiser Wilhelm II was about to embark on the war of all wars. From then on no military mind could ignore the railroads as a potential weapon.

BOER WAR
A train makes its way to the front line. Baden-Powell, the grandson of the locomotive engineer Robert Stephenson, made full use of the railroads during the conflict.

FAITHFUL TO THE END

✦

After their success in Crimea, Samuel Peto and his partner Edward Betts carried on building railroads in England, from Peterborough to Doncaster, Boston to Louth, Oxford to Wolverhampton, Gloucester to Hereford, Oxford to Birmingham and, in 1851, the prestigious line from South London to the Crystal Palace, where the Great Exhibition was to be held. They built lines overseas from Dunaberg to Vitebsk in Russia, Bildah to Algiers in North Africa, the Grand Trunk in Norway between Chistiania and Eidsvold and further afield in Australia. Yet in 1866, when a bank, Overend, Gurney & Co. failed, it pitched Peto into bankruptcy. He spent the last twenty years of his life in Hungary and England and in penury.

Chicago to St. Louis Railroad

Country: U.S.A.

Type: Passenger

Length: 262 miles (421 km)

+ **SOCIAL**
+ **COMMERCIAL**
+ POLITICAL
+ ENGINEERING
+ MILITARY

Train passengers expect some creature comforts in exchange for their ticket: armchair-like seats, a foldaway table, a restaurant car perhaps. George Pullman offered them all on the Chicago and Alton Railroad, and his service set a worldwide trend in luxury rail travel.

DEATH OF A PRESIDENT

When President Abraham Lincoln died on April 15, 1865, a nation prepared to mourn. Shot in the head at Ford's Theater in Washington the night before, the dead Lincoln was to be borne away from Washington back to his birthplace, Springfield, Illinois. Thousands watched in shocked silence as the funeral train departed from Washington. It traveled at a dignified 20 mph (32 kph), a speed it would not exceed for the next 1,600 miles (2,575 km). For George Pullman, the first national commemoration by the railroads of a presidential death was both a personal tragedy and an unexpected business opportunity. Pullman, as a family friend of the Lincolns, provided the funeral car. The event was to put his business into overdrive.

The 35-year-old Chicago entrepreneur had only recently left the business of moving houses (literally raising them with a jack, a method of house moving invented by his father, Lewis) to involve himself in rail-

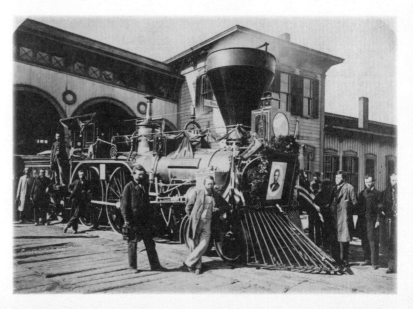

BLACK TRAIN
A Nashville locomotive prepared to draw the funeral train of the assassinated President Lincoln home to Springfield, Illinois. George Pullman leans on the cowcatcher.

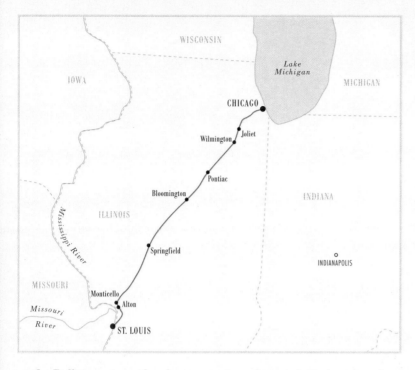

roads. Pullman was said to have experienced a particularly uncomfortable night aboard a sleeping car between Buffalo and Westfield, New
York, the hell-of-a-journey prompting the idea for a luxury car. He took
his plans to the Chicago and Alton Railroad. Pullman proposed to strip
out an old car, refit it and run it on one of the Chicago and Alton's regular routes. Exploiting the notion of providing a little extra comfort for a
few extra dollars, Pullman would charge the Chicago and Alton passengers a small supplement.

The first cars went into service in September 1859 on the Chicago to
St. Louis line and in the early 1860s Pullman launched the *Pioneer*. It
was the most expensive car in America, but unfortunately too wide to
ride on much of the Chicago and Alton Railroad. Then Lincoln was
assassinated and the president's wife, Mary
Todd Lincoln, accepted Pullman's offer to use
the *Pioneer* as the funeral car. The Chicago and
Alton hastily altered the trackside to accommodate it and almost overnight Pullman
became a brand name. (The relationship with
the Lincolns went deep. Their only surviving
son, Robert Todd Lincoln, went on to become
president of the Pullman Company after
George Pullman's death.)

FINAL JOURNEY
An astute businessman,
Pullman loaned his
Pioneer car for the
President's funeral train.

PULLMAN CARS EXPAND

The Pullman cars gained plenty of admirers. Mark Twain traveled in one from Omaha: "After dinner we repaired to our drawing-room car, and, as it was Sabbath eve, intoned some of the grand old hymns—"Praise God from whom," etc.; "Shining Shore," "Coronation," etc.—the voices of the men singers and of the women singers blending sweetly in the evening air, while our train, with its great, glaring Polyphemus eye, lighting up long vistas of prairie, rushed into the night and the Wild. Then to bed in luxurious couches, where we slept the sleep of the just." (*Roughing It*, 1872)

An English journalist with *Harmsworth Magazine* was similarly impressed: "At night a porter appears to convert your two easy-chairs into a berth; the sofa is in like manner transformed; the table is shut up somehow, and whisked away; shelves which you had not noticed before are brought into action so you undress and go to bed like good children, leaving orders as to what time you would like to be called."

The orders were taken by African Americans (Twain referred to "Ethiop waiters"), since Pullman made a point of employing former slaves. Although many African Americans were glad of the work, the policy infuriated social reformers who thought it underlined the servile role of freed slaves.

After forming his Pullman Palace Car Company, Pullman operated almost fifty sleeping cars across the United States and Canada. He diversified into dining cars after an unsuccessful trial with a hotel car where everything from cooking, eating and sleeping took place in the same, somewhat claustrophobic carriage. The new dining cars operated as separate restaurants on wheels, joined to the passenger car by a corridor, a feature later adopted on passenger trains across the world. The first, the *Delmonic*, was named after a renowned New York restaurant. Mark Twain was again impressed. He reported in *Roughing It* how he and his companions onboard the train out of Omaha

WAITER SERVICE
Pullman made it a policy to hire African Americans for his restaurant-car staff. Social reformers critized the practice, but the jobs were readily filled.

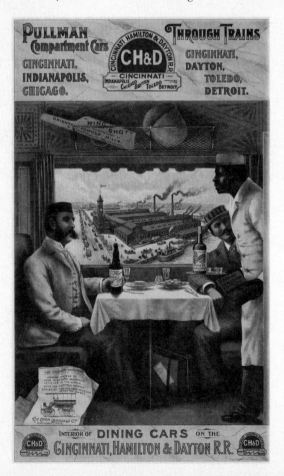

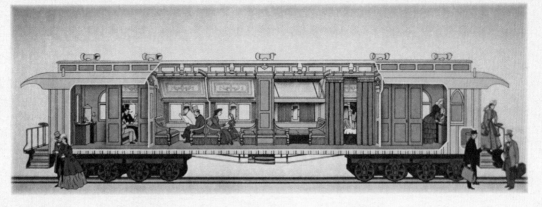

enjoyed "a repast at which Delmonico himself could have had no occasion to blush . . . for in addition to all that ordinarily makes up a first-class chop dinner, had we not antelope steak . . . our delicious mountain-brook trout, and choice fruits and berries." Two days afterwards their "Champagne glasses [were] filled to the brim [and] spilled not a drop."

NAGELMACKERS' WAGONS-LITS

The Pullman empire expanded until there were 7,000 cars running on over 150 railroads. On the eve of making his first million dollars in 1868 Pullman is believed to have met up with a lovesick banker's son from Belgium. This was Georges Nagelmackers, who had been sent abroad to study the railroads after being involved in an unfortunate love affair with a first cousin. Looking for a way to improve family relations, Nagelmackers took a long, cool look at the Pullman business and soon returned home to try to interest his family and friends in his Wagons-Lits company. Like Pullman, Nagelmackers planned to tack luxury carriages onto regular trains and skim off the premium ticket price that wealthy travelers were prepared to pay.

His initial plans for a route between Ostend and Berlin foundered because of the Franco–Prussian war and failed to attract more than a tepid response from his family. But by 1872 and with an injection of cash from the somewhat dubious Colonel William D'Alton Mann, (the American businessman and publisher was known to take bribes to keep people out of the news), Nagelmackers launched his own version of the Pullman.

LE TRAIN BLEU

✦

The midnight blue and gold trim of the sleeping carriages on the express train from Calais to Nice on the French Riviera earned it its name. The luxury service, which began in 1886, was relaunched between the two world wars, leaving Paris in the early evening and arriving in the Riviera sunshine the following morning with such luminaries on board as Coco Chanel, Serge Diaghilev, Georges Simenon, F. Scott Fitzgerald, Charles Chaplin and Agatha Christie. Second- and third-class carriages were added to the train in the 1930s. Its 1945 revival was seriously undermined by the growing speed of air travel and high-speed trains that cut journey times from 20 hours to 5.

He reasoned, rightly, that Europeans preferred their privacy and would be more interested in compartmentalized "boudoir cars." This was certainly the case with one of Nagelmackers' patrons, the Belgian King Leopold II. He was the world's most traveled railroad monarch and his rumored affair with 22-year-old Parisian ballet star Cléo de Mérode (she modeled for both the painters Henri de Toulouse-Lautrec and Gustav Klimt) made Leopold particularly susceptible to the idea of a railroad bedroom. Another client was the Peninsular and Oriental Steam Navigation Company, the P & O, which was charged with ensuring that the Indian mail reached its destination as quickly as possible. Nagelmackers' introduction of Pullman-like dining cars in 1881 meant that the Mail Train was no longer delayed by refreshment stops as it sped through Europe to the Mediterranean ports.

Wagons-Lits constructed special cars for trains that traveled by sea from the port of Dover to France. First-class passengers were not obliged to disembark and special sea locks were created in Dover and Dunkirk so that the trains could connect with the rails on the ferries whatever the height of the tide. (It was said that the clanking of the chains used to secure the trains during the sometimes choppy crossings ensured that passengers were deprived of a good night's sleep.)

Nagelmackers looked for new horizons, in particular the idea of an entire Wagons-Lits train rather than a collection of luxury carriages attached to someone else's train. He dreamed of a fabulous rail journey by express train across Europe, from the gaiety of Paris to the exotic

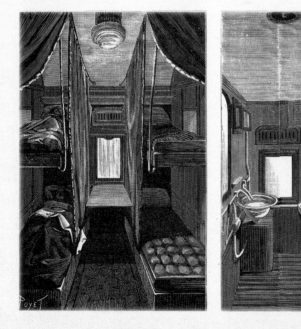

capital of the East, Constantinople. Despite having to negotiate with the eight different railroad companies that operated between the two cities, Nagelmackers, in June 1883, achieved his dream of an Express d'Orient (see box). The trend for de luxe train travel had been established.

In 1885, as special Wagons-Lits trains were re-routed to collect passengers disembarking from the transatlantic liners, Le Train Bleu (see box on p.103) began transporting its dilettante passengers from Calais to the French Riviera. A Sud Express from Paris to Lisbon was launched in 1887, and in 1896 the first Nord Express left Paris, traveling through Brussels and Berlin to reach St. Petersburg 1,341 miles (2,158 km) away. Running a business that crossed continents had inherent risks, and many Wagons-Lits coaches were expropriated during World War I (Germany formed a rival company to take over the Wagons-Lits business) and the Russian Revolution. The period between the world wars, however, saw the popularity of the Wagons-Lits reach its peak. By 1936 a wealthy London couple could buy their travel guide to Baghdad, Cairo or Tehran and, after dinner, catch the night ferry from Platform 2 in Victoria Station to Paris' Gare du Nord. From here they might board the Orient, or the Simplon Orient, Express trains to Istanbul, or the Arlberg Orient Express to Athens, in the knowledge that they shared their journey with royalty, diplomats, wealthy businessmen and even novelists. Graham Greene wrote his *Orient Express* in 1932, while Agatha Christie's *Murder on the Orient Express*, featuring the Belgian detective Hercule Poirot, came out in 1934.

Every time Nagelmackers introduced a new European service, George Pullman, who assiduously guarded his business interests, was there to rival it. Pullman even tried to buy Nagelmackers out in 1882, but in the end the competing Pullman and Wagons-Lits continued operating within their own territories. The two men who had promoted top-class travel died, Pullman in 1897 and Nagelmackers in 1905, while the business of luxury rail travel carried on.

ORIENT EXPRESS

✦

The Orient Express went into service in 1883. It represented the height of railroad luxury with its Moroccan-leather covered chairs, richly carpeted saloons, smoking rooms for the gentlemen and private toilet facilities. Its reputation for edgy glamor was enhanced when, in May 1891, it was held up by bandits. They derailed the locomotive 60 miles (96 km) from Constantinople, kidnapping the driver and five German businessmen who were later released for an £8,000 (200,000 franc) ransom. Famous passengers included the German spy Mata Hari, executed by the French in 1917, and the Bulgarian King Ferdinand, who insisted on driving the locomotive. World War II effectively ended the era (although the service continued for some years, sometimes as no more than a single carriage attached to local trains). A new Orient Express was launched in 1982.

1862

Hannibal to St. Joseph Railroad

Country: U.S.A.

Type: Freight

Length: 206 miles (332 km)

+ **SOCIAL**

+ **COMMERCIAL**

+ **POLITICAL**

+ **ENGINEERING**

+ **MILITARY**

Never mind pork, people, parcels or newsprint, one of the most lucrative cargoes of all was also the lightest: the letter. The railroads revolutionized the mail. It would be a devastating blow when, one by one, they lost the business to their truck and airline rivals in the twentieth century.

RAIL MAIL

The 1860s saw the former Mississippi steamboat pilot Sam Clemens writing for the Virginia City newspaper the *Territorial Enterprise* under his pen name, Mark Twain. Mark Twain was an old depth-sounding expression from his steamboat days, but Sam Clemens was finished with steamboats: "The romance of boating is gone," he declared. Twain, a great exponent of the *mot juste*, held similarly jaundiced views on the railroads. As he told readers of the *Alta California* in 1867, "A railroad is a ravenous destroyer of towns."

Nevertheless it was the railroads that gave Twain a nationwide audience, just as they carried his letters home: the American authorities had designated all railroads as postal routes in 1838 after the company running the Philadelphia to Lancaster Pennsylvania Railroad secured a $400-a-year allowance "for carrying mail on the railroad." The development of the postal rail services also had close connections with Mark Twain's family. The line that bore many of his missives home was the one between St. Joseph and Hannibal, Missouri. Built to supersede the Hound Dog stagecoach trail, plans for the railroad were first signed and sealed in an attorney's office at Hannibal in 1846. The attorney was John Marshall Clemens, Mark Twain's father.

MARK TWAIN
The American writer claimed to be no friend of the advancing railroads.

THE PONY EXPRESS

St. Joseph, Missouri—"St. Joe"—was a frontier town set up by fur trapper Joseph Robidoux. It lay at the end of the railroad line and 2,000 miles (3,212 km) of open territory separated it from the distant West Coast where settlers had a long and frustrating wait for news and letters from back home in the East. That was until April 3, 1860, when a mail package arrived at St. Joe's for delivery by Pony Express. (The packet arrived two hours late at Hannibal and was dispatched on a special one-car train, pulled by the *Missouri* locomotive in record time.)

The Pony Express had been launched by William H. Russell—he advertised for riders who were "young, skinny, wiry fellows not over 18. Orphans preferred." Twain described riding out of St. Joe's aboard a mule-powered mail express to Carson in 1861: "It was a fierce and furious gallop and the gait never altered for a moment till we reeled off ten or twelve miles [16–19 km] and swept up to the next collection of little station huts and stables." Russell's boys aimed to be faster, collecting the mail from the St. Joe railhead and completing the journey in ten days as they pounded across Kansas, Nebraska, Colorado, Wyoming, Utah and Nevada, delivering it safe in its sealed *mochila* or leather pouch to the postmaster in Sacramento, California.

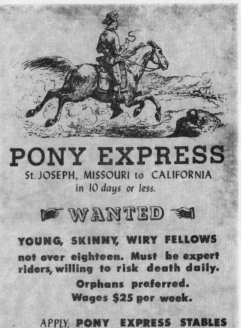

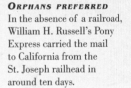

ORPHANS PREFERRED
In the absence of a railroad, William H. Russell's Pony Express carried the mail to California from the St. Joseph railhead in around ten days.

WESTERN MAIL
The Missouri line carried mail from the East to St. Joseph where it was met by the Pony Express riders.

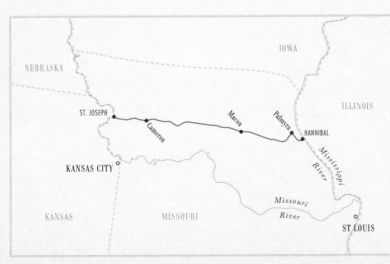

TRAINS AND SHIPS
Railroads provided the
missing link between
the shipping mail routes.
The S.S. *Cathay* worked
between Britain
and Australia.

The Pony Express lasted only until late 1861, but long enough to become a legend. The Hannibal and St. Joe postal services, however, did not rest on their laurels. In 1862 William A. Davis tried out a postal car in which postal workers sorted the mail as they rode between St. Joe's and Hannibal. It broke new ground in mail services until it was interrupted by the Civil War. Two years later, a regular U.S. railroad mail service was set up between Chicago and Clinton, Iowa; similar schemes soon followed around New York, Washington and Pennsylvania. By now Mark Twain had also ridden aboard a mail train: "We sped along at the rate of thirty miles [48 km] an hour, [and all] agreed it was the fastest living we had ever experienced."

GOING GLOBAL

On the other side of the globe in New South Wales, Australia, mail had been carried on the Sydney to Parramatta Railroad since 1855, the postal service sending an armed guard to accompany the mail car. As at St. Joe's, a traveling post office started to operate (although not until 1879) and the business of rail mail continued to build as new lines were laid across the continent. (In 1896 the railroad boasted of "splendid mail vans attached to mainline trains leaving Sydney daily [which] travelled 900,000 miles [1,448,407 km] a year.")

In Britain one Elizabeth Frere, wife of the President of the English Law Society, viewed the lack of a local railroad postal service with annoyance. It was 1838 and she was eager to pass on news of her daughter's wedding. "Susan went to church in the white satin gown, Brussels' veil fastened with a diamond sprig, two sprigs of orange flower in her hair, a gold chain on her neck and a bracelet on her right arm. The servants had a dance in the laundry at night, a neighbor or two, and trades people were asked. They danced till between two and three in the morning but we put ourselves to bed at 10 o'clock and so ended our day." This charming evocation of Cambridgeshire village life was sent by slow mail coach. The British authorities, like the Americans, had legislated for postal services in that year, 1838. Elizabeth Frere, however, would wait another two years before the London to Cambridge railroad line drove through the village (and the family estate). It brought radical

> **"It is hard to make railroading pleasant in any country. Stage-coaching is infinitely more delightful."**
>
> *Mark Twain*, The Innocents Abroad, *1869*

changes to country life, but her letters, at least, now sped to their destination in half the time.

The Liverpool to Manchester railroad had carried the first U.K. mail, and seven years later, in 1837, a post office surveyor, George Karstadt, proposed the first traveling post office. Converted from a four-ton horse box, it ran along the Grand Junction Railway between Birmingham and Liverpool, enabling the Post Office to "duplicate time by travelling and working at the same instant," as a commentator from the *Illustrated London News* put it. A year later John Ramsey, from the Missing Letter branch of the Post Office, sped things up further with a fiendishly clever device that attached to the side of the carriage and swept up a mail pouch from the trackside without the train having to stop. Both the French and Prussian railroads borrowed Ramsey's "drop and grab" contraption, which continued to be used in Britain for over 130 years.

The *News* in 1844 also highlighted the arduous business of fetching the India Mail. The mail, in reality the correspondence relating to "all of the departments of the East," was placed in iron boxes

INDIA MAIL

+

Before the continental railroads arrived, boxes of mail were dispatched from India by steamship over the Red Sea and Mediterranean and by pack horse across Egypt and France to England. But the need to receive reports from the colony as quickly as possible led to an "abstraction" of the important news being rushed to England when the mail boxes reached Marseille where, as the *Illustrated London News* put it, "the race against time and tide in reality commences." The "abstraction" was telegraphed to Paris, then raced to the port of Boulogne by horse and rushed across the Channel, the vessel carrying a warning pennant to alert the station-master at Folkestone to ready his train for London.

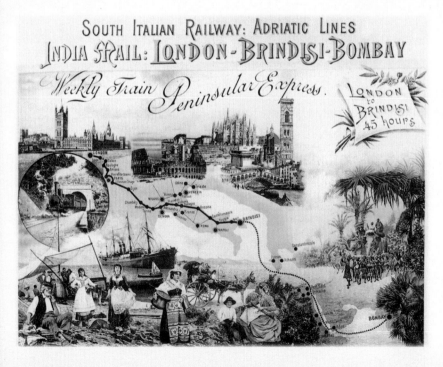

SOUTH ITALIAN RAILWAY: ADRIATIC LINES
INDIA MAIL: LONDON-BRINDISI-BOMBAY
Weekly Train Peninsular Express.
LONDON to BRINDISI 45 hours

INDIAN MAIL
A poster portrays the benefits of taking the Italian mail train between London and Bombay. The journey to Brindisi in Italy took only two days.

in Bombay (Mumbai). Soldered closed (wax seals would have melted), the thirty or forty boxes would be shipped to Suez (the canal had yet to be built), taken overland by cart to Cairo and then Alexandria, across the Mediterranean into France and eventually to England. It was little wonder that the British authorities constantly campaigned for an international railroad system to carry the India Mail.

The Great Western Railway, realizing there was money to be made from mail, ran Britain's first mail-only train between the Paddington district of London and Bristol (and later Penzance) in 1855. In 1907, when Mark Twain paid a visit to England, the mail bags bulged with a new type of mail: the picture post card. The Post Office had finally consented to carrying the cards, producing a flood of "Wish you were here" messages written on the back of pretty landscape scenes.

POST BY NIGHT

The night mails, rushing picture postcards, lovers' letters and business payments across country, evoked the spirit of the rail-post age. The most iconic of the night mails, thanks to an early documentary film, was the British West Coast Postal. Lit by a row of lamps along the carriage steps, it raced through the night like a demented glowworm between London and Scotland, up to forty postal workers feverishly sorting an annual payload of 500 million letters. It drove north, as English poet W.H. Auden put

NIGHT MAIL
Although the railroads carried the mail for well over a century, mail freight came to an end in many countries toward the end of the twentieth century.

it, "crossing the border, bringing the cheque and the postal order." Auden (curiously, a distant relative of the couple whose wedding Elisabeth Frere had described) was a contemporary of the British composer Benjamin Britten. Both men went on to enjoy glittering artistic careers, but 1936 saw them in an unlikely collaboration on what became a classic documentary, *The Night Mail*. It was directed by Basil Wright and Harry Watt, and Watt, drew much of his inspiration from Viktor Turin's film *Turksib* (1929), about the building of the Siberia to Turkestan railroad. (Turin, in his turn, was smitten by scenes of majestic American steam locomotives hammering along the tracks.)

For all the romance of the mail trains, rail mail began to wane in the latter half of the twentieth century. June 1977 saw the final railroad post office running between New York and Washington, D.C. In Britain, the Royal Mail stopped using rail for mail in 2003, while in Australia the New South Wales traveling post office had already come to a halt in 1984 as the Australian Post switched to a fleet of road trucks. The loss of the mail freight was a significant one for the railroads, and a considerable victory for road and airline delivery businesses.

UNDERGROUND

✦

In 2011 a group of illicit urban explorers posted photographs on the Web of an unusual break-in: the City of London's underground postal railroad. They showed empty tunnels, like abandoned catacombs, threading beneath London for more than 7 miles (11 km). Most of the Mail Rail, as it was known, was tunneled 70 feet (21.3 m) below ground. Driverless trains had carried the mail under the city from 1927 to 2003, when the system was mothballed. The idea behind the railroad followed the construction of a freight railroad under Chicago, which operated from 1906 to 1959.

<table>
<tr><td>

1863

</td><td>

Metropolitan Railway

</td></tr>
</table>

Country: England

Type: Passenger, Freight

Length: 3.75 miles (6 km)

✦ **SOCIAL**

✦ **COMMERCIAL**

✦ **POLITICAL**

✦ **ENGINEERING**

✦ **MILITARY**

In the mid-nineteenth century growing city populations were forcing the authorities to reassess their urban polices. The idea of persuading people to avoid the crowds and travel in an open train underground seemed, at first, an unlikely solution.

STAGNANT MASS

Among some strange ideas that appeared in the pages of family magazines in the mid-1800s were sloping roads ("pedestrians could, having applied roller skates to their feet, just stand erect at the top of the slope and allow themselves to travel down without further effort"), pavements in front of shops that were raised at night to "baffle the burglar" and locomotives with wedge-shaped ends: the wedge shapes would mitigate the effect of a head-on collision while "less resistance would be offered to the wind and, therefore, the train would proceed at an easier and quicker pace." (This early proposal for streamlining was not as absurd as it sounded.) Another odd idea was to dig tunnels beneath busy cities and run trains through them.

By the 1850s, however, the authorities in London were ready to look at any scheme that might relieve the growing congestion on the metropolitan streets. Its mainline stations handled over 250,000 passengers a

UNDER LONDON
The success of the overground stations caused greater congestion than ever before in the capital. The solution was to build a subway.

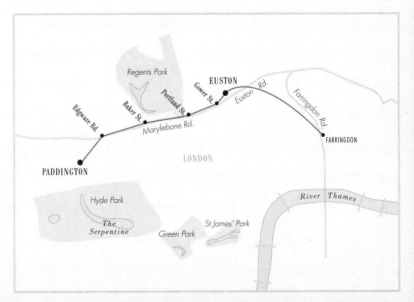

day while 4,000 horse-drawn buses and cabs hurried from the stations to London's financial heart, the City. "Our courts and alleys are crowded with a stagnant mass of humanity," argued the liberal lawyer Charles Pearson. "Families of respectable working men [could] like their masters, if they had the facilities which a Railroad could afford them, live with their families in the country, a few miles from . . . their occupation." He had a point. Horse traffic alone was producing a noxious quantity of flyblown manure. (In 1895 *The Times* predicted the city would be buried under horse dung within fifty years.)

London, considerably bigger than New York and home to more people than lived in the rest of the country, was sick. Tuberculosis killed between 10,000 and 20,000 people a year; smallpox, diphtheria, whooping cough and typhus were endemic, and an 1832 outbreak of cholera finished off 18,000—its cause, Edwin Chadwick of Woodhead Tunnel fame surmised incorrectly, "gases noxious to health."

Pearson's solution was a giant central London station connected by tunnels to surrounding stations. When the authorities banned any further inner-city stations, Pearson petitioned instead for a railroad tunnel linking, as a first step, the City with the northern stations. It would run between Bishops Road, Paddington and Farringdon Street, passing through the two key north London stations, Euston and King's Cross; and it was christened the Metropolitan.

Navvies started in 1860, pulling up the cobbled streets and excavating deep, shored-up trenches—the "cut and cover" method. Most of the early railroad engineers had employed cut and cover, digging an almighty deep trench, laying a railroad line at the bottom, bricking the tunnel over and replacing the roadway above.

In the smarter city districts the Metropolitan Railway went to considerable efforts to enhance the local architecture: amongst the "stagnant mass of humanity" the poor were evicted and their hovels pulled down.

METROPOLITAN LINE
The method of constructing an underground railroad by what was known as the "cut and cover" method had already been tried and tested on railroad tunnels.

CLEAN AIR
A C-class steam engine at Neasden around 1890. Steam eventually gave way to electrically powered engines, creating a clean-air underground.

PADDED CELLS

In May 1862 the great and good, including the Chancellor of the Exchequer William Gladstone and his wife—he sheltering under his top hat, she beneath a bonnet—assembled for the first trip in one of the open carriages. (Viscount Palmerston, the aging prime minister had refused the journey, arguing that he needed to stay above ground for as long as possible). Lit by flickering oil lamps and drawn by coal-burning locomotives fitted with condensers to reduce the steam, the journey was like a trip into Hades. Yet the public flocked to use it, in 1863 more than 30,000 riding the subterranean train. The Metropolitan carried over 9 million in its first year. The signal was clear: the way ahead was underground.

Traveling conditions gradually improved with the introduction of closed carriages (nicknamed "padded cells") with upholstered seats. By now the New York editor of the *Scientific American*, Alfred Beach, had discreetly constructed his own private subway and was running an air-pressure-driven train ferrying passengers between Murray Street and Warren Street on Lower Broadway.

In London railroad tunnelers had acquired a new tool by 1870, a 7-foot (2.1 m) "shield," which was used to tunnel beneath the Thames to create a rope-hauled railroad. A radical improvement on

MIND THE GAP
Despite the primitive, smoky conditions on the early Underground, pictured here in 1863, the public made the most of it.

the disruptive cut-and-cover method, it allowed excavators to mine deep underground "tubes." In 1886 it ground out the first deep-level tube, a 3.5-mile (5.6 km) railroad tunnel on the City and South London Railroad with six stations between the City of London and Stockwell. When the newly developed electric locomotives arrived, the steam trains swiftly departed. Before long a Central London Railroad opened, its bargain "Twopenny Tubes" operating in the comparatively clean air of the Underground.

UNDERGROUND GOES GLOBAL

Other cities waited, watched and then started their own "tubes." Budapest opened the 2-mile (3 km) long Franz Josef Electric Underground in 1896. Glasgow, Scotland, followed in 1897, opening a circular line with trains hauled by wire ropes driven by static steam engines. These 15 mph (24 kph) trains continued working until the 1930s. Boston hosted America's first public subway line in 1898, the same year that Vienna opened its Stadtbahn. Work also began on one of the world's most iconic subway systems, the Paris Métro.

The Métro borrowed its name from the Metropolitan, but the brains behind it were those of the French engineer Fulgence Bienvenüe. He became *le Père du Métro* (the father of the Métro) despite losing his arm in an engineering accident. Bienvenüe's

HARRY BECK

✦

Among the commuters who boarded the Tube at Finchley every day in the 1930s was a London Transport Signal Office draftsman, Harry Beck. In his spare time he worked on a diagrammatic map of the Underground. The map was published in January 1933 as the various private companies that operated the Underground system were merged into London Transport. (Beck was thought to have based the map on electrial circuit diagrams.) The clarity of Beck's pocket map turned it into an instant success. It became a style icon and was adapted by other mass transport systems across the world.

6-mile (10 km) line linking the Place de le Bastille, the Louvre, the Place de la Concorde and the Arc de Triomphe opened in July 1900, the year of the Paris Olympics (when women competed for the first time) and the World Fair. Parisians, enthralled by the fresh face of Art Nouveau, commissioned an architect, Hector Guimard, to create a series of Art Nouveau Metro entrances. Most were later destroyed and Guimard died in relative obscurity in New York in 1942.

In the 1930s Muscovites had similarly grandiose plans for their subway system, the *Metropoliten im. L. M. Kaganovicha* named after its designer Lazar Kaganovicha, and managed to combine the Communist ethic with Art Deco styling. (They sought advice from British engineers and the meeting of minds brought mutual benefits: Essex's Gants Hill station was said to closely resemble a Russian metro station.)

By now Berliners could strap-hang to the zoo from Potsdamer Platz on the *U-Bahn* (opened in the early 1900s), New Yorkers from Times Square to Brooklyn on the subway and Philadelphians on their 4.5-mile (7 km) subway. Hamburg opened a partial underground railroad, as did Buenos Aires. By the 1950s Madrid and Barcelona, Sydney, Tokyo, Osaka and Nagoya, Chicago, Cleveland, Stockholm, Toronto, Rome, Leningrad, Lisbon and Haifa in Israel had all gone underground.

One hundred and fifty years after William and Catherine Gladstone first rode the Underground, congestion and pollution caused by cars and trucks were persuading around 155 million people to use subways every day. The Tokyo subway, part of the Greater Tokyo rapid transit system, became the world's busiest, followed by Seoul. Seoul, with automatic safety doors on every platform, smart-payment ticket systems and carriages equipped with digital TV and heated seats, has been described as the best subway in the world.

ONE UNDER

✦

The underground railroad system proved to be one of the world's safest mass transport systems, safer even than overland rail. The worst loss of life occurred during air raids on London in World War II. In 1940 a bomb hit Balham High Road, the blast rupturing water and sewage pipes and drowning 68 people sheltering in the tube station. At Bethnal Green in 1943, 173 were crushed to death on a stairwell during an air raid. Over the years most Underground fatalities have been due to suicides, known as "one unders" or "jumpers."

ART NOUVEAU
Many of the Paris Métro
entrances, designed by
Hector Guimard, were
pulled down.

Central Pacific Railroad

Country: U.S.A.

Type: Passenger, Freight

Length: 1,087 miles (1,749 km)

✦ **SOCIAL**
✦ **COMMERCIAL**
✦ ***POLITICAL***
✦ **ENGINEERING**
✦ **MILITARY**

I t was not the world's first, but America's first transcontinental railroad revolutionized the U.S. economy and put the romantic old wagon trains out of their misery. It was the railroad that tamed the Wild West and set the pattern for transcontinental railroads across the globe.

GOD-FORSAKEN CALIFORNIA

When the reporter for London's *Cassell's Family Magazine* packed his portmanteau and prepared to board the Pacific Railroad in 1875 he slipped a six-shooter pistol in among his clean shirts. And a Bowie knife. And instructions on how to deal with knife wounds. The reason was that the reporter, known only by his initials, M.A., had consulted his New York friends before embarking on the epic round trip of "THREE THOUSAND TWO HUNDRED AND EIGHTY-SEVEN MILES [5,290 km]," as he put it to his readers. Full of foreboding (or dressing the story for dramatic effect), M.A. repeated one of the warnings he received before his departure: "You are going to California, and you will find it, sir, the most God-forsaken place in the universe."

CROSSING BORDERS
The transcontinental railroad that joined the east with the west opened up the markets and helped America become the world's richest nation.

The transcontinental railroad had been open for six years when M.A. boarded. He was in a state of surprise right from the start. "My little railroad trip lasted just a week of seven days and the country traversed was the entire width

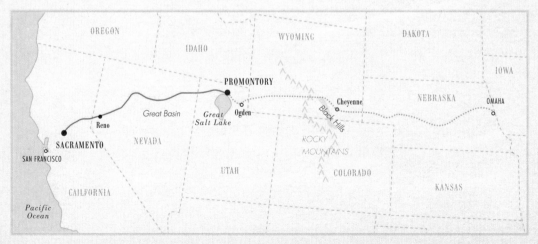

of a great continent," he explained in his piece. Yet the trip was less tiresome than a four- or five-hour journey back home, particularly because of the American contrivances (cars, or as he called them in the British style, carriages). Equipped with drawing rooms fitted out with armchairs, sofas, books, carpets and ornaments, they "lighten[ed] all the inconvenience of travel." He was intrigued to discover that the traveler "whose purse is long enough" could charter a whole drawing-room car in New York and occupy it until San Francisco was reached.

In England, he reported, the duration of a train journey was a terror in itself. In America it was "a distinct element of enjoyment," although he took a while to adjust to the protocol. The passengers who alighted at Chicago, "gentlemen . . . absorbed in business calculations, and as anxious to reach their destinations for purely speculative and money-making purposes," were a different breed from those who boarded—"they were a more miscellaneous company." Yet each and every one seemed to plunge into conversation and become very sociable "within a quarter of an hour." The correspondent was taken aback. Travelers on British railroads (then as now) maintained a chilly friendliness. "Is anyone seated there?"—"No" was as far as it went. Here on the Pacific "a thaw set in the Britisher's reserve" as he traveled with companions, good-natured "to the backbone."

DONE!

✦

The railroad was expected to take ten years, but it was completed in four, the tracks meeting in Promontory Point, Utah on May 10, 1869. Leland Stanford for the Central Pacific and Thomas Durant for the Union Pacific drove the symbolic final spikes home, both apparently missing the mark first time round. A cartoon from the time shows a fanciful hand extending from each locomotive, offering one another what looks like a high five (despite the custom apparently originating a century later). The indigenous buffalo and the Native Americans, meanwhile, flee in terror. A telegraph line had been run along the railroad and the first message sent along the wire read simply: "Done."

M.A. chose not to labor his account with the first "insignificant run of a thousand miles [1,609 km] through Pennsylvania, Ohio, Indiana, by the southern limits of Lake Michigan." This section of the route he judged no more interesting, in landscape terms, than that between London and Rugby on the journey from the English capital to the Scottish Highlands. For him the real journey began in Chicago, "this wonderful corn and cattle emporium as the boundary between east and west." The extent of Chicago's vigor was fully described by one of M.A.'s fellow passengers, "a genuine American with whom silence was an absolute impossibility." The city had recently risen from its own ashes after a devastating fire in October 1871. M.A.'s informant explained how he had "lost every cent in the world in the fire . . . and now I have doubled what I had before." More than 17 miles (27 km) of railroad had been built around Chicago's stockyards and now, M.A. understood, the beasts (21,000 cattle, 75,000 hogs, 22,000 sheep and 350 horses) were better accommodated than the "wretched poor" at home in Britain.

This was a reference to the Irish Problem, as the Irish potato famine was sometimes called. The famine had been widely reported in America, which had received many of the 2.5 million migrants created by the famine (prompting one garden author, E.A. Bunyard, to comment: "No one will regard the potato as a mere vegetable, but rather as an instrument of destiny.")

SCRAPPED LOCOMOTIVES

✦

Neither of the historic locomotives, *No. 119* and *Jupiter*, which met on that May day at Promontory Point in 1869, were preserved. *No. 119* carried Thomas Durant and had been built at the Rogers Locomotive Works in Paterson, New Jersey. Leland Stanford arrived aboard the *Jupiter*, which had been built at the Schenectady Locomotive Works, New York, and then sailed round to San Francisco by ship. (Stanford was due to travel on the *Antelope*, but it was damaged by a falling log.) Both locomotives were scrapped between 1903 and 1909.

Benefiting "Savages"

Asa Whitney, a New Rochelle, New York, resident and dry-goods man, had also been aware of the problem when, in 1849, he outlined the idea for a transcontinental railroad in his pamphlet, *A Project for a Railroad to the Pacific*. A railroad enthusiast, Whitney had visited the Liverpool and Manchester Railway in England and was convinced of the efficacy of "a communication between the Atlantic and Pacific Oceans, by means of a Canal or Railroad, at Panama, Nicaragua, and Tehuantepec." He promoted the concept like a quack doctor with a patent medicine: the railroad would benefit "yourselves, your country . . . the destitute over population of Europe, and the savage, on whom the blessings and lights of civilisation and Christianity have not Shone; for the Chinese, who, for want of food, must destroy their offspring; for the aged and infirm, who deliberately go out and die . . . and for all the human family."

Whitney's railroad became something of an obsession. He explored possible routes himself, stumbling on places that had "never before been traversed except by savages." He also traveled further afield, to China, Japan, India and Polynesia, looking at what he regarded as immense trading possibilities. Whitney viewed the situation from a

BLOOMER CUT
The railroad blasted its way through the 800 feet (244 m) Bloomer Cut, close to Newcastle, California, in 1865.

VALLEY CROSSING
A trestle bridge under construction on the Central Pacific Railroad in 1868.

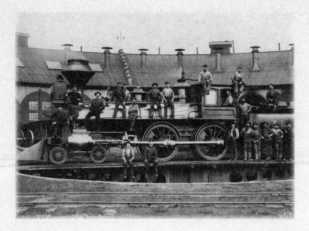

SALT LAKE CITY
Railworkers with their locomotive on the Mormon-built Utah Central Pacific Railroad in 1885, the first line built in the state after the "Trans" went through.

geocentric point of view: "Here we are with more than 2,000 miles [3,219 km] in extent, of unoccupied wilderness land in the center of the globe; Europe, with a starving, destitute population . . . on the one side of us and all Asia on the other side . . . still more destitute, seemed to demand the accomplishment of this great work."

A possible route for a transcontinental railroad had been explored during President Thomas Jefferson's administration, but that involved a combination of rail track and river with a little wagon work thrown in. Boats and rail cars would have made an unhappy union. Whitney, who insisted that no "mature plan" for a communication "directly across the continent by means of a railroad or otherwise, was presented before my proposition," estimated the distance from Lake Michigan to the Pacific Ocean at 2,030 miles (3,267 km). Using "heavy rail of 64 lb (29 kg) to the yard, and on a gauge or width of road not less than six feet," he estimated the work at $20,000 per 1 mile (1.5 km) with additional costs for machinery and repairs. What's more, he wrote, the whole enterprise could be done with "not one dollar . . . asked for from the treasury." This, of all his predictions, was a hollow promise.

The U.S.A., destined to become the world's richest country, was blessed with sufficient exploitable resources to make it economically self-sufficient, but, as Whitney had pointed out, the affluent East was cut off from the West, from California, Oregon and Washington, by deserts, plains and the Rocky Mountains. Abraham Lincoln, from the early days of his presidency, recognized that the nation risked splitting economically into an East and a West, just as the Civil War threatened to divide it into two nations, North and South. Lincoln, like Whitney, was convinced that a railroad would bridge the divide, and he pushed the 1862 Congress' Pacific Railroad Bill through.

> "We are grateful to the train, as to some god who conducts us swiftly through these shades and by so many perils."
>
> *Robert Louis Stevenson*, Across the Plains, *1892*

However, the Civil War (and Lincoln's assassination at the hands of a Confederate sympathizer) delayed for another seven years the realization of America's "manifest destiny." This was the notion, widely held at the time, that it was the inalienable right of the white settler to conquer and control the West.

Grants Dished Out

The task of uniting the nation was given to two companies, the Union Pacific Railroad in the East and the Central Pacific Railroad of California in the West, the government helping both along with generous land grants. The railroads were handed an area of land that, in total, was bigger than the state of Texas, in a checkerboard pattern along both sides of the track. Much of the land was Native American territory and their rights were ignored. In 1872 the artist John Gast portrayed Native Americans slinking away from the advancing railroads: in *American Progress* he pictured Columbia (the symbol of America and womanhood until she was usurped by the figure of the Statue of Liberty) striding across country from the illuminated East to the darkened West bearing the fruits of modernization—plows, books, railroads and a telegraph wire—in her wake. M.A. may have known the painting. He certainly noted "the occasional Indian, a dismal red-skin, half heathen, half Christian [who] has looked stolidly at us as we passed." Where, he wondered, was the "noble savage who ruled the wigwam and made glorious the warpath?"

MANIFEST DESTINY
John Gast painted the ethereal Columbia accompanying the railroads and advancing across America, driving away the Native.

THE "BIG FOUR"

M.A. celebrated the role of the "hardware merchants, wholesale grocers, and dry-goods men, all living in Sacramento, [who] conceived the idea of linking the east and west. Their pride cannot be too great for an enterprise which is worth a prominent page in the history of courageous undertakings."

These were the "Big Four": Leland Stanford, Collis Huntington, Charles Crocker and Mark Hopkins. Stanford, elected governor of California (and founder of Stanford University), was the railroad's public politician; Huntington kept his distance, but retained his financial interest; Hopkins was the impassive bookkeeper who, like the other three, was provided with the means to build his San Francisco mansion; and the line's construction boss was Charles Crocker. He appointed James Harvey Strobridge to do the job.

Meanwhile the Union Pacific in the East drove toward them, their surveyors followed by an army of general laborers, graders, bridge builders and blacksmiths. Small towns like Julesberg, Cheyenne and Laramie, Wyoming sprang up in the wake of the railroad and the establishment of new settlements along the railroad line proved to be a feature of virtually every transcontinental railroad from here on. "We don't wait for population," explained one gentleman from Omaha who was interviewed by M.A. during his journey West. "We lay down a pretty steep project and work it straight up. That's how we had a railroad [the TransAmerican] from Omaha to Frisco. The people follow it like sheep after a bell-wether" (the castrated ram with a bell that the flock trails after).

BIG FOUR
Charles Crocker, Mark Hopkins, Collis Huntington and Leland Stanford, the men behind the idea of linking East and West.

The Union Pacific eventually met the Central Pacific at Promontory Summit in Utah. The ceremony marking the occasion was carefully stage-managed: a symbolic "last spike," cast in gold, was driven home by Leland Stanford before being hurriedly whipped away and replaced with a regular iron spike, on May 10, 1869. The two locomotives were then driven together until their cowcatchers touched. Workmen scrambled on board to pose for the photographers. (Their toasting bottles of liquor were often erased from later prints in order not to upset temperance supporters.)

Although Promontory Summit would be bypassed by the railroad in the early 1900s, this could not diminish the historical significance of eastern and western America being joined by rail. As M.A. pointed out to his readers, the transcontinental railroad, often referred to simply as the Overland Route, had "opened up the mountains, valleys and plains of the Far West" which could now be "reached with ease." And, he conceded, with some satisfaction:

"At the close of my little railroad trip, the six shooter was never taken from its mahogany case [and] the civilisation of San Francisco struck me as far superior to that of New York: California is the richest and most beautiful of the United States of America."

Port Chalmers Railway

Country: New Zealand

Type: Freight

Length: 7.5 miles (12 km)

While Americans were devising methods of shifting frozen meat on the railroads, a little New Zealand line was making its own contribution to history thanks to a zealous railroad supporter, Julius Vogel.

+ Social
+ **Commercial**
+ Political
+ Engineering
+ Military

FROZEN MEAT TRADE

New Zealand's governor opened the new railroad that led from Dunedin down to Port Chalmers in 1873. The job should have been given to the new premier, Julius Vogel. Vogel was a visionary, as enthusiastic about railroads as he was about women's suffrage. He had recently borrowed heavily on the London money markets to fund a national railroad network in the hope of kick-starting the New Zealand economy. It worked.

Nine years later an unusual-looking clipper ship was hauled up in Port Chalmers harbor. The *Dunedin*, named after the capital province of Otago (New Zealand's South Island), (and the Gaelic name for Edinburgh) and with a funnel between her sails, looked like a half-steam, half-sail ship. The steam power, however, was to work a freezer unit that the operators hoped would keep the cargo frozen all the way to London. The Port Chalmers railroad swung into action. Sheep, lambs and pigs were slaughtered near the railhead on the Totara Estate then, covered in ice, transported to the dock by train. The railroad also shipped in hares, pheasants, turkeys, chickens, butter and 2,200 sheep tongues. With the meat packed in calico bags and loaded on board, the *Dunedin* set sail. When she docked in London just under 100 days later the New

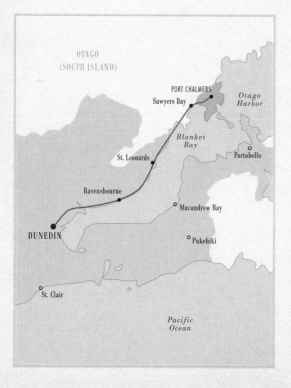

NEW ZEALAND
The short stretch of railroad leading to the seaport near Dunedin on South Island had a historic role to play in the frozen meat trade.

Zealand meat was as fresh as the day it had been killed. The owners banked a healthy profit, having launched New Zealand's international frozen meat trade. (The *Dunedin* and her crew were not so fortunate: the ship sank without trace in 1890.)

Some years earlier Gustavus Franklin Swift had been working in America on an idea for carrying meat in special freezer cars. Swift was a man who knew his meat. The former butcher's boy had worked the cattle drives, herding beef animals to market. But the business of running livestock was not profitable enough: animals died or lost weight, despite using the old trick of denying them water toward the end of their journey so they drank deeply on arrival and weighed in well on market day.

In the mid-1870s Swift moved to the railroad capital, Chicago, to work at the Union Stock Yard. This was the pivotal rail link between the Great Plains, where the cattle were raised, and the markets to the east where they were eaten. One newspaper reported: "There are seventeen miles [27 km] of railroad connecting the Town of Beasts with the city of Chicago [and] in 1869 we sent through Chicago nearly five hundred thousand head of cattle, and more than a million and a half swine." Swift devoted his energies to designing a car that could deliver some of this meat to the east as fresh as it was when it left the west.

His early experimental boxcars, or *reefers*, worked well in winter only. Others were fine until the train took a bend and the carcasses all shifted at once, derailing the train. His reputation for producing problem cars preceded him: when he finally launched an insulated and well-balanced car (the ice was stored above the meat), no rail company would touch it. Swift sidestepped them all, persuading the Grand Trunk to deliver his meat through Michigan and into Canada, before setting up his own Swift Refrigerator Line. It was soon shifting 3,000 carcasses of meat into Boston a week. Railroads had transformed the meat business.

PACKING INSPECTIONS

✦

The combination of dead meat, chilled transport and railroads not only revolutionized the farming markets of New Zealand, Australia and the U.S.A., but nations such as Argentina and Brazil too. The new business was not without setbacks. In Chicago accusations of tainted meat and poor quality control created a customer backlash when writer Upton Sinclair worked in a meat-packing plant to research *The Jungle* in 1906. It became a bestseller and, having exposed some dubious practices, led directly to legislation and regular inspections of the meat packing industry.

1885

Canadian Pacific Railway

Country: Canada

Type: Passenger, Freight

Length: 2,000 miles
(3,219 km)

+ SOCIAL
+ COMMERCIAL
+ **POLITICAL**
+ ENGINEERING
+ MILITARY

NORTH AMERICA
The Canadian Pacific
Railway with Vancouver
as its western terminus
was the first of the
nation's transcontinental
railroads.

British Columbia joined Canada in 1871 on one condition: that they were united by a railroad. Canada's first transcontinental railroad was completed six years ahead of schedule. It not only quelled a rebellion, it also promised to unite the nation.

ACROSS THE CONTINENT

Canada is bounded by the Pacific Ocean in the west, the Arctic in the north and the Atlantic in the east, and embraces part of the Rocky Mountains, the Great Lakes and the vast Hudson Bay, named after the English explorer who disappeared after he was set adrift by a mutinous crew in 1611. The world's second-largest country occupies a generous piece of the globe.

In the opening days of the railroad age Canada, destined to become a federation of ten provinces crossed by three transcontinental railroads, was still finding its constitutional feet. The country came into being after France lost her North American territories to the British, under the British North American Act of 1867. While the Act created a full Dominion of Canada, there were parts missing: one was the place that had been "bought" by the Canadian government from the Hudson Bay Company for £300,000 in 1870. Queen Victoria graciously named the territory British Columbia.

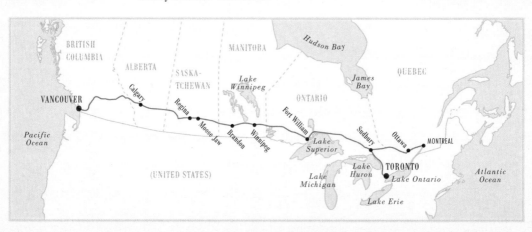

Burdened by bad debts in the aftermath of a gold rush, and keenly aware of how well their territories would look as part of an American west coast running from Washington to Alaska, the British Columbians signed up to be part of Canada on the condition that they would be linked with the rest of the nation by a railroad. (There was an implicit understanding that debts would be shouldered by the mother country.)

In July 1871 they became the sixth province to join the federation. In 1885, their umbilical railroad, the Canadian Pacific, opened when the final spike was driven in between the two lines on Eagle Pass near Craigellachie in the Rocky Mountains.

Canada's first prime minister John A. Macdonald, had promised the railroad would unite the country "instead of making us tributary to American bondage, to American tools, to American freights, to all the little tricks and big tricks that American railroads are addicted to for the purpose of destroying our roads." The Old Chieftain, as he was known (he was also nicknamed "Old Tomorrow," a reference to his fondness for a wee dram), liked to make political capital out of a Canadian David facing up to the American Goliath. The railroad, however, was not going to be a smooth ride either for its builders or Macdonald. An intercolonial railroad linking Britain's North American colonies in the East had been

LAST LINK
A bearded Donald Smith (Lord Strathcona) drove the final spike home on the Canadian Pacific Railway at Craigellachie in British Columbia in 1885.

completed by 1876, but while the Pacific Line was started in 1874, Macdonald and his government were forced to resign over financial shenanigans involving generous contributions to his election campaign.

As for the railroad men, they faced 1,000 miles (1,609 km) of rocky wasteland in northern Ontario, another 1,000 miles (1,609 km) of deserted prairie beyond Winnipeg, and the formidable Rockies.

Back in office again, Macdonald insisted in January 1881 that the world's longest railroad "is going to be built and be proceeded with vigorously, continuously, systematically and successfully until the fate of Canada then, as a dominion, will be sealed." His promise rested on the backs of two men in particular; the grandson of a Scottish crofter, George Stephen, and the far broader back of the well-built American William Cornelius Van Horne, brought in to prop up the faltering operation.

Stephen, who had set up in business after emigrating to Montreal, had, with his business associates, turned around a struggling railroad in Minnesota and sold it at a profit. Now he and his partners (they included Donald Smith from the Hudson Bay Company and James J. Hill, an expansionist railroad builder from America) formed the Canadian Pacific Company and turned to the transcontinental effort.

NATURAL GAS

✦

In 1883, as temperatures dropped to -130 °F (-55 °C), the *Calgary Herald* described an unusual discovery. "At Langevin, 4th siding west of Medicine Hat, a rather singular phenomenon has presented itself. The well-borers have reached a depth of 1,120 feet (340 m) without finding water, but a gas which rushes out of the tube, which, on taking fire emits a flame sufficient to light up the surrounding country. They still propose going deeper for the water, but have given up working at night, not considering it safe." Boring for a water supply for their steam locomotives, the Canadian Pacific engineers had stumbled on natural gas.

Two surveyors, Sandford Fleming (see box on p.132) and Major A.B. Rogers, had looked at the 2,000 miles (3,129 km) of forest, river, boggy muskeg, and mountains with some trepidation, knowing that in order to maintain a level gradient the railroad builders would have to bridge every valley.

Thousands of laborers from Europe were drafted in to build the railroad. In winter they worked in temperatures of -104 °F (-40 °C); in summer they were plagued by swarms of black flies and mosquitoes that brought sickness and disease. Nine thousand Chinese migrant laborers joined the European navvies. They were nicknamed "coolies" after the Hindu term for a hired laborer, although conditions for most of them verged on those of slave laborers. They were paid less, worked on the more dangerous parts of the line, often handling explosives, and, if they were injured, received no compensation. If they died on the job, their families only heard the news through fellow workers. When the railroad was finished there was yet more discrimination: the Government reneged on a promise to let their families join them. (In 2006, the Government formally thanked the Canadian Chinese for their work on the transcontinental).

"Until this great work is complete, our dominion is little more than a geographical expression."

John A. Macdonald, Canada's first prime minister

TOWERING TIMBERS
A steam locomotive crosses the railroad bridge at Mountain Creek in British Columbia. Erected in 1885 it contained more than 2 million board feet (4,719 cubic meters) of timber.

CRUSHING THE REVOLUTION

As the muskeg swallowed up the railroad's floating foundations (in some places 40-foot [12 m] long ties were used to spread the load), the railroad soaked up its government subsidies along with Donald Smith's and George Stephen's fortunes. The government was only persuaded to pitch in with a rescue package after an unexpected turn of events in Saskatchewan. A resistance leader, Louis Riel, founder of the province of Manitoba, returned from exile to lead an uprising of the aboriginal Métis people. Anxious to quell the rebellion, the government was persuaded by Van Horne to use the railroad. Hastily laying down temporary track ahead of the militia, the men from the Canadian Pacific helped crush the revolution. The grateful government found the cash to complete the line and Riel was hanged, despite pleas for clemency, nine days after the railroad was completed in 1885.

By now the Company's coffers were almost empty. They began to fill with the first trains, and the Company branched out into steamships, paddle-steamers, hotels and natural gas (see box on p.130). Slaughterhouses, airlines, buses and forestry followed, and a century after opening Canada's first transcontinental railroad the Canadian Pacific was the nation's second-largest company.

RUNNING REPAIRS
The Canadian Pacific Railway opened its own locomotive manufacturing shop at Angus, Montreal in 1904. The shop also repaired and restored rolling stock.

TRAVEL BY TRAIN

Canadian Pacific

The Canadian Pacific had begun the process of settling western Canada, their overseas agents selling complete Canadian Pacific packages that included cheap land holdings and transportation on its ships and trains in special colonists' cars (see p.135). Some crossed the second border, heading for the U.S.A., but once the U.S. transcontinental railroad had reached San Francisco and the West had settled down, the American border was closed to migrants from Canada in 1890. That left western Canada as "the last best west," as their emigration advertisements described it.

Premier John A. Macdonald had given the Canadian Pacific generous concessions in land and cash to help populate the region, especially the Fertile Crescent, the prairie lands that lay between Edmonton, Alberta, Regina, Saskatchewan, and Winnipeg, Manitoba. The Canadian Pacific made out well in the settler trade and helped convince William Mackenzie and Donald Mann to buy up land and railroad lines for a second transcontinental railroad. The Canadian Northern Railroad planned to run a route from Vancouver Island in British Columbia to Cape Breton Island in Nova Scotia. They purchased steamships on the Great Lakes, swallowed up several smaller railroads and constructed Montreal's Royal Tunnel and a line through Hells Gate in British Columbia. (It caused a major environmental accident when blasting triggered a landslide that partially blocked the Fraser river and its ancient salmon runs.) In January 1915, the final spike was driven home. A third transcontinental route now entered the fray: the Grand Trunk Railroad.

PONT DE QUÉBEC
When it finally opened in 1919, the Quebec bridge dwarfed shipping passing beneath on the St. Lawrence River. It was the world's longest cantilevered railroad bridge.

By 1867 the Grand Trunk had accumulated more than 1,277 miles (2,055 km) of track mainly along the eastern seaboard. At the time it was the world's largest railroad. Its transcontinental line was to run west to a new town, Prince Rupert, north of Vancouver. Battling against the familiar elements of severe winters, the muskeg and surveyors who went out into the wilderness and never returned, the line was also dogged by the double failure of the Quebec Bridge over the St. Lawrence River (see pp.180–181). It opened finally in 1914.

CAPITAL INJECTION

The capital for this transcontinental railroad came from London investors and its driving force was Charles Melville Hays. Hays had started on the railroads at seventeen, working on the railroads between his hometown, St. Louis, Missouri, and Tulsa, Oklahoma. Now, in his late forties, Hays forged his way through the obstacles to create the third transcontinental railroad. He died before it opened, returning from a London business trip in 1912 on the R.M.S. *Titanic* when the ship struck an iceberg. He drowned after helping women into a lifeboat. (Another railroad official who died on the *Titanic* was John Thayer of the Pennsylvania Railroad. His wife and son were rescued.)

All three of the transcontinental railroads brought settlers to the "prairie provinces," Manitoba, Saskatchewan and Alberta, where would-be farmers were given 160 acres if they "proved up," that is, paid their $10 registration fee, turned the sod and lived on the land for three years. The hard times for farmers who had hewn their homesteads out of the aspen parkland were made easier during the 1890s by a boom in wheat prices and improved seed and machinery.

Hays' Grand Trunk, denied the government handouts given to the Canadian Pacific, nevertheless made capital from setting up new towns every 10–15 miles (16–24 km). Each was a mirror of the last, laid out on standard street grids. Inventing names for them all was a casual affair as railroad officials worked their way through the alphabet.

The railroads also introduced the "prairie sentinels," towering grain elevators (based on Oliver Evans' designs) to replace the long railside warehouses that took as long to fill as they did to empty. (The grain business persuaded Stephen and Van Horne to set up the Lake of the Woods Milling Company with its famous Five Roses brand.)

Almost 2 million immigrants from Britain alone were lured to build the railroads between 1901 and 1921. British workers were given priority over "undesirable" Asians, who ironically had helped build the railroads in the first place. A special head tax was introduced to prevent Chinese and Japanese immigrants, while red tape was used to obstruct direct passage immigrants from India.

By 1921, as Canada nationalized its railroads, the process of immigration was almost complete. Canada had come of age thanks to the railroads.

COLONIST CARS

+

A number of special trains appeared on the Canadian transcontinental railroads, including the funeral trains that carried the late prime minister John A. Macdonald in 1891 and the Canadian Pacific president, Cornelius Van Horne, in 1915. British King George VI traveled aboard a leviathan *Royal Hudson* in 1939. The colonists' cars were more basic. Made from former first-class cars that had been stripped out by the railroad companies, they were refitted with oiled-wood floors, slat seats that folded down into berths, and a toilet at each end to serve the needs of the seventy-two people in each car. There was also a little heating and cooking stove. Rudimentary though they were, many marriages and lifelong friendships were founded within their walls.

LAST BEST WEST
Laying tracks across the plains. The railroads opened up the interior for migration and many of the railroad builders themselves would settle in the new country.

Jerusalem to Jaffa Railway

Country: Israel

Type: Military, Passenger, Freight

Length: 54 miles (87 km)

✦ **SOCIAL**
✦ **COMMERCIAL**
✦ **POLITICAL**
✦ **ENGINEERING**
✦ **MILITARY**

The Jaffa to Jerusalem line, constructed in one of the world's hotspots, fell victim not to political expediency, but to the automobile. And yet, a century later, it came to symbolize a new age for railroads in the Middle East.

PILGRIM ROUTE

Jerusalem, one of the world's oldest cities, did not enter the railroad age until trains had run for almost a century. Even then they made a slow start. The first line reached the old port of Jaffa, and the Middle East's first station, in 1892. Jerusalem was important to Jews, Muslims, and Christians alike and the line should have benefited from pilgrim traffic. Yet the station was closed and the line abandoned in 1948.

The British financier, Moses Montefiore, had constantly promoted the idea of a Jerusalem railroad. His first visit to the Holy Land in 1827 persuaded him to lead a more orthodox life (from now on his personal kosher butcher was to accompany him on all his travels) and to lobby the British Prime Minister, Lord Palmerston, for a Jerusalem to Jaffa rail link. Jerusalem's ruling Ottoman regime remained unsupportive especially when a British survey team estimated costs at £4,000 per kilometer.

Montefiore did not give up. He had a railroad engineer reassess the route in 1857. His proposal, and similar ones from American, French and German engineers, failed to gain support. Finally, in 1885 a shrewd rabbi's son from Jerusalem, Joseph Navon, persuaded the Ottoman authorities to agree to a railroad. Navon rushed his concession

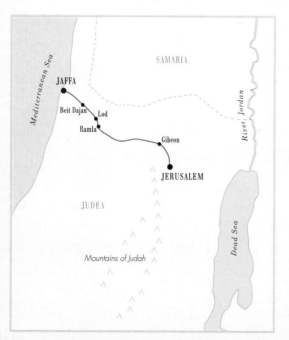

HOLY LANDS
A rail line from Jaffa to Jerusalem was heavily promoted by the British banker Moses Montefiore.

to Paris and sold it for a million francs to Bernard Collas and his Société du Chemin de Fer Ottoman de Jaffa et Prolongement.

With a Jewish promoter, Turkish approval and French funding, the line promised to be a cooperative project. The list of contributing nations lengthened as work began: there were Swiss and Austrian navvies, canny British coal merchants and rail makers from Belgium (although Ferdinand de Lesseps was rumored to

be selling his old Panama stock). Pennsylvania's Baldwin Locomotive Works sold them their engines, while France supplied everything else including half a dozen of Gustave Eiffel's iron bridges (he had completed his famous Paris tower). When the first locomotive steamed into Jerusalem, draped with the French Tricolor and the Stars and Stripes, 10,000 people turned out to cheer it.

The opening in September 1892 was a brief success. The three-hour train took almost as long as the coach journey and, while freight traffic rose and some villages settled along the track, the tourist trade remained thin. One traveler wrote of being able to step down from the dawdling train and harvest flowers for his botanic collection without losing the train.

In World War I the Turkish and German Central Powers tore up part of the line to save its being shelled by Allied ships off the coast. The track was raided to provide a new line to connect with the Hejaz Railroad between Damascus and Medina. (T.E. Lawrence—Lawrence of Arabia—and his Arab guerrillas subjected the Hejaz line to constant sabotage.) When the army retreated they blew up all the bridges. The line was restored by the British, but it continued to decline until, under the auspices of Israel Railroads, it was closed.

That would have been the end of the story, but for the emergence of high-speed rail and the problem of traffic congestion. In 2001, as rail passenger numbers almost tripled in a decade, Israel embarked on a flagship project for a new high-speed railroad. The Jaffa to Jerusalem line acquired a new lease of life.

> **"That wretched little Jaffa—Jerusalem line."**
>
> *Theodore Herzl, Jewish leader*

HIGH-SPEED PROGRESS

✦

Many countries, including Israel, began planning new, high-speed rail links in the twenty-first century. Modern railroad builders had to contend with environmental considerations and, on the Jaffa to Jerusalem line, construction teams had to minimize the environmental impact on the Yitla Stream, a place of Biblical significance. Meanwhile, as tensions rose in the Middle East, some commentators speculated that Israel's high-speed railroad could one day rival the Suez Canal by linking the Red Sea with the Mediterranean.

1898

Highland Railway

Country: Scotland

Type: Freight, Passenger

Length: 240 miles (386 km)

R ailways, warned commentators in the nineteenth century, would empty the provinces and alter the traditional city markets for ever. They were right, but the changes turned out to benefit people in both town and country.

+ **SOCIAL**

+ **COMMERCIAL**

+ **POLITICAL**

+ **ENGINEERING**

+ **MILITARY**

CONFUSION AND DISTRESS

"[Railroads] will give an unnatural impetus to society, destroy all the relations which exist between man and man, overthrow all mercantile regulations, overturn the metropolitan markets, drain the provinces of all their resources and create, at peril of life, all sorts of confusion and distress." One can hear the infuriated thump of the whisky decanter as the editor of the popular Sunday newspaper, *John Bull*, finished his broadside against the railroads in 1835. He was not to know that his glass of Scotch whiskey, together with his favorite beef and mustard dinner, would benefit hugely from the railroad age, nor that the journey to Edinburgh, which then took 43 hours, would shortly be cut by the railroads to just under 11 hours.

SCOTTISH PRIDE
The Scots and Scottish distilleries were quick to exploit new, more lucrative markets for their local produce once the railroads reached the Highlands.

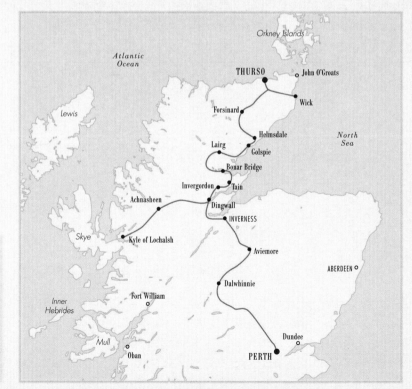

The editor's attack on the railroad menace made no mention of the ills of society at the time. The Industrial Revolution and the railroads, like magnets passing through iron filings, drew country people to the cities where, to begin with, they were mostly inadequately housed and poorly fed. As late as 1913 the military was dismayed by the poor health and stature of their inner-city recruits, who were often underweight, undernourished and disabled by tuberculosis and rickets. Had it not been for the nineteenth-century railroads their health would have been considerably worse.

Train services delivered fresh food into the metropolitan districts. *John Bull's* editor, lived a very different life from the inky-fingered printer who fetched his galley proofs and yet, by the mid-1800s, virtually everything on their respective dinner plates came courtesy of the railroad. Railroads put money back into the rural districts; and they altered the face of the countryside as different districts developed their more marketable specialities. The changes rippled out across the world with the railroads. Just as Kent became the famous "England Garden," so Brazil became famed for its coffee, Cuba for its cigars and Argentina its beef.

The Highland Railway was a supplier of fresh beef and fresh fish. The Inverness and Nairn Railroad, initially sponsored by the townspeople of Inverness itself, had opened in November 1855. It was soon linked to Perth in the south (and the mainline routes to the rest of the country) and north to Dingwall, Invergordon, Bonar Bridge, Golspie, Helmsdale, Wick and Thurso as well as the Kyle of Lochalsh on the west coast of Scotland. By 1898 the lines were complete (branch lines, added over the previous forty years brought the length of track up to just over 240 miles [386 km]). Tourism boosted traffic, especially during the "Glorious Twelfth," August 12, when bombastic editors might join the gentry to shoot grouse on the Scottish moors, but the Highland lines made the most of their freight.

HIGHLAND WAY
The viaduct over Culloden Moor, the longest in Scotland, lay just east of the site of the Battle of Culloden. It crossed the River Nairn outside Inverness.

"Does anybody mean to say that decent people would consent to be hurried along through the air upon a railroad?"
The editor, John Bull *newspaper, 1835*

Scottish distillers appreciated the line from the outset. In 1895 the Balbair Distillery in the county of Ross relocated to the railside, while famous distilleries such as Glenfiddich and Glenmorangie were made more famous still by the expanding market offered by the railroads. The meat trade, too, transformed by the railroads, saw carcasses of Highland beef hurried down to the capital. Even the contents of the mustard pot came courtesy of the railroad. In 1823 a Norfolk miller, Jeremiah Colman, who had started blending crushed mustard seed into a paste, set up business to challenge the great mustard makers of Dijon, France. Around thirty years later he moved the business to a site with its own sidings beside a Norfolk Railroad (which was by this time part of the Eastern Counties Railroad). The business took off. Colman's distinctive yellow powders were shipped around the globe, freshening the palates of British empire builders from Bombay to Sydney. (Jeremiah's efforts persuaded other food processors to follow including Richard and George Cadbury with their chocolate factory beside Birmingham's Stirchley Station, sugar refiners Henry Tate and Abraham Lyle in Silvertown, London, and, in 1923, Philadelphia's pickle maker Henry Heinz in Willesden.)

CITY MARKETS

Neither beef nor whisky was affordable to the average East London family. Even those with jobs relied on the "pop shop." "The people who ran the pawn shop, they knew the plight of other people," recalled a soldier's daughter, Katy Deem, in the early 1900s. "You'd get half a crown on a big bundle of clothes . . . then you had to find half a crown on the weekend to fetch it all back." The health of children like Katy was improved by a regular glass of milk. An outbreak of cow fever, rinderpest, in the 1860s decimated London's city cows, which many of the poor kept in backstreet stables to supply themselves with milk.

The milk started to trickle in by train. Dairies in country areas like Carmarthenshire, Pembrokeshire, Devon, Cornwall and Cheshire began to structure their operations around the milk trains. Even former railroad men themselves became involved. One Welsh borders lad, Edward Matthews, left for America in 1833, and drove steam locomotives between Chicago and New York before returning home to do the same between Cardiff and Shrewsbury. When he was injured in a rail accident he took his compensation, bought a dairy cow for £14 12s 6d and delivered milk in his neighborhood from a wheelbarrow.

At the turn of the twentieth century the Highland Railway was making the most of the new city markets. Midway through the Victorian age the Friday fish supper, derived from the traditional Catholic abstention from meat, had become a staple even in poor households as "silver darlings"—herrings—were shipped south by the barrel. In 1903 a light railroad, the Wick and Lybster, was opened to move the fish faster. So much tonnage was carried in rail cars that the drizzle of fish oil created slicks on the tracks and caused problems with braking and traction.

The Highland was not the only means of supply. In the 1880s, having been taken over by the Manchester, Sheffield and Lincolnshire Railroads, the Grimsby Docks railroad station in Lincolnshire carried an esti-

EXPRESS DAIRY TRAINS

✦

The railroads helped establish London's Welsh dairies, family businesses that bottled and sold milk in the capital. The milk was supplied by dairy farms in west Wales, often through family connections. The cows were milked on the farm, the milk placed in churns and then taken by cart to the nearest Great Western Railway station where it was shipped, still in churns, to London and the Welsh dairies. The businessman George Barham had greater ambitions. He launched his London "express" dairy company, the milk arriving by Great Western and Southern Railways express trains at his bottling plant in south London.

MILK TANKER
Businessman George Barham used express trains to ship country milk from the south and west to the London markets.

mated quarter of all the fish in the
country. This rapacious combination of
steam trawlers and steam locomotives
was unsustainable. Just as the whalers
overkilled their own prey, the trade would
decimate North Sea fish stocks, but not
before giving rise to the fish and chips
supper. Early fish and chips shops opened
in northern England in the 1860s, but a
meal of fried fish and "tatties" was familiar to many coastal country people. It was
only when the railroads carried the fish and the potatoes (around 2.2
million tons mostly from the Midlands and Lincolnshire, by 1920) that
the traditional fish and chips supper came into being.

NATIONALIZED BREWS
One pleasure afforded to both rich and poor was the jug of porter.
Porter, allegedly named after the strong-backed men who hauled the
brewers' hogsheads, was a strong, dark ale, heavily hopped to preserve
it longer and blended with lighter ales for taste. Also known as "entire,"
it was one of the first industrialized beers and could be carried far on
the railroads.

While local breweries still predominated in the late 1800s (many pubs
brewed their own beer, a feature that would return in the late twentieth
century), a lot of beer was being "nationalized"—brewed in one place
and dispatched by rail to the outlets. Britain's beer capital was Burton

TROUBLE BREWING
The beer trade boomed in
the railroad age, the railroads
helping the big brewers
dominate domestic and
export markets. Many
smaller breweries were
taken over.

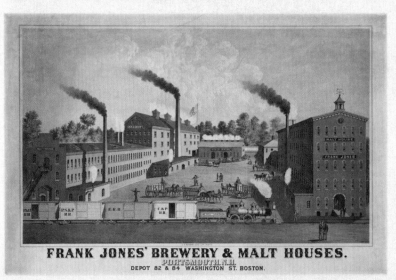

FRANK JONES' BREWERY & MALT HOUSES.
PORTSMOUTH N.H.
DEPOT 82 & 84 WASHINGTON ST. BOSTON.

BEN VRACKIE
A Highland Railways
"Ben class" steam locomotive
behind a coal wagon at
Dingwall Station.

on Trent, where private rail lines snaked around big breweries such as Bass and Arthur Guinness & Son to deliver their beer to the main railroad lines. The railroads not only carried the beer and the hops, they also transported the hop pickers to the hop yards. In the late 1800s there were over about 70,000 acres (283 sq km) of hops growing in England, centered around the Kent hop "gardens" and Herefordshire and Worcestershire's "hopyards." Every autumn, special trains collected families of hop pickers from poorer urban areas—east London, the Welsh coal mining valleys and Birmingham—to harvest the crop.

There was no great demand for beer to be transported to the Highlands, except to the troops stationed in Scotland during the two world wars. The Highland Railway played a key role in both. In World War I with the British naval fleet stationed at Scapa Flow off the Orkney Islands, men, munitions and supplies were trundled across country. The line suffered badly from overuse and restricted maintenance in both wars, and many of the branch lines had already closed when, in 1963, the Highland Line itself was scheduled to be erased from the railroad map on the advice of Lord Beeching. In the end the rail routes were returned to the basic network of 1898. The milk, beef, and whisky traffic, meanwhile, had virtually all been taken over by trucks.

COUNTRY STATIONS

✦

Farmer Arthur Bellamy recalled how life in the 1950s revolved around the village station, Fawley. "We had six passenger trains a day. Everything went by train, all our stock, cattle, sheep, pigs, hay, straw, sugar beet and our feeding stuffs and mineral, cake, and slag." Fawley station, and the line between Ross-on-Wye and Hereford, closed in the 1960s when rail chairman Richard Beeching presided over the axing of 2,000 stations. Fifty years later, as passenger numbers rose and country villages were blighted by car and lorry traffic, there were many who lamented the loss of the Beeching railroads.

Valtellina Railroad

Country: Italy

Type: Passenger

Length: 66 miles (106 km)

Over the course of two centuries trains have been moved by just about any means from people power, horses and sail to the steam locomotives. But the exciting new power source of the twentieth century was electricity.

+ SOCIAL

+ **COMMERCIAL**

+ POLITICAL

+ **ENGINEERING**

+ MILITARY

GALVANIZED INTO ACTION

The burglars who broke into a rail shed in Scotland in the 1840s were not interested in the cash box. They were steam-railroad men and they were looking for the *Galvani*, an electric locomotive built by Robert Davidson. When they found it they pounded it to pieces.

Davidson had named his machine in honor of the Italian Luigi Galvini, a Bologna-born physician who married his university professor's daughter. That secured him a post at Bologna University and the chance, in the 1770s, to discover bioelectricity and the startling effect of electrical impulses on the nervous system, in particular the twitching legs of the dead frog he was dissecting.

The Aberdeen inventor Robert Davidson had, like the Vermont, U.S.A. blacksmith Thomas Davenport who patented an electric motor in 1835, taken a creative approach to Galvani's concept of electricity and applied it to a four-wheeled, battery-powered locomotive. Tested on the Edinburgh to Glasgow line, it drove at a reasonable 4 mph (6.4 kph).

LOMBARDY
It was inevitable that locomotives would eventually be powered by electricity. The Hungarian engineer Kálmán Kandó helped it happen on this northern Italian railroad.

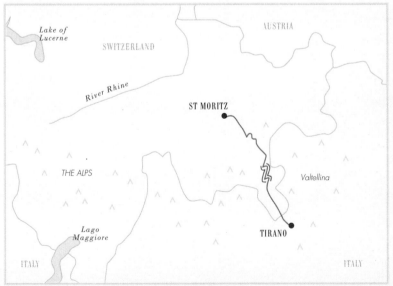

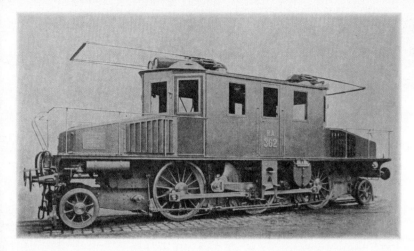

Despite the fears of Luddite railroad workers, however, the *Galvani* posed no serious threat to steam locomotion. That threat arrived at a little railroad in a park next to Lehrter Station in 1879 for the Berlin Exhibition. While steam passenger trains pounded out of the imposing Lehrter Bahnhof to Hannover, German families in their Sunday best toured the park on the electrically driven train. The uniformed driver, like a jockey astride his steed, sat at the front over a brass plate: "Siemens and Halske Berlin."

Werner von Siemens, who founded his company in the 1840s, had a solid reputation for his long-distance telegraph lines, often placed alongside railroad tracks. He would shortly introduce the world's first electric street lighting in Godalming, in Surrey, England, while the success of his electric tractor led to the launch of Berlin's first electric tramline in 1881. Two years later Magnus Volk, a Brighton engineer, launched his own electric train (see box on p.147), and a month afterward Austrians were patronizing their electric tram and railroad at Mödling near Vienna.

The Swiss, who were short of coal, but blessed with plenty of hydroelectricity, monitored developments. After nationalizing their railroads by common consent, they trialed a complicated-looking electric locomotive called *Eva* in 1904 on the line between Seebach and Wettingen. The year 1913 heralded the opening of the most spectacular electrified railroad lines through the Alps, the Bern–Lötschberg–Simplon, and in 1919 the Swiss moved to electrify the whole network. They abandoned first class carriages in the 1950s and, in the 1980s, introduced the *Taktfahrplan*, the clock-faced timetable designed to rationalize train departures.

> **"The days of my youth extend backwards to the dark ages, for I was born when the rushlight, the tallow dip or the solitary blaze of the hearth were the common means of indoor lighting."**
>
> *Joseph Swan, inventor of the patent electric filament lamp*, The Electrician, *1893*

There were occasional problems: in 2005 a power cut shut the whole system down, temporarily stranding 1,500 trains and 200,000 passengers.

Back in America in the 1890s, the smoke- and steam-filled Howard Street tunnel caused such problems to the Baltimore and Ohio Railroad that they ordered some electric locomotives, nine times heavier (and nine times more powerful) than their nearest rivals. It was a huge development for a main line. The New York Central followed their lead in 1902. By then another engineering firm working closely on electric-powered trains, the Budapest-based Ganz, had landed a job on Italy's railroads.

Ganz's Kálmán Kandó was one of the early engineers to appreciate that, for an electric train to be efficient, it had to draw power from the public network, rather than attempt to generate all its own power. In 1902, a few years after Siemens' electric train trundled around the Berlin Exhibition, Kálmán Kandó was enjoying the mountain air of the Valtellina Valley in Lombardy, near the Swiss border in northern Italy, as he installed the first high-voltage, mainline electric railroad.

Italy's railroads had been through troubled times. They had struggled to keep pace with other parts of Europe in the initial nineteenth-century race for rail. The first line, between Naples and Portici, which bought a locomotive from Robert Stephenson, simply linked the residence of Ferdinand II, king of the Two Sicilies, with his barracks 5 miles (8.5 km) away. It was not until after Italy's disparate kingdoms were united in 1861 that construction began on just over 1,000 miles (1,609 km) of new track to add to the existing 1,335 miles (2,148 km). Appreciating that railroads united nations, the Italians offered generous subsidies to private companies to build more. Railroads were soon being rolled out across the country: Naples to Rome in 1863, Florence to Milan in 1864, Rome to Florence in 1866 and Verona to Galvani's hometown, Bologna, and beyond to Innsbruck in Austria in 1867. The construction standards were not the best, contractors being more interested in capturing profits than in spending serious

amounts of money on the tracks. In a bid to rectify the matter the government grouped the railroads under three companies, the Upper Italy Railroad, the Rome Railroad (responsible for the central network and the Florence–Rome–Naples line) and the Calabrian to Sicily Railroad. As an afterthought a fourth, the Strade Ferrate Meridionali, was charged with opening a new line down the Adriatic coast and, during the 1860s, another from Bologna to Lecce in the heel of Italy. Three years after the Valtellina Railway opened, the old companies (two had already been replaced after running into financial difficulties) were taken over by the state as the Ferrovie dello Stato. The Valtellina line would successfully operate for the next thirty years. Italy's love affair with electric trains, however, was not over.

Both Ganz and Siemens and Halske continued to develop electric trains. In 1903 a Siemens and Halske electric-powered train EMU (electric multiple unit) tore along the Marienfelde and Zossen line in Germany at 131 mph (211 kph). (The company also launched an early electric car in Berlin in 1905). In 1937 the Ferrovie dello Stato unveiled its new *Elettrotreno*. With a streamlined front like an aerodynamic cricket, the *Elettrotreno 200* zipped into the record books at speeds of 126 mph (203 kph) along the Pontenure and Piacenza line between Bologna and Milan. Word went round that the driver was no less than the portly Italian dictator Benito Mussolini himself. It was, like the story that Benito made Italy's trains run on time, false. Mussolini did, however, dispatch his national pride to the World Exposition in New York where it shared the limelight with Pennsylvania's huge experimental locomotive, dubbed *The Big Engine*. The *Elettrotreno's* development was stopped in its tracks by the war, many being destroyed by Allied bombing. The war also claimed the life of the *Elettrotreno's* interior designer Giuseppe Pagano. He left Mussolini's Fascists for the Resistance movement and was tortured and killed in a German concentration camp in 1945. In the post-war period Italy's stylish electric trains, once the fastest in Europe continued to serve the nation into the 1990s.

VOLK'S ELECTRIC

✦

Volk's Electric Railway in Brighton, England, credited with being the world's oldest operating electric railroad, opened on August 3, 1883. It was developed by Brighton Corporation's electrical engineer, Magnus Volk. He also designed the electricity generating station that powered the train along its tracks. The Volk's Brighton train proved popular with the public. Five weeks after it opened, an electric railroad run on hydroelectricity started operation at the Giant's Causeway in Portrush, Northern Ireland.

1904

Cape to Cairo Railway

Country: Africa

Type: Passenger, Freight, Military

Length: 1,641 miles (2,641 km)

+ **SOCIAL**
+ **COMMERCIAL**
+ **POLITICAL**
+ **ENGINEERING**
+ **MILITARY**

If Cecil Rhodes had achieved his dream of an African Trunk Line, it would have been the world's longest railroad. His plans, however, were destined to fail.

FIRST RACE

John Ruskin, one of the Victoria era's most influential thinkers, did not care for railroads. Their speed depressed him. "A fool always wants to shorten space and time, a wise man wants to lengthen both," he once remarked. And he was quick to support his friend, the poet William Wordsworth, in opposing plans to bring the railroads into his beloved Lake District.

Yet Ruskin managed to inspire one of Africa's most ambitious railroad builders, Cecil Rhodes, through an inaugural speech he gave at Oxford University. Speaking on the subject of Imperial Duty he warned the undergraduates that if England was not to perish "she must found colonies as fast and as far as she is able . . . seizing every piece of fruitful waste ground she can set her foot on, and . . . teaching her colonists that . . . their first aim is to be to advance the power of England."

Cecil Rhodes was born the sickly child of a Hertfordshire clergyman in 1853. He thrived under the African sun. He arrived in Durban (in modern South Africa) in 1870 to work on his older brother's cotton farm and when

RHODES COLOSSUS
Punch magazine in 1892 portrayed Cecil Rhodes joining Cape Town to Cairo with a telegraph line that would run alongside his proposed 1,641-mile (2,641 km) railroad.

that venture failed, went to the diamond fields of Kimberley in the north of Cape Province. He began buying up smaller holdings and mines, gradually amassing a minerals portfolio that allowed him to launch the De Beers Mining Company. At one time it controlled 90 percent of the world's diamond market.

Rhodes harbored plans for a hugely ambitious trans-African railroad and he was very much of the same mind as Ruskin. As he put it: "If there be a God I think that what he would like me to do is paint as much of the map of Africa British red as possible." His trans-African dream, 5,700 miles (9,173 km) in a straight line, would start in the south at Cape Town, snake through what is now South Africa, Botswana, Zimbabwe, Zambia, Tanzania, Uganda, Sudan and into Egypt to arrive at the capital of the Arab world, Cairo. At the

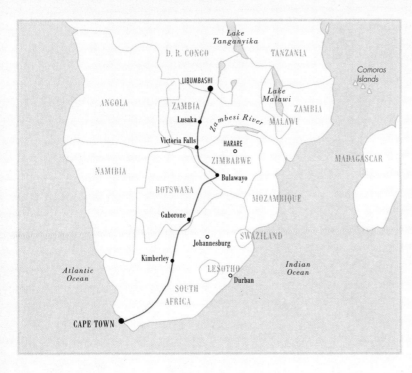

time British interests were strong throughout much of that region, but
the Germans, Portuguese and French were also busy acquiring pieces of
the continent. In the African land grab these conflicting colonial squabbles would eventually defeat Rhode's planned railroad.

In April 1904 Cecil Rhodes' first Cape to Cairo train reached the Victoria Falls. The journey from the Cape, which had taken six months by
bullock cart, was now possible in a matter of days. The Cape to Cairo
experiment, however, was virtually over.

AFRICAN TRUNK LINE

For Rhodes, Africa was the last great colony. It was a source of considerable mineral wealth and the railroad was to be the means of removing
this into the pockets of Europeans. The African people were to be servants in that process. As Rhodes wrote in his will: "I contend that we are
the first race in the world and that the more of the world we inhabit the
better it is for the human race." His will was read even before the railroad reached the celebrated Victoria Falls in 1906. Rhodes died in 1902
and his obituaries celebrated his political contributions (he was prime
minister of the Cape Province), significant fortune, and the fact that
Rhodesia had been named after him. But, as the *Manchester Guardian*
newspaper noted: "Rhodes' last great task, a task that has so far not
been completed, was the Cape to Cairo Railway."

He started the Cape to Cairo when he approached an old friend from Oxford, Charles Metcalfe, now working in South Africa, to survey a line from Kimberley to Vryburg. The state-owned Cape Government Railroad, which had taken over a mere 57 miles (92 km) of private lines in 1874, built a railroad line between the Kimberley diamond fields and Cape Town, 647 miles (1,041 km) away, in 1885 (they also added 1,243 miles [2,000 km] of railroads in the Cape Province).

Rhodes and Metcalfe saw the Vryburg extension as the start of what they called the "African Trunk Line." (It was an editor of a London newspaper, the *Daily Telegraph*, who coined the phrase "Cape to Cairo.") Metcalfe was in full accord with Rhodes' ambitions: "The passage of the iron track ... must ultimately join the Cape with Cairo, and carry civilisation through the heart of the dark continent," he declared. After completing the Vryburg line in 1893, Rhodes gave the contract to extend it to Mafeking, 96 miles (155 km) away to George Pauling.

Grinding to a Halt

Like Metcalfe and Rhodes, Pauling was another newcomer to Africa. A big man with a taste for champagne and grand meals, the 20-year-old arrived in Africa with his brother in 1877 and by 1881 had completed a 65-mile (105 km) railroad in the Eastern Cape, the Port Alfred. He was on hand to resolve the problem of a 200-foot (61 m) tunnel between Worcester and Beaufort West (he was also asked to consider a tunnel under the sea between England and France) and was never short of railroad work. Over the next eighteen years he would build almost 1,550 miles (2,500 km) of the Cape to Cairo through modern Botswana, Zimbabwe, Zambia to Elisabethville (Libumbashi) in the Congo where the railroad finally ground to a halt.

After driving the line through to Mafeking, Pauling tackled the next obstacle, the stretch to Bulawayo. Before the railroad, the quickest way to make the journey was onboard Doel Zeederberg's pioneering coaches. The

Victoria Falls

✦

Once the Cape to Cairo reached Victoria Falls, Cape Town Railroads began advertising luxury rail travel through "darkest Africa," persuading travelers to leave behind the boredom of the Baden-Baden and ride instead on the *Imperial Mail,* the *Zambezi* or the *African Express* to Victoria Falls. Here the Zambezi plunged over the precipice into the rainbow-streaked mists below. At night the roar of wild game might be heard from the balconies of the Victoria Falls Hotel: by day the sight of giraffes and purposeful herds of elephants (into which the train occasionally ran) gave the journey an extra frisson of excitement.

BUSH STAGE
Before the railroad joined
Mafeking to Bulawayo
the journey was made by
Zeederberg stagecoach.
It could take up to five days.

South African Zeederberg dispatched his American-built stagecoaches into the bush from the Mafeking railhead two hours after the Cape Town train arrived. Up to twelve passengers paid an expensive nine pence to one shilling per 1 mile (1.5 km) for five or six days of extreme discomfort as a team of mules (an experiment with zebras had been judged a failure) lugged them off to Bulawayo. Journey times depended on the number of times the coach capsized and the political situation amongst the rebellious Matabele.

When George Pauling rode the coach, the drivers took nine days to reach Bulawayo, traveling after dark through the Matabele strongholds. "We could see their fires on the hills, but although the prospect was disquieting, no attempt was made to stop us," Pauling declared later. The journey was made more intolerable by the stench of thousands of dead or dying cattle, ravaged by an outbreak of rinderpest. The outbreak not only devastated the native economy, it also sent the cost of transporting people and equipment from Mafeking to Bulawayo soaring. The European settlers needed a railroad more than ever before and George Pauling was the man to build it.

Rhodes leaned on Pauling to complete the connection as quickly as possible and in November 1897 the last stretch of line between Francistown and Bulawayo was made. The Zeederberg coaches gave up and the Cape

CECIL RHODES
A cartoon of the founder of the De Beers diamond company, Cecil Rhodes, from *Vanity Fair* magazine. Rhodes was an ardent supporter of British colonial rule in Africa.

Government began advertising its rail journeys from Cape Town to the wide boulevards of Bulawayo. (The streets had been widened by Rhodes' own British South Africa Company to accommodate a nine-beast mule train turning in the street.) They took a mere five and a half days.

KITCHENER'S RAILROAD

In the north of the continent, meanwhile, Britain's Lord Kitchener set out to avenge the death of General Charles Gordon and retake Khartoum with his railroad route out of Cairo. After the British occupation of Egypt in 1881, Gordon and his garrison had taken the Sudanese capital, Khartoum. They were attacked and put to the sword by the forces of Mahdi Muhammed Ahmad in 1884. Four years later Kitchener's 576-mile (927 km) railroad reached Omdurman and the general, with the aid of his new Maxim machine guns, slaughtered Ahmad's successor, Abdullah al-Taashi, and his fighters.

The first line on the continent had been built by Robert Stephenson in 1856 from Alexandria to Cairo. Now, in 1896, Kitchener was driving his Sudan Military Railroad south toward Khartoum, and not on the expected narrow gauge. Kitchener had met Rhodes only a few weeks before starting construction and was persuaded to adopt the same gauge as Pauling had done on the Cape to Cairo. He had also "borrowed" several of Rhodes' locomotives—or rather, Kitchener's Canadian engineer, Edouard Girouard, so did as he battled across the Sahara in temperatures that touched 104 degrees. After Kitchener quit the Sudan, the railroad line was continued south for 1,240 miles (1,965 km) south to Kosti.

COMMON GAUGE
After a meeting with Cecil Rhodes, Lord Kitchener adopted the same gauge as the Cape railroad when he built his Sudan Military railroad toward Khartoum.

Pauling, meanwhile, had continued the line north to Victoria Falls, but progress was faltering after the Boer War and Rhodes' death. The completion of the Victoria Bridge across the Falls in 1905 attracted crowds after word spread that it would probably collapse. The bridge, built in sections by a British company, Cleveland's of Darlington, another beneficiary of the race to build rail in Africa, was reassembled on site and, apart from modifications to cope with the heat and consequent expansion of the metal ribs, opened on April Fool's Day.

Pauling went on to push the line farther into central Africa (initially funded by Scottish mining engineer, Robert Williams, who had discovered valuable copper deposits in Katanga). By 1906, having founded the township of Lusaka, Pauling was 2,000 miles (3,218 km) from the Cape. He carried on alone taking the Cape to Cairo as far as Bukama in the Congo. And there it stopped.

As a straight line scribed across the African map the Cape to Cairo was an impressive achievement, even if the two ends failed to meet. (Rhodes, perhaps, never intended that they should, expecting steamships and ferries to complete the connections). It also spawned a plethora of new lines, as Rhodes had predicted, such as the 240-mile (386 km) Matadi to Kinshasa line and the Benguela Railroad across Angola, used to cart Williams' copper out in 1932.

The Cape to Cairo was the first transcontinental railroad that failed to reach completion. The collapse was partly due to conflicting colonial interests: Germany in East Africa, Portugal in Angola and Mozambique, and France in North Africa. After Germany's defeat in World War I Britain secured the territories it needed to complete the line, but the political will was absent. Although plans were drawn up to restore Africa's north-south transcontinental railroad, the Cape to Cairo dream was at an end.

PRECARIOUS CROSSING
A steam train edges across a ford on the Shashu River near Francistown on the Botswana and Zimbabwe borders.

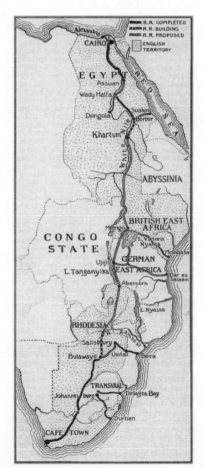

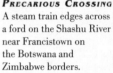

UNFULFILLED DREAM
Cecil Rhodes' plans for a north to south transafrican railroad finally foundered in the early 1900s.

Jingzhang Railway

Country: China

Type: Passenger, Freight

Length: 121 miles (195 km)

+ **SOCIAL**

+ COMMERCIAL

+ **POLITICAL**

+ ENGINEERING

+ MILITARY

In the twenty-first century, the Chinese railroads carry more people and freight than any other. Yet when the first Chinese railroad was opened in 1876 it triggered riots.

ALL-CHINA RAILROAD

An unseasonably heavy snowfall during *Chunjie*, the Chinese New Year, in January 2009 left 100,000 travelers stranded in the mainline station at Guangzhou. It took the army and reservists to clear the tracks and secure the running of the trains in China's southern province.

Traveling during Chunjie has never been easy. The week-long public holiday traditionally signals the start of two billion rail journeys by students starting their vacation and others trying to reach the family home for the annual reunion. (To put the figures in perspective, the population of China numbered less than 1.5 billion in 2009.) Even extra trains, buses and temporary ticket stations set up in city squares cannot alleviate the strain of New Year train travel.

One development that did ease the journey in 2010, provided passengers could find a reasonably priced ticket from one of the ticket scalpers, was a high-speed train. The world's fastest train sliced 7.5 hours off the 10.5-hour journey between Wuhan and Guangzhou, traveling at average speeds of 199 mph (320 kph) as it covered the 609-mile (980 km) route.

JINGZHANG RAILWAY
Zhan Tianyou (third right, front row) built his line two years ahead of schedule. It earned him the title "Father of the Railroads."

It beat even the record set by France's TGV (see p.212). Based on Siemens and Kawasaki technologies, the high-speed train was all Chinese-made and, in spite of a high-speed crash in Wenzhou that interrupted its development, was a matter of great national pride and significance.

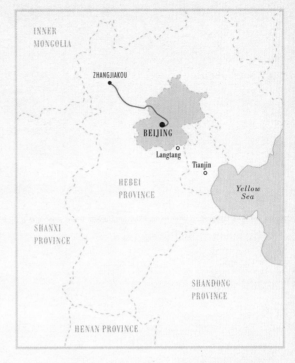

The official story started with the nominal "Father of the Railroads," Zhan Tianyou, a Chinese engineer who built the Jingzhang Rail, the all-China railroad from Beijing to Zhangjiakou (formerly Peking to Kalgan) in 1909. It was a masterful piece of engineering, completed two years ahead of schedule despite Zhan Tianyou having to build a special switchback to cross the mountainous region north of Peking near to the Great Wall. Zhan Tianyou's railroad achievements earned him great respect, a burial site at the railroad station in Qinglongqiao and a statue to his memory outside the Zhangjiakou station.

Curiously, Zhan Tianyou's influence and education was closer to that of an American teenager than a boy from Guandong. At the age of twelve he had been sent by officials from the ruling Qing dynasty to study in America. He secured a place at Yale University and, in 1881, shortly before being hastily recalled to China (the mandarins had changed their minds about the benefits of a foreign education), was awarded a degree in railroad engineering. Despite his qualifications he was dispatched to the navy, but by chance fell in with a railroad engineer named Claude Kinder. Kinder's background was even stranger than his own.

CHINA
The Jingzhang Railway, formerly the Imperial Peking to Kalgan Railroad, was the first section of the Beijing to Baotou Railroad. It reached Baotou in 1923.

OLDEST LINE IN USE

Kinder was the son of an Englishman, the director of the Imperial Japanese Mint. He had studied railroad engineering at St. Petersburg in Russia, and in 1873 had been appointed director of the Imperial Japanese Railroads. When he was forced to leave, he headed for Shanghai. Destined to become the largest city in China and, in population terms, the largest in the world, Shanghai was, briefly, the site of China's first railroad (see box on p.156). When Kinder arrived, local traders were still seething at the loss of their railroad after the last journey of their locomotive, *Victory*. The tracks had been torn up and dumped in a rust-

CELESTIAL EMPIRE

✦

China's first railroad between Shanghai and Wusong opened in 1876 and closed in 1877 after running down a pedestrian. It was built by local merchants to avoid the Wusong sandbars, maritime obstructions at the approach to Shanghai's harbor, which business people regarded as unholy obstacles to trade. The conservative Chinese officials saw them as heaven-sent barriers to foreign invaders. They did not support the idea of a railroad either, and the line was conceived with much secrecy. When the 5-mile (8 km) line opened in June 1876, steam locomotives hauled six trains a day, packed with passengers. But the accident triggered local riots and officials shut the line after the final train, the *Celestial Empire* (a traditional name for China.

ing heap on a beach in Formosa (now Taiwan). (There were similar local objections to the use of telegraph lines, said to play havoc with the *feng shui*.)

Kinder moved on. He had come into contact with a Cantonese merchant, Tong King-Sing, who gave him a post at the China Mining Company in Tangshan near Kaiping. Mindful of China's implacable opposition to railroads, Kinder secretly built a locomotive, the *Rocket of China* (the first to be built in China), and in 1881 ran it on a 6-mile (10 km) line from Tientsin to the Tangshan coal mines.

The railroad, which had been described to officials as a "tramway," prospered, eventually becoming not only the second major railroad line in the country, but, after many extensions and innumerable name changes (it was variously known as the Peking to Mugden or Beijing to Harbin), the oldest line still in use.

CONTINUED EXPANSION

Zhan Tianyou, delighted after his collaboration with Kinder on the line, went on to successfully complete a private rail line for the Empress Dowager Cixi. The powerful former concubine, who deftly controlled the Qing Dynasty for almost fifty years, wanted a means to visit the tombs of her ancestors. With her support the engineer moved on to build the Beijing to Zhangjiakou line. Following the death of the Empress in 1908, the collapse of the Qing dynasty and the Xinhai Revolution that hastened its end in 1911, the railroads became a Nationalist aspiration. Sun Yat-Sen, one of the revolutionary leaders and a railroad enthusiast, was put in charge of planning the

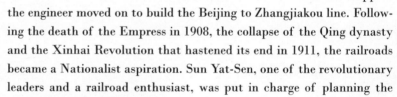

TRADE SECRET
Claude Kinder built the
Rocket of China from scrap
materials and used it to haul
coal from the Kaiping mines.

nation's rail network after the revolution. When in 1949 Mao Tse-Tung's Revolutionary Red Guards defeated the old Nationalist order, China still had only around 17,000 miles (27,359 km) of railroad, almost half of it in Manchuria. Mao was as enthusiastic about national railroads as the reactionary Sun Yat-Sen, although for political rather than economic reasons. As America had done in the 1800s,

China expanded its railroads at an extraordinary pace after 1949. In a decade 12,000 miles (19,000 km) of new railroads were built and 4,000 miles (6,437 km) were modernized. There was the Chengdu to Kunming line, 600 miles (965 km) in the southwest, requiring over 400 tunnels—some of them spiraling through the rock to cope with the gradient—over 650 bridges and the lives of more than 2,000 workers. Started in 1958, it was finished twelve years later in 1970. In 1964, work began on the 569 mile (916 km) line from Xiangfan to the former capital Chongqing; it, and the 716 bridges and 400 tunnels needed, were completed in 1979 as the demands for rail freight peaked at sixteen times their 1949 levels.

"Railroads would only be beneficial to China, when undertaken by the Chinese themselves and conducted under their own management."

Viceroy Li Hongzhang in 1863

The arrival of China's first diesel, the *Dongfeng*, in 1959, signaled a long and protracted end to steam: China built the world's last steam locomotive factory and at least one main line was running a steam locomotive in 2005. Aside from its high-speed trains there was one more chapter in China's railroad story: the Chinese Imperial Railroad to Tibet. The 1,215-mile (1,956 km) line, first considered by Sun Yat-Sen in 1917, reached Golmud from Xining in 1984 and Lhasa in 2006, after engineers had worked out a method of crossing the permafrost. Running over the Tanggula Pass made the line the world's highest; Tanggula Station also went into the record books as the world's highest and the trains, each accompanied by a doctor, were equipped with oxygen for the passengers. China's railroads had come a long way since Zhan Tianyou's 1909 all-China railroad from Beijing to Zhangjiakou.

DONGFENG
China's first diesel-powered engines appeared in the 1950s.

Grand Central Terminal

Country: U.S.A.

Type: Passenger

Length: 33 miles (53 km)

✦ SOCIAL
✦ COMMERCIAL
✦ POLITICAL
✦ ENGINEERING
✦ MILITARY

Aman bids a brief goodbye to a woman on a smoky northern English station to the nostalgic strains of Sergei Rachmaninov's Piano Concerto No 2. Noel Coward's *Brief Encounter* marked a sea change in the romance of the station— but none could match the majesty of New York's Grand Central.

TABLES IN THE WILDERNESS

There are plenty of contenders for the world's most historic station: the hired room at the Ashby Road Hotel at Bardon Hill that, in 1832, served the first passengers on England's Leicester and Swannington line; or the Gare du Nord in Paris, Europe's busiest station, where in 1940 the platforms thronged with German troops arriving to occupy the city. Bombay's Victoria Station, a fusion of empire and native styles; Milan Station, a monument to Benito Mussolini's Fascist followers; or St. Pancras in London, a fruitcake of Victorian Gothic, all fall into the category of what the nineteenth-century Frenchman Théophile Gautier called the "cathedrals of the new humanity."

Railroad stations were places of joyful reunions and stomach-churning partings. Musing on the scene at one station, the English poet Thomas Hardy (1840–1925) noted in his *In a Waiting Room* (1901):

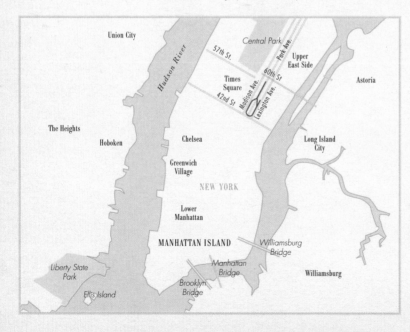

NEW YORK
The Grand Central Terminal took shape on land between 42nd and 48th Streets, Lexington and Madison Avenues. It opened for business in 1871, but was soon to be redeveloped.

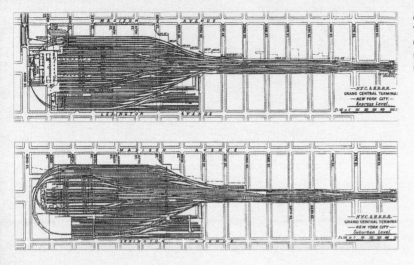

GRAND PLAN
The tracks leading into
Grand Central were built on
two levels, the suburban and
the express.

A soldier and wife, with haggard look
Subdued to stone by strong endeavor
And then I heard
From a casual word
They were parting as they believed for ever.

David Lean's 1945 film of Noel Coward's *Brief Encounter* was pure
fiction, but the poignant final moments between two lovers as the station
clocked ticked off the time moved cinema audiences. Following the film's
release, moviegoers made pilgrimages to the station where it was filmed,
Carnforth on the London, Midland and Scottish Railroad, to relive the
moment when Trevor Howard's Alec left Celia Johnson's Laura behind.
The film inspired a public campaign to
save the station and its railroad clock
(see box on p.160).

Carnforth was opened in 1846 when
the early stations on the American
transcontinental railroad were often no
more than a rudimentary halt by the

> "There is probably no vehicle of such
> importance to the country house as the station
> car, because it forms the last link with town
> life, its conveniences and its supplies."
>
> *Meryvn O'Gorman*, Country Home Magazine, *1908*

railside. One journalist discovered only a long, low log cabin with a table
and chairs set out in the mud and a couple of wagons nearby waiting to
pick up any people or parcels. Although it was basic, the writer reported
that in the Rocky Mountains he enjoyed railroad meals of "buffalo, elk,
grouse, prairie fowl, antelope, turkey, and other small deer" on the section of line where "snow-sheds and snow-fences appear suggestive of
severe winter storms. Sometimes," he added, "a party of us united in
telegraphing to some station ahead, and then we found seats reserved,
and a bounteous table spread in the wilderness."

As railroads started to appreciate the opportunities afforded by the captive, hungry and often bored passenger, they allowed restaurants and book-stalls to set up business in the stations. England's Great Western, taking marketing advantage of the refreshments offered at Swindon Station, unwisely signed a 99-year lease that required every train to stop for refreshments. Eventually, and expensively, they had to buy themselves out of the contract. The "youthful maidens" serving in Swindon happened to turn the head of Francis Head, author of *Stokers and Pokers* (1849), but he was less impressed by the hungry tide of humanity that swept from the train at Wolverton Station. "The confused crowd of passengers simultaneously liberated from the train hurry towards [the refreshment room] . . . with a velocity exactly in proportion to their appetite." It seems to have been a healthy one, since travelers consumed around 190,000 Banbury and Queen's cakes a year, washed down with copious quantities of coffee, soda water, tea, lemonade and ginger beer and an impressive 3,000 bottles of gin, rum and brandy.

A BUSY STATION

Charles Dickens (who had an unfortunate experience when the train he was traveling on crashed) was unimpressed by the service at Peterborough (England) Station in 1856 where "the lady in the refreshment room . . . gave me a cup of tea, as if I were a hyena and she my cruel keeper with a strong dislike to me." Another Victorian author, Anthony Trollope, in *He Knew He Was Right* (1869), raised the perennial subject of the English sandwich: "We are often told in our newspapers that England is disgraced by this and by that . . . but the real disgrace of England is the railroad sandwich, that whited sepulchre, fair enough outside, but so meagre, poor and spiritless within."

According to the American Edward Dorsey it was not the sandwich that made life difficult in Britain's stations, but the signage. "As station advertising is carried to a great extent throughout England it is

very difficult to recognize the station sign from the hundreds of advertisements, equally conspicuous, of Pears Soap, Lorne Whiskey, Colman's Mustard, etc., surrounding the name of the station." Dorsey once traveled 114 miles (183 km) from London to Gloucester "without being able to find out the destination from the car I was in." Dorsey was looking at both railroads and stations in his *English and American Railroads Compared* (1887). He was critical on both accounts. Take luggage control: "Baggage checks, like our through check system over many distinct lines, are still unknown in England. [Luggage] is placed in a baggage car without any distinctive mark of ownership, and subject to the call of the first claimant." (He did concede: "One seldom hears of its loss. This speaks well for the honesty of the English people.")

Dorsey was writing sixteen years after New York's Grand Central Station first took shape amidst the city sprawl of rail yards, breweries, slaughterhouses and shacks in 1871. New York had suffered the arrival of the New York and Harlem Railroad in 1831, its stables and offices situated on Fourth Avenue, 26th and 17th Streets. (P. T. Barnum later bought the station and yards, converting it into the first Madison Square Garden.) Later arrivals added to the congestion: the New York and New Haven and the Hudson Railroads during the 1840s. The pollution was so bad, the city banned steam locomotives from huffing through the crowded streets: New York needed a new terminal.

Commodore (as he liked to be known) Cornelius Vanderbilt, who had made good as a New York ferry boy and was now a wealthy shipping owner, had bought out the Hudson River Railroad in 1864, added the New York Central Railroad to his portfolio and linked Spuyten Duyvil and Mott Haven (which allowed the Hudson River trains to arrive at an

GRAND CENTRAL
The New York terminal lived up to its grandiose name. It was to become the biggest station in the world.

East Side terminal). He also bought up as much of the property as he could between 42nd and 48th Streets, and Lexington and Madison Avenues and opened his Grand Central Terminal in 1871. It was a chaotic creation serving three lines (The New York Central, Hudson River and New York and Harlem), each with its own ticket office and baggage area.

In 1898 Grand Central was reborn with a glass and steel train shed to rival Paris' Eiffel Tower and London's Crystal Palace, and a classical façade surmounted by a row of 1.5-ton cast-iron eagles, emblematic of America's strength, majesty and long life. They failed to survive the final rebuild, which was given added impetus by a fatal two-train wreck in the murky air of the 2-mile (3.2 km) Park Avenue tunnel. New York Central was obliged to go electric and Grand Central was once again redeveloped.

The opening in February 1913, despite (or perhaps because of) a whiff of scandal over the nepotistic choice of contractors, attracted 150,000 people who gazed up in wonder at the famous Beaux-Arts frontage and the starry hall inside. (The depiction of the night sky in gold leaf and electric lights was created by French artist Paul Helleu who pictured not the American, but the French sky at night—and, for reasons best known to himself, in reverse.) The opening also attracted the developers who, purchasing the "air rights," could start altering the skyline with steel, glass and concrete towers such as the 54-story Lincoln, the 56-story Chanin and the 77-story Chrysler Buildings. Grand Central hosted an art gallery and an art school, a movie theater dedicated to newsreels, a railroad museum and, by 1947, transit facilities for over 65 million people, 40 percent of the U.S. population. When plans were put forward to pull it all down (as had happened to New York's original Pennsylvania Station, demolished amid protests in the 1960s), famous figures including Jacqueline Kennedy Onassis helped defeat them.

TICKETS PLEASE

✦

Printers earned a considerable income from the work of the railroads. Britain's North British Rail Company ran their own print shop, but most contracted with printers to produce sequentially numbered tickets, which were dated on sale by the ticket office. When the ticket-holder finished their journey the ticket was collected at the barrier gate and sent for sorting by railroad clerks. Their calculations not only provided useful marketing information, but also exposed the use of fraudulent tickets.

FLYING SCOTSMAN

Grand Central served some of the great trains of the era, from the *Twentieth Century* to the *Broadway Limited*. In terms of historic turning points, however, Doncaster Station in Yorkshire, England, witnessed the introduction of what were arguably the world's two most famous trains, the *Flying Scotsman* and the *Mallard* (see p.242). Doncaster lay on the line of the Great Northern Railroad where freight trains hauling the black gold, coal, from the Barnsley coal seams to London passed by at the rate of almost one an hour.

The station had opened in 1849, followed by its railroad engineering factory, "The Plant," in 1853. The town's population rose by 3,000, and the railroad company built schools and chipped in for a new church before launching a series of famous steam locomotives. In the 1870s there were the Stirling Singles, characterized by enormous driving wheels and capable of hauling up to 26 passenger carriages at an average speed of 47 mph (76 kph). Then in 1923 the *Flying Scotsman* emerged from Doncaster. Five years later, in 1928, it hauled the first ever nonstop train from London to Edinburgh in eight hours. It went on to tour the U.S.A. and Australia (where it traveled 422 miles [679 km], then the longest nonstop distance run by a steam locomotive) before being mothballed. The Doncaster locomotive was eventually saved for the nation by public donations and a gift from the train entrepreneur Richard Branson.

STIRLING SINGLE
These locomotives, characterized by their huge drive wheels, emerged from The Plant at Doncaster.

STEEL HIGHWAY
Cecil Allen's evocative picture of the *Flying Scotsman* (third left) together with the *Leeds Express* and the *Scotch Express* at King's Cross Station.

Trans-Siberian Railway

Country: Russia

Type: Passenger, Freight

Length: 4,627 miles (7,446 km)

+ SOCIAL
+ COMMERCIAL
+ **POLITICAL**
+ ENGINEERING
+ **MILITARY**

It promised to be the world's longest railroad journey. But Russia's Trans-Siberian not only bridged the continent, it bridged the era between the tsarist regime and revolution.

FABERGÉ SURPRISE

The fireman on board the American-built steam locomotive 293, a 4–6–0 Class Hk–1 heading for St. Petersburg in April 1917, wore a wig and carried false identity papers. Riding the footplate of the locomotive they nicknamed the *Big Wheel Kaanari* was one of the architects of the Russian revolution, Vladimir Lenin. After slipping into Russia from Finland he threw off his disguise to be welcomed by a brass band and a cheering crowd of gun-bearing, red-flag-waving Bolsheviks at St. Petersburg's Finlyandski Station. His compatriot Leon Trotsky, meanwhile, was about to set off aboard his armored train to drum up support for the revolution amongst units of the Red Army. "The train linked the front with the base, solved urgent problems on the spot, educated, appealed, supplied, rewarded, and punished," Trotsky later wrote in his memoir, *My Life*.

Lenin's locomotive was presented to premier Nikita Khrushchev in 1957 and parked in a glass cage at Finlyandski Station while his statue,

RUSSIAN REVOLUTION
The Trans-Siberian Railway was the longest in the world and proved to be a dauntingly difficult line to build.

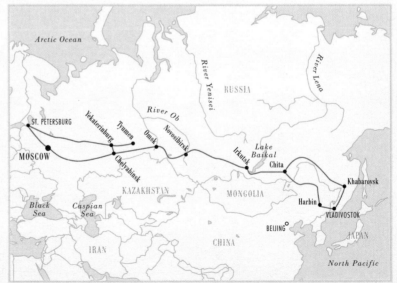

pictured standing on the gun turret of the armored train, was erected in Lenin Square outside. In 1917 railroads and the Russian Revolution were close partners.

Lenin would shortly issue the order sealing the fate of Russia's last emperor, Tsar Nicholas II, and his family. They were shot and bayoneted along with family servants in July 1918 at Yekaterinburg, a significant city stop on the Trans-Siberian Railway. It was two years since the completion of the world's longest railroad ride from Moscow to Vladivostok in the far east. Nicholas II had been appointed chairman of the construction committee that built the line after his father Tsar Alexander had given it his royal consent in 1891. Nicholas even attended the start of construction at Vladivostok in May of that year, dropping in for the ceremony at the end of a round-the-world trip designed to broaden his horizons.

In 1900 the Russian jeweler Peter Fabergé created a special Trans-Siberian Fabergé egg for the tsar. The gold and silver egg opened to reveal a map of the Trans-Siberian engraved in silver. Fabergé designed an additional surprise: a miniature clockwork replica of the Trans-Siberian train with five carriages and a golden key to wind up the mechanics. The tsar would also be treated to a film of the Trans-Siberian Panorama, exhibited at the Paris World Fair in 1900 along with the Eiffel Tower (completed in 1889) and Rudolph Diesel's new engine. Like the *Shinkansen* (see p.202) at Britain's York Railroad Museum where would-be passengers could sit aboard and watch a film of the journey, visitors to Paris could sit in a wagons-lits taking caviar and borsch from waiters while painted scenes of Siberia rolled past their train window. The Panorama was shown again at the St. Louis World's Fair in 1904. In fact the line had yet to be completed.

LENIN'S LOCOMOTIVE
Vladimir Lenin arrived in St. Petersburg two years after the Trans-Siberian was opened. His locomotive was put on show at Finlyandski Station.

GOLD TRAIN

✦

In the 1920s the Soviets paid in gold for an order for locomotives from the Swedish firm Nohab. The source of the bullion was a mystery, but during the Russian Revolution in 1919 a trainload of gold, from the empire's gold reserves at Kazan, had been shipped east along the Trans-Siberian by Lenin's enemies. Despite being guarded by Czech soldiers, part of the bulky cargo went missing and historians have been trying to find out what happened to it ever since. One theory suggested that Lenin's Bolsheviks were given a portion of the gold, but the train carrying it hit a landslide at Lake Baikal and the freight car plummeted into the lake. Investigators claim to have discovered the remains of a carriage in the lake.

GIFT FOR A TSAR
The Trans-Siberian Fabergé egg contained a clockwork replica of the train.

LABORIOUS CONSTRUCTION

The Trans-Siberian, covering a distance equivalent to that between London and Cape Town, was a huge undertaking. Rails and rolling stock had to be shipped almost halfway around the world to Vladivostok to start the line. The western end of the line was begun at Chelyabinsk in the Urals, over 4,500 miles (7,242 km) away, in July the following year, rails, ties and rolling stock being sailed up Siberian rivers when they were not frozen over.

Siberia was Russia's Wild East. Invaded by Russian Cossacks in the sixteenth century against the resistance of the resident Tartars, it would become the hostile home for Russia's twentieth-century exiles. Its 5 million square miles (8 million sq km) made it larger than the United States and Europe put together. The railroad line would have to cross the three great rivers, the Ob, the Yenisei and the Lena, and the world's deepest inland water, Lake Baikal. Eight bridges, each one over 1,000-feet (305 m) long (one measured almost 3,000 feet [914 m]), had to be built before the line reached the great lake. During the lake's winter freeze tracks were laid across the ice, the engineers being careful to lift them before the spring thaw. When the waters were passable again a pair of British-made ferries with ice-breaking prows were commissioned to carry trains from one side to the other. Eventually a line was cut around the cliffs of Lake Baikal and the ferries were retired from service (one, the *Angara*, being put on show at Irkutsk).

The railroad was dauntingly difficult to build and territorial tensions in the east, with China and Japan, made matters worse. One section of the line ran through Manchuria on the Chinese Eastern Railroad.

> "During the most strenuous years of the revolution, my own personal life was bound up inseparably with the life of the train [as the Chairman of the Revolutionary Council]."
>
> *Leon Trotsky*, My Life, *1930*

Between 1898 and 1903 Japan, which had acquired southern Manchuria, was forced to surrender its Manchurian territories and Russia swept in, investing vast amounts of roubles in the port towns of Dalian and neighboring Lüshun for the Trans-Siberian. During the ensuing Russo-Japanese War the Trans-Siberian, which had only been built as a single-track line, created major logistical problems as the Russians tried to ferry troops and munitions in, and empty trains and injured troops out. The bottleneck cost Russia the war as well as Dalian and her South Manchurian line. In what was the first serious conflict of the twentieth century the West was shocked to see the Russian superpower defeated by little Japan.

By 1916, apart from the section around Lake Baikal, laborers, prison convicts and Russian troops completed the construction of the line. It brought the Russian rail network to about half its eventual total. The locomotives, like some of the distances involved, were big. Although the Russian Revolution temporarily halted the import of 200 American-built Decapods, (one Baldwin Decapod, built in 1886, was reputedly the biggest locomotive of its time), the Soviets were soon building their own, often based on American designs, in St. Petersburg. One 1934 leviathan, the longest non-articulated steam locomotive ever built, was so huge it straightened the curves on tracks and had to be scrapped.

When its armada of steam locomotives was finally retired, diesel-driven trains took the strain until 1991 when Boris Yeltsin seized power and the political pack of cards that had been the Soviet Union collapsed. The Trans-Siberian was 75 years old and Russia's railroads, by then the second largest in the world, were moving 3.5 million passengers a year.

WHYTE'S WHEELS

✦

Lenin was borne to his grave aboard a Russian-built U–127, but arrived at Finlyandski Station on a 4–6–0 Class Hk–1. The numbers separated by hyphens refer to the number of leading, driving and trailing wheels, respectively, and were first used to describe steam locomotives by a New York railroad man, Fred Whyte in 1900. The locomotive class referred to a group of locomotives built to a common design. There was inevitably a *Joseph Stalin* Class. Individual locomotives were also christened, such as the *Felix E. Dzerzhinsky*, named after a former head of secret police.

RED STAR
Most of the Soviet Union's steam locomotives, such as this U.S.-built "Russian Decapod," were phased out in the 1980s.

Allied Railroad Supply Lines

Countries: France, Belgium

Type: Freight, Passenger

Length: 397 miles (638 km)

+ **SOCIAL**
+ **COMMERCIAL**
+ **POLITICAL**
+ **ENGINEERING**
+ **MILITARY**

The opening of hostilities in Europe in 1914 saw railroads used as never before. The major powers had embarked on one of the most devastating wars in history, but the rail invention of a French farmer, and the timely intervention of the U.S. in 1917, finally turned the tide of war.

NARROW GAUGE ON THE WESTERN FRONT

In the summer of 1914, on the eve of the Great War, English poet Edward Thomas took the train to Gloucestershire. He was rejoining his friends, the Dymock poets, who included Rupert Brooke, Eleanor Farjeon (author of the hymn "Morning has Broken") and the American Robert Frost. Thomas had been considering an invitation from Frost to escape the war and leave for America.

The train halted momentarily at a little Gloucestershire village. In the simmering silence with a blackbird calling nearby, Thomas sketched the first line of a new poem: "Yes, I remember Adlestrop." His poem would become a wistful recollection of rural England, made more evocative to men and women touched by the horrors of trench warfare.

In the war between the Allied Powers (Britain, France, Russia, Japan, Serbia, Italy, Portugal and Romania) and the Central Powers (Germany, Austria–Hungary, Ottoman Turkey and Bulgaria), Germany planned to use the railroads to strike first. During the Franco–Prussian war of 1870, Field Marshall Helmuth von Moltke, an early advocate of rail power, had used the railroads to launch attacks on several fronts simultaneously. Even as Thomas traveled to Gloucestershire, Moltke's nephew, now chief of staff of the German forces, was mobilizing his army to be delivered on scheduled trains through Belgium into France. Once the French had been knocked out, the troops were to entrain to an eastern front and deal with the Russians.

CONQUERING RAILROADS
German troops lay a railroad to cross boggy ground near Ypres in 1917.

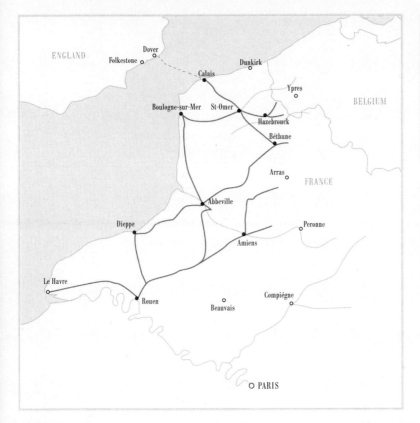

EUROPEAN CONFLICT
The railroads extended the supply lines over previously unimagined distances in World War I. By 1917 munitions for the front line were being manufactured in Glasgow.

This was the Schlieffen Plan, named after its originator Count Alfred von Schlieffen, and it relied on Germany's superior rail power. But the Central Powers underestimated the French railroads and the fighting spirit of both the French army and the British Expeditionary Force. The German advance was checked at the Battle of the Marne in September 1914 (which also featured the morale-boosting arrival of 10,000 French reservists in 600 taxis commandeered in Paris). Moltke is said to have told his leader, Kaiser Wilhelm II: "We have lost the war."

Both sides dug in, creating a meandering line of trenches that straggled north and south for over 470 miles (756 km). "The questions of transportation lay at the root of . . . keeping up the fight," wrote the German general Erich Ludendorff in his postwar memoirs. "These questions, in their turn, depended on locomotives, wagons, staff, and were closely bound up with coal supply. We had prepared for a short war, and . . . had to reshape ourselves to meet a long one."

Trucks, trains, horses and light-gauge rail supplied the trenches. Long before the advent of steam power, light, or narrow-gauge, rail had been used by miners and quarrymen. In 1875 a frustrated French farmer, Paul Decauville, had constructed ready-made rail sections to haul a crop

of sugar beets mired in one of his rain-sodden fields. Even as he began marketing Decauville rail, the military was purchasing stock for its campaigns in Madagascar and Morocco.

The Central Powers were ahead of the game. Anticipating the conflict in Europe, they stockpiled huge quantities of German-built Orenstein and Koppel light rail and rolling stock. (Ironically the Orenstein family shares would be seized during the "Aryanization" of Nazi Germany in World War II.) Only the British lagged behind, their generals still advocating the use of farm horses and trucks even as they were being swallowed up by the mud and blood of the Western Front.

The light railroad networks led back to railheads and refilling stations, established up to 10 miles (16 km) behind the front lines. They were served by the mainline rail routes, which were initially under French control. It caused chaos and confusion. A British infantry battalion, for example, would entrain in England aboard two trains that could travel to the port steaming at a steady 25 mph (40 kph). In France the battalion would transfer to one long, slow train, which, at best, could manage 12 mph (19 kph). The Allied rail supply lines improved when the military took control. By 1917 over 70,000 British railroad men were working (and sometimes losing their lives) on the lines.

LAST MESSAGE

✦

A whole district of Halifax, in Nova Scotia, was destroyed in 1917 when the S.S. *Mont Blanc*, loaded with explosives, ran into a Norwegian ship, the S.S. *Imo*, in Halifax harbor. The stricken *Mont Blanc* drifted toward the shore before exploding and killing an estimated 2,000. The death toll would have been higher, but for railroad man Vince Coleman. He was leaving the station when he heard about the impending explosion. Returning to his post he telegraphed a warning to a passenger train approaching from New Brunswick: "Ammunition ship afire in harbor making for Pier 6 and will explode. Guess this will be my last message. Goodbye boys." It was. The train, however, stopped in time.

Ten million troops were killed in the war, most of them by artillery shells:

"Bombed last night, bombed the night before,

Going to get bombed tonight if we never get bombed anymore,"

as one music hall lament put it. In the early years of the conflict, however, the Allies were using the wrong type of shell.

MUNITIONS WORKERS

One May morning in 1915 the *Daily Mail* informed its readers that Lord Kitchener, the face on the "Your Country Needs You" recruitment posters, was starving the army of high-explosive shells. "The admitted fact is that Lord Kitchener ordered the wrong kind of shell." Kitchener never had to face his critics: he drowned in 1916 on his way to a diplomatic meeting in Russia when his ship, H.M.S. *Hampshire*, struck a German mine off the Orkney Isles. The fiery Welsh politician and future wartime prime minister, David Lloyd George, was appointed Minister of Munitions in his place and tasked with sourcing the right kind of shell. He would make full use of the railroad network, and the as yet untapped resources of women munitions workers.

Lloyd George had great faith in women war workers. He gave financial support to a suffragette march through London under banners

DANGEROUS WORK
Dubbed the "Canary girls" because exposure to high explosives stained their skin and hair yellow, women munitions workers labored overtime after the Great Shell Scandal.

demanding: "Mobilize [the] Brains and Energy of Women"; he tackled the Clydeside ship workers' union and their entrenched opposition to "dilution"—the training of unskilled or semi-skilled workers (mostly women) to do jobs normally done by its members; and, once he had won them over, he built a string of new munitions factories on, or close to, the railroad lines. The last to be built, the Scottish Filling Factory, was re-christened Georgetown in his honor.

The factories were equipped with cafeterias, restrooms and first-aid stations, facilities that would become a benchmark for postwar industry. The women workers, paid a fair wage on Lloyd George's insistence, relied on the railroads. East Londoner Caroline Rennies, whose recollections were recorded at the Imperial War Museum, London, explained how they traveled from London Bridge Station to a munitions plant in Deptford outside London aboard open-sided "Adam trains." ("We used to say it was built when Adam was made [because] every time it rained the rain used to come in").

"There comes a time when locomotives are more important than guns."

General Erich Ludendorff, The Coming of War, *1934*

Women who filled the artillery shells were nicknamed "canary girls," because of the jaundice-like stains, caused by contact with high-explosive powder, on their skin and hair. "At night we'd come off these Adam trains with our hair ginger and our faces bright yellow." Boarding the trains home, crowded with soldiers, the station porters would sneak them into the First Class compartments. "They knew we were munition kids and they used to open the carriage and say: 'Go on girl, hop in

CAMPAIGN FOR SUFFRAGE
Six women munitions workers from the Bethlehem Steel Company at Newcastle, Pennsylvania lobbied President Woodrow Wilson to support the Suffrage Bill.

there.' " The chillier their reception, the more inclined they were to tease their fellow passengers. "Perhaps you'd have an officer one side of you and, being tired, you'd lie your head on [his] shoulder."

Bold as brass, they were not afraid to die. "The old boys on the trains used to say you only had two years to live [on shell filling]," remembered Caroline. "We'd shout back: 'We don't mind dying for our country.' "

Inevitably many did die. More than 130 women were buried in a mass grave in 1918 after they were killed in an explosion at Filling Factory No. 6, built in Chilwell, Nottingham because of its proximity to the railroad. Chilwell earned the dubious distinction of becoming the site of Britain's worst-ever wartime accident and yet Chilwell's canary girls were back at work the day after the explosion, feeding the guns for the final Allied advance.

By 1917 America had joined the fray after the transatlantic ship *Lusitania*, was torpedoed by the Germans and Germany was found to have offered military assistance to Mexico if it declared war on the U.S. The U.S. shipped extensive railroad equipment and steam locomotives from the Baldwin works, among others, to carry artillery to the Western Front. When Germany finally conceded defeat, the Armistice was, fittingly, signed in a railroad carriage. (See box). The war had been a battle of resources with the Allies better resourced than the Germans, thanks to the munitions workers. (Their efforts contributed to British women over the age of twenty-one securing the vote in 1928.)

Back in 1914 the poet Edward Thomas had decided against escaping to America. Instead he enlisted in the Artists' Rifles and was killed by an artillery shell at the Battle of Arras in 1917. His friend, the poet Rupert Brooke, had already died near Gallipoli in 1915, having written his poem "The Soldier":

If I should die, think only this of me:
That there's some corner of a foreign field
That is for ever England.

Wagon de l'Armistice

+

One of Nagelmackers' Wagons-lits carriages was brought out of commercial service and converted to provide office accommodation for the Allied Commander, Marshall Foch, during the war. When Germany capitulated the wagons-lits was taken to a railroad siding in the Forest of Compiègne outside Paris for the signing of the Armistice on November 11, 1918. The German leader Adolf Hitler regarded the act as an insult and, when France capitulated to the Germans in World War II, he insisted the signing take place in the same carriage, at the same place. Germany's S.S. would later destroy the *Wagon de l'Armistice* when it became clear that the Allies were going to win the war.

Kalgoorlie to Port Augusta Railway

Country: Australia

Type: Passenger, Freight

Length: 1,052 miles
(1,693 km)

✦ **Social**
✦ **Commercial**
✦ **Political**
✦ **Engineering**
✦ **Military**

F reight was the driving force behind the early railroads, but in the Australian outback the Slow Mixed carried everything a family could need, from fresh meat and vegetables to all-important water.

SLOW MIXED

The first role of the railroads was to shift goods, not people. The showman Phineas Barnum used the Pennsylvania Railroads to send his circus around America in the late 1870s. The Russian Orthodox Church preached to its flock from cattle cars converted into mobile churches on the Trans-Siberian, until the Soviet Union outlawed religion. And many European missionaries set out to recruit their African brethren from the altar rail of a refurbished freight wagon. The *Slow Mixed* No. 5205, however, aimed to do just about everything except preach to the railroad workers living along the Trans-Australian.

The *Slow Mixed*, nicknamed the "Tea and Sugar," operated for almost 80 years between Kalgoorlie in Western Australia and Port Augusta in South Australia. It carried its own butcher (the only non-railroad man on the train), fresh vegetables and other foods including the nearly essential tea and sugar. There was a traveling health clinic and sometimes in the 1950s a cinema on wheels to entertain the 345 track maintenance workers and their families living at eleven stops along the way. Above all there were the water tankers to fill the families' reservoirs. The *Slow Mixed*, like the other trains that traveled the Trans-Australian Railroad, had to carry its own water since there was none on the land.

The railroads had reached Kalgoorlie from Perth in 1897 after gold was discovered in the interior. The impetus to carry the line on to Port Augusta across the Nullarbor desert came in 1901 when the six colonies, Western Australia, Northern Territory, South Australia, Queensland, New South Wales and Victoria, were federated into the Commonwealth of

COMMONWEALTH TIES
The impetus behind the Trans-Australian was to give Western Australia closer links with New South Wales.

Australia. Just as the Canadian government had persuaded the British Columbians to rally to the flag with the promise of a trans-Canadian railroad line, Western Australians were to be lured to the fold by the promise of a railroad linking them to Port Augusta and on to Sydney.

The big obstacle was the Nullarbor (*nulla* "no," *arbor* "tree"), the largest single piece of limestone in the world and a formidable piece of Aboriginal territory. A clergyman's son, Edward Eyre, walked 1,250 miles (2,000 km) across it on foot with the Aboriginal guide Wylie in 1841. Twenty years later another clergyman's son, Colonel Peter Warburton, crossed it with a troop of camels, which, he reported were "unmanageable when alive, and almost uneatable when turned into meat." In 1896 an enterprising cyclist, Arthur Richardson, rode across it. In the 1900s it was the turn of railroad men to survey the route of the Trans, including in their calculations the longest stretch of straight track, 297 miles (478 km), ever. The Trans took five years to build. Because the connecting tracks at either end were still on different gauges, the Trans ran its own trains such as the *Slow Mixed*.

The line from Perth to Kalgoorlie was served from 1938 by *The Westland* overnight, with its water bags cooling from the carriage railings and bundles of firewood provided for the onboard stoves. Then in 1969, when the tracks were finally regauged, the *Indian Pacific*, a shiny, stainless-steel passenger train with room on board for no more than 144 passengers (the maximum that could be accommodated in the restaurant car in three sittings), began the first direct service between Perth and Sydney.

Although the Trans went on to become one of the world's must-do passenger journeys, it also continued to be an important freight route between east and west.

"I said to my missus when we came out here first, I've heard of damn all, but this is the first time I've seen it."
Railroad man on the Trans-Australian, 1954

INDIAN PACIFIC
Once the Trans had been regauged, a regular service could run from Perth to Sydney, a route including the longest straight stretch of rail in the world.

THE GHAN

✦

It took over 125 years to complete Australia's north-south transcontinental railroad between Port Augusta and Darwin by way of Alice Springs. The Port Augusta to Government Gums Railroad, better known as the Afghan Express or Ghan for short, had reached Oodnadatta by 1891. For the next twenty-two years the journey to Alice Springs had to be completed by camel. Even after the line reached Alice in 1929, the business of joining the whole 1,851-mile (2,979 km) route together would not happen for another seventy-five years.

Sydney City Railway

Country: Australia

Type: Passenger

Length: 3 miles (4.9 km)

F or many years the world's widest long-span bridge, the Sydney Harbor Bridge was built to complete part of the city's subway system. As the railroad age advanced, big bridges sprang up on the other inhabited continents. It was only when, occasionally, they fell down that they made big news.

+ **Social**

+ **Commercial**

+ **Political**

+ **Engineering**

+ **Military**

LES CORNES DE LA VACHE

Aside from gephyrophobics, those stricken with a fear of bridges, we are drawn to cross bridges, to gain a new view of the shore or gaze complacently into the abyss below. Great bridges are things of beauty: the Ponte Vecchio in Florence, the Pont du Gard at Avignon, France, both Italian masterpieces, and the Charles Bridge in Prague; the masterful Brooklyn Bridge in New York, or the vertiginous Salazar Railroad Bridge over the Tagus in Lisbon, Portugal, hastily renamed the Ponte 25 de Abril after the fall of the Portuguese dictator. Some of the most inspired engineers were bridge builders at heart.

Jean-Rodolphe Perronet founded the first school of engineers, the École des Ponts et Chaussées. He also put into practice his theory that slender, curving pillars could support significant weights (*les cornes de la vache*, the cow-horn concept) on his 1771 brick and stone Pont de Neuilly across the Seine in Paris. At the start of the railroad age bridge engineers

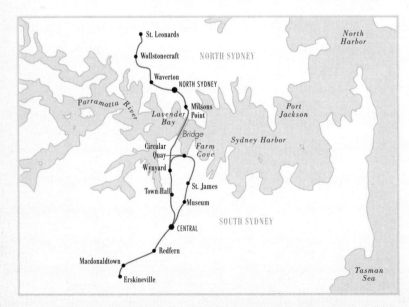

NEW SOUTH WALES
Australia's iconic Sydney Harbor Bridge, nicknamed the Coathanger, was the vital railroad link between the North Shore and Sydney's Central Business District.

had at their disposal a wondrous new material to play with: iron. The first cast-iron bridge at Coalbrookdale in Shropshire, England, was built in the late 1770s. "This extraordinary metal, the soul of every manufacture, and the mainspring perhaps, of civilised society," was how Samuel Smiles put it in *Invention and Industry* (1884). And mainspring it was, for iron's great benefit was its compressive strength. Thomas Paine, signatory to the American Declaration of Independence, had explored ideas for wrought- and cast-iron bridges as had James Finney, a judge in Fayette County, Pennsylvania, who employed the material on a rigid suspension bridge over Jacob's Creek in 1800, patenting his idea in 1808.

CAST IRON
The first iron bridge, at Ironbridge in Shropshire, proved to be the "mainspring of civilised society," according to Samuel Smiles.

The first railroad bridge, however, had been built of brick over a little English valley called Causey Burn on Squire Dawson's land in 1725. The local mine-owning conglomerate employed a stonemason, Ralph Wood, to bridge the gap and he did so with Dawson's Bridge (later the Tanfield or Causey Arch), unwittingly entering the record books with what, when it was completed a year later, became briefly the world's longest single-span bridge. (As late as the 1980s, the Tanfield Railway was still running steam locomotives across it, making it the world's oldest railway bridge still in service at the time.) Ralph Wood apparently had so little confidence in his structure that he leapt to his death from its parapet on the day it opened.

CAUSEY ARCH
The first railroad bridge served the local mines in County Durham. The stonemason was said to have jumped to his death when it opened.

The year 1845 marked a lull in the rush to build railroads in Britain. A count revealed that the nation had almost doubled the number of bridges since the opening of the Liverpool and Manchester line. Most, but by no means all, remained standing. The trouble with trains was that they imposed a brief, but heavy moving load on a bridge. Trains could, literally, shake a bridge to pieces: a suspension bridge, built over the Tees by Samuel Brown for the Stockton and Darlington Railway, lasted only a matter of months for this reason.

The early American railroad bridges, towering timber structures that prompted Abraham Lincoln's remark about "nothing but beanpoles and cornstalks," did not inspire confidence in everyone: "It is shaky trusting them . . . for there is no way of telling what may be done with trestle work," remarked a dubious Mark Twain. Yet America, as befitted the go-getting nation of the nineteenth century, went on to build some totemic river crossings. One of the most dramatic was John Roebling's Niagara Falls railroad bridge, a double-decker construction with trains on top and horse-drawn carriages on a deck below. The suspension bridge opened in March 1855 and was subjected to such a continuous stream of traffic that it was worn out by 1897 and was replaced. Roebling's triumph was the 1883 rail and road Brooklyn Bridge in New York. (He did not live to enjoy it: a landing ferry crushed his foot and he died of tetanus.) The Brooklyn remained the world's longest suspension bridge until the early 1900s. Another record-breaking American bridge builder was James Eads, a self-taught St. Louis, Missouri boy who had spent the Civil War building "ironclads," armored ships for the Union. Having made a small fortune raising wrecks from the riverbed, he knew the Mississippi and, when he was given the contract to

NIAGARA FALLS
The bridge over the Falls
in 1855 was the world's
first railroad suspension
bridge, seen here from the
Canadian side.

build St. Louis' first rail bridge across the river, constructed the longest arched bridge the world had ever seen. He made sure it worked too, weight-testing his design with fourteen locomotives.

SYDNEY HARBOR BRIDGE

The designers of the iconic Sydney Harbor Bridge almost sixty years later were even more cautious, conducting a track weight test with over ninety locomotives at a time. It was easy to see how the Harbor Bridge earned it its casual nickname, the Coathanger, yet this was the biggest, widest, and certainly the most famous steel arched railroad bridge in the world. The bridge opened in 1932, the ribbon being unexpectedly slashed with the sword of a uniformed cavalryman opposed to the government's policies, who burst in on the ceremony astride his horse. The bridge was designed to link the North Shore with Sydney's central business district and join up Sydney's City Railroad, started in 1926 and completed thirty years later by John Bradfield although, with more lanes for cars than train tracks, it marked the ascending fortunes of the automobile. (The bridge's two tram lines, abandoned with the trams in 1961, were also turned over to trucks and cars.)

One of the British engineers behind the Harbor Bridge was Ralph Freeman, who in 1905 had been responsible for the Victoria Falls Bridge (see p.149). Freeman followed in the footsteps of bridge builders like John Rennie and the self-taught Thomas Telford. Both had been building road bridges when the railroads came along, Rennie working with steam-engine manufacturer Boulton and Watt while Telford was constructing the Pont Grog y Borth in 1826, an elegant suspension bridge that took the mail coaches over the Menai Strait in North Wales to the Irish ferry. If his commission had come ten years later he would have been building a railroad bridge. As it was, the job of constructing the rail bridge over the Strait fell to Robert Stephenson who, along with Isambard Kingdom Brunel and Joseph Locke, were the three key railroad bridge builders of the early 1800s. Having journeyed to North Wales and drawn out

BRADFIELD'S BRIDGE
John Bradfield, the brains behind the Sydney Harbor Bridge, believed the city's economy would be stimulated by a railroad that joined the North and South.

designs for his innovative Britannia Bridge (he was using wrought-iron tubes), Stephenson had to subject a scale model to a test weight of 86 tons before his detractors would countenance the idea that such a bridge could safely carry the mail train. In 1850 Stephenson himself drove the final rivet (of 2 million) home and trains continued to run across his bridge for the next 120 years until a fire in 1970 forced a rebuild.

Joseph Locke was eclipsed by both Stephenson and Brunel (and yet he was the man behind several major lines including the Paris to Le Havre). Brunel was a prodigious bridge builder. As his Great Western Railway crept westwards across England into the rolling downs of Avon and Somerset and then the plunging valleys of Devon and Cornwall, Brunel designed eight viaducts for the West Cornwall Line, thirty-four for the Cornwall Railroad between Plymouth and Truro, and the bridge across the Tamar River named after Queen Victoria's consort, Prince Albert, who opened it in May 1859. Four months later the dying Brunel (he had suffered a stroke) was borne home across his bridge.

Bridges that stayed standing, such as the Tamar, made less of an impact on history than those that fell down. None seemed so ill-fated as the Quebec Bridge over the St. Lawrence River on Canada's Grand Trunk transcontinental railroad (see p.134). The central 1,800-ft (549 m) long cantilevered section had been part-built by August 1907 when a site engineer noticed a slight buckling of some supporting plates. A message was sent to the aging designer, Theodore Cooper (he had been James Ead's chief engineer on the St. Louis), who ordered work to stop. His

BRUNEL'S BRIDGE
The revolutionary new Albert Bridge across the Tamar opened on the Great Western Railway in 1859. The dying Brunel was carried over the bridge shortly afterwards.

instruction was never relayed to the work team and the bridge collapsed suddenly while eighty-five men were working on it. Only eleven survived. In September 1916, as the new Quebec Bridge neared completion, disaster struck for a second time. The central section dropped into the St. Lawrence as it was being raised into position, killing another eleven workers. The St. Lawrence was finally conquered a year later.

Britain's most infamous rail disaster involved the collapse of Scotland's Tay Bridge. The man who built it, Thomas Bouch, became a "Sir" after Queen Victoria crossed what was then the world's longest bridge in 1879. The British Empire might have been very different had she taken the mail train that set out across the bridge one stormy December night later that year. A signalman reported seeing the rear car's red light dimming into the gloom as storm winds howled around the bridge. It was the last sighting of the mail train. The bridge's central section had collapsed and the train with all seventy-five passengers on board plunged into the Tay. No one survived, although the locomotive was recovered and restored to active service. The subsequent inquiry found that Bouch, now deprived of his knighthood, had made a simple miscalculation. Future bridge builders were bound to be more circumspect.

JOSEPH MONIER

✦

Builders of the concrete railroad bridges had the French gardener Joseph Monier to thank for their building material. Monier, dissatisfied by the brittle nature of his traditional clay pots, patented an idea for combining the plasticity of wet concrete with the reinforcing qualities of steel: reinforced concrete was born. He took his ideas to the Paris Exhibition of 1867 (where they were exhibited alongside cattle trucks from Belgium and a locomotive called the *America*, built by Grant Locomotives of Paterson, New Jersey) and later built a concrete bridge for a client at Chazelet.

Berlin to Hamburg Railway

Country: Germany

Type: Freight, Passenger

Length: 178 miles (286 km)

✦ SOCIAL

✦ **COMMERCIAL**

✦ POLITICAL

✦ **ENGINEERING**

✦ MILITARY

Steam ruled the railroads for more than a century. But it was to meet its match with an invention by Dr. Rudolf Diesel and the arrival in the 1930s of the *Flying Hamburger*.

ARRIVAL OF ELECTRIC DIESEL TRAINS

In 1934 the Union Pacific Railroad launched a train that would change the nature of rail travel across America. That February all 93.5 tons of the *M–1000*, with its Darth Vader-like nose and curvaceous rear, heaved out onto the tracks of the Union Pacific for a coast-to-coast demonstration. Rebranded as the *City of Salina*, it was designed to go into service between Kansas City, Missouri, and Salina, Kansas, carrying the mail and just over 100 passengers in air-conditioned comfort. It was also going to be the first diesel-electric high-speed train.

Unfortunately its diesel engine was not quite ready and the rival *Pioneer Zephyr* took the record for being the first in America. As the Union Pacific's first working diesel locomotive, the train sped off on the 508 miles (817 km) of track between Cheyenne, Wyoming, and Omaha, Nebraska, at an average speed of 84 mph (135 kph). Its replacement, the *City of Portland*, ran 2,270 miles (3,652 km) from Chicago to Portland, Oregon, slicing a healthy 18 hours from the previous schedule

GERMAN DIESEL
The Berlin-Hamburg Railway made headlines in the 1930s when it carried the fastest regular passenger service with the diesel-powered *Fligender Hamburger*.

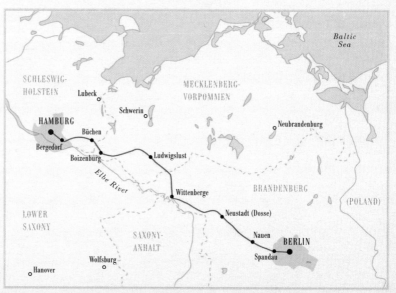

of 58 hours. It stimulated demand for speedy rail travel just at a time when America's love affair with the automobile was beginning to impact on travel habits. The railroad followed up with 11- and then 17-car streamliners such as the *City of Los Angeles* and *City of San Francisco*.

The streamlined *Pioneer Zephyr*, which had eclipsed the *M–1000*, was put to service on the line between Kansas City and Lincoln, Nebraska. The fastest train between the two cities had been the steam-driven *Autocrat*, which had averaged a reasonable 37 mph (59 kph) in the early 1930s. The journey time, just under 28 hours for the 1,015 miles (1,624 km), was pared down to 13 hours on May 26, 1934 when the stainless-steel, articulated *Pioneer Zephyr* swept through at an average speed of 78 mph (125 kph). It was headed, appropriately enough, for the Chicago's Century of Progress exhibition. The *Zephyr* captured the public imagination particularly because of a concentrated public relations exercise surrounding the launch. Rail staff were posted at the railroad crossings and Boy Scouts stood on duty at the stations for the dawn-to-dusk dash.

Diesel-electrics like the *Zephyr* were expensive trains to manufacture, but the capital costs were offset by relatively low running costs (compared to the coal-burning steamers), while passengers not only enjoyed air-conditioned cars, but radio reception, reclining seats, an observation lounge and a buffet. The original 72-seater train (mail and freight took up a third of the space) accumulated a total of 3,000,000 miles (1,609,300 km) before it was retired to Chicago's Museum of Science and Industry. The aluminum-bodied *M–1000*, meanwhile, was usefully recycled into aircraft and munitions parts during World War II.

The Pioneer Zephyr–Daddy of 'em All
FIRST DIESEL STREAMLINE TRAIN IN AMERICA
1934 – TENTH ANNIVERSARY – 1944

SILVER STREAK
The stainless-steel *Pioneer Zephyr* raced between Denver and Chicago to set a dawn-to-dusk speed record of 77 mph (124 kph).

BO BO & CO CO

✦

The conventional way of referring to steam locomotives by their wheel arrangements (see p.167) did not apply to the new breed of diesel or electric locomotives. Instead, letters were used to denote the driving axles and the number of non-driving, or carrying, axles. *A* stood for one driving axle, *B* for two, *C* for three and *D* for four. The classification became more complicated when axles were grouped together, each one being separately driven, and the letter *o* was added, leading to some endearing notations such as *Bo-Bo*s and *Co-Co*s.

SHARP AND FAST

Streamlining swept across America and Europe in the 1930s. It started out as a technical term for increasing aerodynamic efficiency, but it came to symbolize speed and power. Heavily influenced by the German Bauhaus and Art Deco movements, streamlining made its mark on a number of 1930s trains including the *Pioneer Zephyr*, the *Fliegender Hamburger* and Britain's *Duchess of Hamilton*, which was later rescued from the scrap heap by vacation camp owner Billy Butlin. It was not a new idea: "It is suggested that the fronts of engines shall be wedge-shaped, somewhat after the manner of a ship . . . the supposition being that the train . . . would proceed with less expenditure of energy," had suggested James Cott in 1895.

There was no air conditioning on the original diesel invented by Germany's eponymous Dr. Rudolf Diesel. But for a twist of fate, drivers might today be referring to their Ackroyd-Stuarts, after the Australian-born engineer who patented a similar engine in 1890. Instead the French-born Diesel patented his invention in 1892, made a million, and then mysteriously disappeared on the boat train S.S. *Dresden* as it crossed from Antwerp to Harwich in 1913.

Engineers had experimented with other forms of power since the inception of the railroads. Gasoline and kerosine proved too explosive while Ackroyd-Stuart's and Diesel's engines could run on cheap, crude-grade oil. It was not entirely safe: Diesel was lucky to survive the explosion of one test machine. The disadvantage of diesel was that it had to be heated before it could perform. As engineers worked on the problem, Munich in 1898 witnessed the first public demonstration of the rumbling engine.

Fifteen years later Diesel, heading for a company meeting in London, boarded the overnight boat train and ordered a morning call. He was not seen alive again. His coat was found folded on deck and his cabin was undisturbed. Later the crew of a Dutch boat hauled a body from the sea, removed personal items later identified by his son Eugen as belonging to his father, and returned the body to the

DOCTOR DIESEL
Having invented one of the most successful engines of all time, Rudolf Diesel disappeared under mysterious circumstances.

"[Vegetable oils] may become in course of time as important as petroleum and the coal tar products of the present time."
Rudolf Diesel

depths. Had money worries driven him to suicide? Was he murdered? Conspiracy theories included his being killed by German agents (he may have possessed useful information in the build-up of hostilities between Germany and England) and oil men (he hoped to achieve his aim of running his machine on vegetable oils, a move that would have jeopardized the profits of the petrochemical industry). The mystery remained unsolved as the diesel engine went into development across the world.

HAMBURGER
The *Fliegender Hamburger* was the world's fastest passenger service before World War II.

Canadian National Railroads in 1925 built eight diesel-electric railcars and sent one off across country from Montreal to Vancouver with instructions to the driver: "Leave her running." The engine did not falter for 67 hours and 2,930 miles (4,715 km).

Seven years later in 1933, Germany, without acknowledging the amusement its name might cause elsewhere, launched its diesel-powered *Fliegender Hamburger* (Flying Hamburger). Its performance did not amuse its rivals. The two streamlined, cream and violet cars, each with its own driver's cab, raced between Berlin and Hamburg at speeds of 100 mph (161 kph). Germany was running the fastest regular railroad trains in the world. The *Hamburger* was removed from service during World War II, then taken by the French as war reparations. The French continued to run it until the late 1940s.

The Hamburg to Berlin travel speeds would not be bettered for almost 65 years and, as diesel and electric locomotives continued to edge out steam trains, General Motors began mass-producing diesel-electric locomotives. These were standardized units, designed to be linked together like building blocks: a single unit for light loads, four units for extra-heavy ones. Diesel engines seemed to be firmly established as the power of the future. But it was not the end of the story: in 1985 Germany's Deutsche Bahn started testing a newer, faster train, the ICE (see p.217).

SHAPE OF THE FUTURE
All-purpose U.S.-built diesel-electric locomotives powered across continents and hastened the end of steam power.

<table>
<tr><td>

1939

</td><td>

Prague to Liverpool Street Station, London

</td></tr>
</table>

Countries: Czechoslovakia, Germany, the Netherlands, England

Type: Passenger

Length: 805 miles (1,296 km)

+ **SOCIAL**
+ **COMMERCIAL**
+ **POLITICAL**
+ **ENGINEERING**
+ **MILITARY**

Removing vulnerable members of the community from danger has a long history, but before the advent of universal air travel, ships and trains offered the only means of carrying large numbers of people to safety.

RAILROAD CHILDREN

The Railroad Children, written by Surrey socialist Edith Nesbit in 1905, featured Bobbie, Peter and Phil who wait in vain for their father to return from far away. Between the book's publication and the end of hostilities in World War II the railroads would evacuate as many as seven million "railroad children."

Removing vulnerable children and their mothers to a place of safety has a long tradition, but the twentieth-century rise of fascism in Europe, and the opportunity for the mass movement of people offered by the railroads, gave it an added urgency. Among the first were the Basque refugees, children evacuated from northern Spain when their homes came under attack from fascist forces under General Francisco Franco, later president of Spain. In 1937 German bombers from the Luftwaffe's Condor Legion conducted an experimental *blitzkrieg* on the defenseless town of Guernica. It prompted Pablo Picasso to create his monumental protest painting, *Guernica*, and the start of what became known as "the Basque refugees." Children as young as five were sent to Britain, Belgium, even Mexico and the Soviet Union for the duration of the war. Those sent to stay with Soviet families were forbidden to return by either the Russian leader, Joseph Stalin, or President Franco.

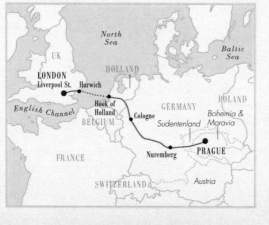

ESCAPE ROUTE
Nearly 10,000 Kindertransportee children escaped the Nazis, but left without their parents before the war closed in.

More than 4,000 were put on board the steamship *Habana* with identity labels marked *Expedición a Inglaterra* tied to their lapels, and shipped to Southampton, England. After being entrained to a temporary camp at nearby North Stoneham they were dispatched to new homes across the country. ("I remembered these dark haired, dark skinned girls suddenly appearing at our school: they taught us strange new nursery rhymes," recalled one English schoolgirl.)

German bombing raids on British cities precipitated the largest evacuation of children by train. At the outbreak of war in 1939 an estimated 4.8 million were expected to move to safer country areas, but as it transpired, only around 1.5 million were sent by train to the rural shires. The numbers involved were large, yet no two railroad children's stories were the same. When nine-year-old Pamela Double was evacuated with her eleven- and three-year-old brothers the train arrived late at night at a country station. She was separated from her brothers and sent to live with a vicar's gardener and his wife. "I don't think she was that pleased to have a nine-year-old girl to stay," she recalled.

Evacuee numbers surged again when France fell and a German invasion of Britain seemed imminent. As German bombing reached its peak in the early 1940s, so too did the numbers fleeing the cities. Mavis Owen, ten years old, her hair in pigtails and dressed in her Sunday best, was one of them. She remembered being led through the bombed-out streets of Liverpool to the railroad station in 1941. "Our Mums weren't allowed on the platform with us children in

> **"I hereby charge you to carry out preparations for a total solution of the Jewish question in all the territories of Europe under German occupation."**
> *Hermann Göring, July 1941*

FINAL JOURNEY

✦

In 2009, seventy years after the *Kindertransportee* started, a historic train left Prague Central Station bound for Liverpool Street Station in London, commemorating the journeys that Nicholas Winton had helped organize. The journey took four days with six different steam locomotives, from the *Green Anton*, a Slovakian locomotive, to the *Tornado*, a new mainline steam locomotive built in 2008. The carriages included the luxury state saloon of Czechoslovakia's first president, Tomáš Garrigue Masaryk, built to serve the *Golden Arrow* boat train in 1951.

HERO'S TRIBUTE
Flor Kent's sculpture of Nicholas Winton, the London stockbroker who helped children escape from Germany in 1939.

case they were too upset. So the Dads put us on board and I cried bitter tears because I thought I would never see my Mum or Dad again."

The train trundled through mid-Wales until the disorientated children disembarked at Llandrindod Wells. Mavis was taken to a little farmstead in the village of Clyro. "I went to stay with Mr. and Mrs. Evans at a farm called Paradise and the smallholding was true to its name." In 1944 Mavis joined the Women's Land Army. "After the war I went back and never returned to Liverpool."

The opportunity to return to their homes and families after becoming wartime railroad children was not an option for most of Germany's Kindertransportees. One was Ruthchen (Little Ruth) Michaelis, born in Berlin in January 1935. Her mother was not Jewish, but her father Robert was, and even at the tender age of three Ruthchen sensed that society was turning against her race. "I knew bad things were happening because I can remember frightening feelings and not knowing what they were about."

In February 1939 she, her mother and her seven-year-old brother boarded a train at the Zoo Station, Berlin. She would not see Berlin again for a decade. "When we got out of the car I threw a tantrum because I wanted to go to the zoo and not to England." Instead they boarded the train to one of the Channel ports. "I remember the seemingly endless train journey . . . and then it was dark and we were being walked along a quay beside a gigantic boat."

They crossed the Channel, and arriving at the customs desk in England, her mother handed her Christine, her favorite doll. The customs officer tried to examine it, but Ruthchen, screaming in protest, made a fuss and it was handed back after a cursory inspection. The doll contained her mother's family jewels, smuggled out of Germany.

"After the boat docked we had another long train journey to London. By then I had had enough of trains." But there was another train ride ahead, to a new foster home at Maidstone, Kent, where her mother tucked the children into bed, wished them good night and disappeared. She had returned to Germany. There was no goodbye. "I just decided she must be dead."

STOPPED IN ITS TRACKS

As one of the 10,000 Jewish Kindertransportees, Ruthchen Michaelis' identity papers were stamped "Person of No Nationality." She set her mind to becoming the English Ruth. It was not easy. Ruth went through three foster families and a hostel until, aged fourteen, she was back on the train to Germany. It transpired that her father had escaped to Shanghai during the war while her mother, having joined the Rosenstrasse in Berlin, a dangerously public protest against the imprisonment of their Jewish husbands, had managed to hide out in Berlin. Ruth initially refused her father's request to return to Germany and had to be subpoenaed to return. But by now the traumatized teenager could not accept another life change and she returned to live in Britain.

Ruth's train, in 1939, had succeeded in leaving Europe. Others were not so fortunate. On September 3 a group of 250 Kindertransportees boarded the train for England at Prague Station. The trip had been one of many organized by a London stockbroker, Nicholas Winton, who, visiting Prague on the eve of war, had set up office in his Wenceslas Square hotel to aid the Kindertransportees. He had helped over 600 to escape, many of whose parents were later murdered as Jews. The final group, however, never reached its destination. By then Germany had invaded Poland, the train was stopped and the children returned to their fate under the Nazis. As the railroad child Ruth Barnett wrote in her memoir *Person of No Nationality:* "We Kinder, the children who survived, will always remember that more than a million children in continental Europe didn't get the chance to escape and were killed. I still can't help thinking that one of those children might have become a famous musician or discovered a cure for some life-threatening disease."

WINTON'S TRAIN
A special train shown here leaving Prague Station for London celebrated the anniversary of the Kindertransportees in 2009. Several of the former children traveled on board.

1941

Southern Railway

Country: U.S.A.

Type: Passenger, Freight

Length: 987 miles (1,585 km)

+ **SOCIAL**
+ **COMMERCIAL**
+ **POLITICAL**
+ **ENGINEERING**
+ **MILITARY**

The sound of the steam locomotive was a gift to musicians, but no one could have anticipated that one song would put an American railroad station on the world map of popular music.

WOMEN AND HORSES

John Henry was a hard man. In the story that survived him he pitched his muscle against that of a steam-driven hammer and died in the attempt. John Henry may have been a run-of-the-mill steel driver working on rail tunnels. He may, as residents of Talcott, West Virginia, believe, have been slaving away on the Big Bend Tunnel nearby during the construction of the Chesapeake and Ohio Railroad. Whatever the true story John Henry, like Casey Jones (see box) became a folk hero, outlived by the "Ballad of John Henry."

The railroads inspired some stirring songs. One of the earliest was the romping "Carrollton March" written to mark the opening of the Baltimore and Ohio Railroad. It made curious comparison with the "music" of British sound recordist Peter Hanford who, in the 1950s and 1960s, recorded trains in the closing days of Britain's steam era. The

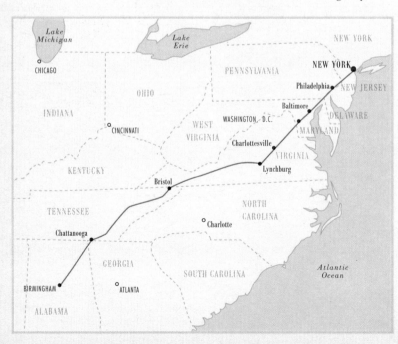

PARDON ME, BOY
Harry Warren and Mack Gordon's "Chattanooga Choo Choo" put the Tennessee railroad town firmly on the world's music map.

SOUTHERN BELLE
The evocative sounds of trains like the *Southern Belle*, which ran from Kansas City to New Orleans, inspired musicians and composers.

Swiss composer Arthur Honegger set the sound of steam locomotion to music in his evocative *Pacific 231* of 1923. (231 refer to the French method of describing a locomotive's wheel arrangement, as opposed to the Whyte notation (see p.167) which would have classified it as Pacific 4–6–2.) Honegger, who spent most of his creative life in Paris, intended his composition to record "the progressive gathering of speed . . . of a train of 300 tons hurling itself through the night at 120 miles an hour [193 kph]," he said in one interview. "I love [locomotives] as others love women or horses."

The great operatic composer Gioacchino Rossini, like the waltz composer Johann Strauss the Younger, infinitely preferred women and horses, having an inherent dislike of rail travel. Rossini wrote his *Un Petit Train de Plaisir Comico-Imitatif* (A Little Excursion Train), a piece, he explained with some satisfaction, which ended in a railroad collision. Rossini and Strauss were in a minority. Other musicians enjoyed the huff, puff and clackety-clack rhythm of railroad travel. The French composer Marie-Joseph Canteloube wrote his hauntingly beautiful *Chants d'Auvergne* (Songs of the Auvergne) on one long French train journey, while the Brazilian Heitor Villa-Lobos took a more literal approach in his *O Trenzinho do Caipira* (the Little Train of Caipira), replicating the sound of train horns and steam traction. Like Honegger he was entranced by the

CASEY JONES

✦

Train accidents were a favorite theme for railroad songwriters. Aside from "Wreck of the Old '97" and Carson Robison's and Robert Massey's "Runaway Train" (1925), one of the most enduring was the "Ballad of Casey Jones." John Luther Jones, from Cayce, Kentucky, was killed trying to halt the No. 4 train from Memphis to avoid a collision with a freight train at Vaughan, Mississippi, in April 1900. He was reputedly found under the cab still holding the broken cord of the whistle.

Come on, Casey,
and blow the whistle,
Blow the whistle
so they all can hear.

tempo of train travel, giving his two-minute piece, which he premiered in 1930 playing the cello, a Latin-American lilt.

Pieces such as *Pacific 231* were favorites on the play lists of North America's first national radio network, which was broadcast from 1923 to 1932 by the Canadian National Railroads. The service led to the creation of the Canada Broadcasting Corporation, modeled on the lines of the British Broadcasting Corporation (BBC), the first and only example of a railroad-inspired national radio station. Listeners to the BBC's Paul Temple detective stories in the 1930s, meanwhile, were given another evocative musical interpretation of steam travel. The Paul Temple theme tune was composer Vivian Ellis' *Coronation Scot*, an exhilarating celebration of the streamlined, crimson and gold express that raced from London to Glasgow in a record six and a half hours during the 1930s. It turned out that the inspirational train was not the Scot, but the *Cornish Riviera*. "The rhythm of the train came from the train journey between my country cottage in Somerset and London," Ellis admitted later.

At the start of Ellis' *Coronation Scot* the orchestra let out the low growl of a train whistle, an acknowledgment that whistles and bells were as integral to a piece of railroad music as the syncopation of the steel wheels running over the track joints. American steam locomotives developed their own orchestra of steam whistles, from the Pennsylvania Railroad's banshee wail to the husky hoot of the Norfolk and Western Railroad. Whistles were cast into multi-chambered bells that produced several notes at once and the mournful howl of the Southern Railway's three-chime whistle was enough to evoke sad goodbyes and the open plains. Some railroad songs simply evolved on the back porches of the Midwest and it was left to folk music collectors such as John Lomax in the 1930s to rescue songs like *The Rock Island Line* (attributed to the Chicago, Rock Island and Pacific Railroad).

When steam whistles gave way to the practical, but less evocative, two-toned diesel horns, the more musical engine drivers were said to be able to render the opening notes of Beethoven's Fifth Symphony or the more vernacular Yorkshire folk song, *On Ilkley Moor baht at* (On Ilkley Moor With No Hat).

For African American musicians the combination of railroads, jazz and the blues introduced a whole new repertoire, from Harry Raderman's 1921 *Railroad Blues* to Muddy Waters' 1951 *Still A Fool*

("Well there's two trains a-runnin' "). None, however, approached the popularity of Glen Miller's *Chattanooga Choo Choo*. "Chattanooga" had been written by Italian Harry Warren (he also wrote *On The Atchison, Topeka and Santa Fe* sung by Judy Garland in the 1946 musical film *The Harvey Girls*) and Warsaw-born Mack Gordon on the Southern Railway's Birmingham Special. The Special ran from Birmingham, Alabama, to New York by way of Chattanooga and the 1941 song brought fame to both Miller and the town (which became the home of the National Model Railroad Association). Miller died when his plane, possibly brought down by "friendly fire," disappeared during a flight from England to Paris in December 1944. After the war the German jazz singer Billy Buhlan performed his own version, the ironic *Kötzschenbroda Express* that highlighted the problems of rail travel when there was little coal and no carriage seats.

A yet more evocative wartime piece, although it was not written until 1988, was *Different Trains*, written for string quartet and recorded tape by Jewish composer Steve Reich. The experimental composition featured recorded speech taken from interviews with different people including Holocaust survivors. Reich, an American Jew, regularly traveled the train between New York and Los Angeles during the war. He composed the music after reflecting that, as a Jew in Europe, his train journeys would have been very different.

**"Oh Mr Porter, what shall I do?
I wanted to go to Birmingham
And they've taken me on to Crewe."**

Music hall song

**CHATTANOOGA
CHOO CHOO**
The *Birmingham Special*, credited with being the train in Glen Miller's hit song, ran between Birmingham, Alabama and New York on the Southern Railway.

1942

Auschwitz Spur

Country: Poland

Type: Passenger, Freight

Length: 1 mile (1.7 km)

I n World War II the Deutsche Reichsbahn transported millions of children, women and men to death camps. It was the most shocking use of mass transport the world had ever witnessed.

✦ **SOCIAL**

✦ **COMMERCIAL**

✦ **POLITICAL**

✦ **ENGINEERING**

✦ **MILITARY**

FINAL SOLUTION

In September 1941 Jewish people in Germany were instructed to allow other passengers to board the trains first, to travel third class and to take a seat only after all "Aryan" passengers had done so. It was the beginning of the most shameful chapter in the history of the Deutsche Reichsbahn.

The state railroad Deutsche Reichsbahn had recovered from the damage and debts that it had inherited from World War I. When Adolf Hitler came to power, the Reichsbahn was running one of Europe's most efficient railroads.

In 1941 the military leader Heinrich Himmler ordered the construction of a death camp at a little place in German-occupied Poland, Auschwitz. It lay on the double-track main line serving trains from the north and east to the southwest. The death camp was reached by a spur just west of the Reichsbahn station in Auschwitz.

The mass extermination of Jews, Gypsies and other "undesirables" started in 1942. (Trains had already taken thousands to the forests of Riga and Minsk where they were shot.) The meticulous planning relied on the railroads. Having mastered the process of mass murder, where people were herded into chambers that were then filled with

DIE ENDLÖSUNG
Nazi Germany's "Final Solution" was designed to annihilate non-Aryan peoples. The railroads were a central part of the Solution.

poison gas, the Germans built new death camps at Belzec, Sobibor, Majdanek and Treblinka. The locations were chosen because they were secluded, yet close to a railroad. Initially two cottages at Auschwitz were converted into gas chambers. The children, women and men were marched from Auschwitz station to their deaths. Later the camp was provided with a special railroad siding and a shunting locomotive used to push the train onto the sidings. The rail staff left the train while the people were driven into the camp.

Staff, however, knew what was happening. According to Alfred C. Mierzejewski (*Hitler's Trains*, 2005), Walter Mannl, chief of operations at Kattowitz, which oversaw Auschwitz Station, was told in 1942 about the building nearby that was used to kill Jews. The Reichsbahn traffic section's Paul Schnell assigned passenger cars for the killing trains: those in Germany or occupied Europe were marked *Da*, those in the former Polish territory, *PKr*.

Officials calculated the bill for transport as "freight extras," third-class passenger cars with 50 passengers in each, and 20 cars to a train. (Later as many as 5,000 were carried on a train.) The "special" rate was half the standard third-class fare for group rates (400 passengers or over). Eventually freight cars were used to transport the victims.

The railroad also carried as freight the possessions of the dead. Himmler received a list in February 1943 of 825 freight cars filled with clothing, bed feathers and rags. It was returned to Germany from Auschwitz and Lubin. One car contained 6,614 pounds (3,000 kg) of women's hair.

At Christmas 1942 railroad staff organized a temporary suspension of the trains while troops returned home by rail for the holidays. From January 1943 to the end of March, 66 trains carried 96,450 people to Auschwitz. By July 1944, 147 trains had brought in 450,000 Jewish people. Other trains arrived from Croatia, Greece, Belgium, Italy, France (see box) and the Netherlands.

After the war some argued that the Reichsbahn was a victim of Nazi oppression, but it cooperated with the government's anti-Semitic policies and profited from the work. It was the rail network that made genocide on this scale possible. On January 27, 1945 Russian forces broke into Auschwitz; the date became Holocaust Memorial Day.

FREIGHT EXTRAS
Railroad officials charged for the service to deliver the state's victims to the gas chambers.

LA MARSEILLAISE

✦

In 1943 one train into Auschwitz carried people singing the French national anthem, *La Marseillaise*. The train was from Paris, the only one to leave the French capital carrying, not Jewish people, but women combatants who had been arrested for taking part in the Resistance movement. The co-operation of the French police led to 230 women, including Charlotte Delbo, being sent to Auschwitz. One of 49 who survived, Charlotte Delbo wrote *Auschwitz and After*.

Burma to Siam Railway

Country: Burma, Thailand

Type: Military

Length: 263 miles (423 km)

* ✦ SOCIAL
* ✦ COMMERCIAL
* ✦ POLITICAL
* ✦ ENGINEERING
* ✦ **MILITARY**

SOUTHEAST ASIA
The Japanese built the wartime railroad to supply troops fighting in Burma. It failed to turn the war in their favor.

Built to supply the Japanese army in Southeast Asia during World War II, the railroad from Siam into Burma, the Death Railroad, cut short the lives of thousands of Allied servicemen and Burmese and Malay villagers.

DEATH RAILROAD

The Bridge on the River Kwai, director David Lean's 1957 epic film featuring the construction of a railroad bridge by the Japanese using prisoners of war labor, was a work of fiction (see box). The story was based on the infamous Burma to Siam (Myanmar to Thailand) Railroad built by the Japanese army between 1942 and 1943. Dubbed the Death Railroad, a life was said to have been lost for every tie laid.

In the early 1940s after its lightning conquest of most of Southeast Asia, the Japanese army's supply lines became increasingly stretched. Military planners decided to build a connecting railroad through Burma, between Ban Pong to the west of Bangkok, through the jungle and over the Three Pagodas Pass to Thanbyuzayat, south of the Burmese capital, Rangoon. The Japanese had taken Singapore in February 1942. They had also captured thousands of British, Australian, Dutch, New Zealand, American and Canadian troops and civilians. (Singapore's fall featured in the J. G. Ballard's novel *Empire of the Sun*.) These prisoners of war were to be used as slave labor to build the railroad.

The British in India had considered building the line, but abandoned the project partly because of the cost and partly to keep peace with the ruler of Siam, Chulalongkorn (portrayed in the 1956 film *The King and I*). The British timescale for such a line was five years. The Japanese took just 15 months to build it despite the deaths of the survey team, killed when their plane hit a mountain. The line was built on the backs of 60,000 prisoners of war and as many as 180,000

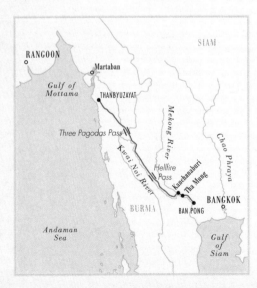

local people. An estimated 100,000 Asians and Allied prisoners died during its construction. The figure may have been higher still.

The line was completed in October 1943, six months before the critical defense of Kohima and Imphal, on India's northeast border. The Japanese had planned an audacious attack on the Indian border towns, a first step toward the invasion of India. However it turned into Japan's worst defeat to date, many of its 13,500 casualties, dying of starvation rather than enemy fire. The Death Railroad had failed to deliver. The Japanese had expected their Class C–56 steam locomotives to be hauling 3,000 tons of food and ammunition a day to provision their soldiers in the north. But the Burma line was jinxed. There were landslides, and breakdowns caused by prisoners who had managed to sabotage their own work. Supremacy in the air allowed Allied aircraft to disrupt the trains. The line managed little more than an estimated 500 tons a day. No one knows for sure since most of the records concerning the Burma Siam line were destroyed shortly before the country surrendered in August 1945. Within weeks Allied servicemen and surviving prisoners of war rode back along the railroad tracks on elephants in a bid to recover as many human remains as possible. They were reinterred at three war grave sites, Kanchanaburi, Chungkai and Thanbyuzayat.

Soon after the war the line was cut at the Burma border, the British fearing it would be used to bring supplies to Burmese freedom fighters. The southern section through Thailand was destroyed, then later rebuilt to Namtok, 130 miles (220 km) from Bangkok.

The Bridge over the River Kwai was a literary invention of the Frenchman Pierre Boulle who wrote the novel on which the film was based. However the Thailand State Railroad erected a "River Khwae" rail bridge 85 miles (137 km) from Bangkok at Kanchanaburi. This adopted memorial became the place of pilgrimage for relatives of those who died on Death Railroad.

THE BURMA LINE
The Bridge over the River Kwai was loosely based on the building of the bridge over the River Mae Klong (Khwae Yai).

<table>
<tr><td>

1944

</td><td>

Dutch
Railways

</td></tr>
</table>

Country: Netherlands

Type: Passenger, Freight

Length: 2,175 miles
(3,518 km)

✦ **SOCIAL**

✦ **COMMERCIAL**

✦ **POLITICAL**

✦ **ENGINEERING**

✦ **MILITARY**

The railroad bosses' relations with their workers were, in the early days, paternalistic and authoritarian. The inevitable strikes and unionization that followed resulted in both America's Labor Day and Britain's Labour Party. In the war-torn Netherlands, however, German military rule and a rail strike led to the *Hongerwinter*.

NETHERLANDS' RAILROAD RESISTANCE

There was silent applause from the audience watching the little dancer perform in their midst in the Netherlands in 1944. It was unwise to draw attention to themselves: as members of the Resistance movement they risked being shot by the occupying German forces. The girl was Audrey Ruston, soon to become the Hollywood film star Audrey Hepburn. She danced well despite being so hungry. In fact, she and children like her were starving. It was the *Hongerwinter*, the "hungry winter," and their mothers had resorted to grinding tulip bulbs into a powder to make into "bread."

The Hongerwinter was triggered by a rail strike. Most railroad stoppages were caused by men trying to improve their working conditions. The Dutch strike was different. By 1944 the German occupation of the Netherlands was looking increasingly tenuous. Three years earlier the Germans had invaded the Soviet Union and declared war on the United States, but they had now been defeated in North Africa and at Stalingrad. As Dutch hopes of an Allied invasion grew, the occupiers tightened their grip on the civilian population. Identity papers were issued to everyone over the age of fourteen and the unions were placed

THE NETHERLANDS
When railroad workers went on strike in the Netherlands, the occupying Germans' blockade and a severe winter caused widespread famine.

RAILROAD STRIKE
The Pennsylvania Railroad
strike of 1877 developed
into the U.S.'s first national
strike. The Union Depot at
Pittsburgh was burned
down during the strike.

under the control of the German National Socialist movement. Dutch
resistance grew. Many Catholic and Protestant church ministers who
had advocated, from the pulpit, that their congregations should assist
the Allies, now called on parishioners to cancel their union membership.

By now 107,000 Dutch Jews were being rounded up and sent by train
to the death camps (almost 80 percent were murdered) as, in 1943, the
Germans summarily shot workers who embarked on a series of lightning
strikes. Finally in 1944, Allied troops landed on the Normandy coast of
France. By September they had reached Brussels and Operation Market
Garden (see box on p.200) was launched to liberate the Netherlands.
Using secret radio broadcasts and undercover couriers, the Dutch
government in exile in London called on the Dutch railroad workers
to strike.

Operation Market Garden foundered on the banks of the Rhine at
Arnhem. The Germans brought in their own trains to transport their
troops and began to stop food and fuel being sent into the Netherlands.
By now the occupying force was using to *deskandidaten*, death candi-
dates, who were held in prison until a resistance attack after which they
were taken out and executed in public. Despite the dangers almost
30,000 Dutch railroad workers went into hiding.

NATIONAL STRIKE
Railroad workers had begun organizing themselves into guild-like
brotherhoods and societies in the 1870s. Workers in Pennsylvania were
well enough organized by 1877 to trigger America's first national strike.
During the financial panic caused when one of the U.S. banks heavily

involved with the railroads, Jay Cooke & Co., went bust, almost a quarter of the nation's 360 or so railroads went broke. When the Baltimore and Ohio Railroad cut wages for the second time in a year men at Martinsburg, West Virgina, and Cumberland, Maryland, stopped the trains. The National Guard was sent in, opening fire in the streets of downtown Cumberland. The strike went viral. When the coal workers came out in sympathy, the Pennsylvania dispute turned into a national strike. In the end President Rutherford Hayes used federal troops to stamp out the fires of insurrection.

Railroad bosses, especially those in the Pullman empire, were no wiser when it came to labor relations under two decades later. George Pullman was a genius at fitting out luxury cars, but lacked imagination when it came to social engineering. He had built the community of Pullman, in Chicago, for his workers who were happy to rent their new homes until 1893 when the Philadelphia and Reading Railroad went under. The rents were still due as workers began to be laid off. Four thousand went on strike. The socialist Eugene Debs, signing the strikers up to his union, demanded arbitration. Pullman refused and eventu-

OPERATION MARKET GARDEN

✦

Attempts by the Allied Forces to bring the fighting in Europe to its conclusion faced fierce resistance from the Germans in the winter of 1944 and Operation Market Garden ground to a halt when Germany held the key crossing over the Rhine at Arnhem. The consequences for the striking Dutch railroad workers and the civilian population, trapped behind the German blockade, were disastrous. As a harsh winter closed in, freezing the canals and making barge traffic impossible, the people simply ran out of food and fuel.

BRIDGE OVER THE RHINE
The Nijmegen railroad bridge over the Rhine was one of the key objectives during Operation Market Garden.

ally 250,000 workers across nearly thirty states responded by withholding their labor. Once again the railroads ground to a halt and the army was called in. When the strikers went back to work, Debs was given six months in jail (where he spent the time reading up on the teachings of Karl Marx). It took President Grover Cleveland the same length of time to announce a conciliatory new public holiday on the first Monday of every September, Labor Day.

RAIL UNIONS

Europe's railroad families regarded May 1 as the traditional as Labour Day and members of the Amalgamated Society of Railroad Servants had special cause to celebrate it in the early 1900s after their victory against the Taff Valley Railroad. The Taff Valley ran from Merthyr to Cardiff in Wales. In 1901 the Society of Railroad Servants had come into conflict with the line's owners. A ten-day strike ensued, the workers resorting to greasing rails on the hillside tracks and, as the train wheels began to lose traction, slipping out from the trackside undergrowth and uncoupling the cars. The company took the Society to court and successfully sued it for £32,000, an enormous sum of money at a time. The Society's defeat set a legal precedent that threatened to prevent working people from ever striking again. The judgment persuaded a group of Labour men to stand for Parliament. (Some were supported by railroad workers: in 1899 a Doncaster railroad man, Thomas Steels, had first proposed sponsoring parliamentary members.) The Taff Valley furor helped twenty-nine new Labour men to power, enough to form a Parliamentary Labour Group. They went to work on the Taff Valley judgment and had it overturned.

FOOD SHORTAGES
The young Audrey Hepburn, destined to become a Hollywood film star, was among the children who suffered deprivations during the Hongerwinter.

Union Is Strength:
All Men are Brethren
Nineteenth-century banner of the Amalgamated Society of Railroad Servants

Over the years railroad unions continued to battle against unfair practices. (The unions were also responsible for adhering to some inflexible working conditions that delayed progress and innovation.) In 1944, however, the Dutch railroad workers faced a greater threat than the loss of wages. Forced underground to escape arrest, they sabotaged the railroad network alongside the Dutch Resistance. The Germans responded by bringing in their own rolling stock and stopping food supplies from reaching those in the western Netherlands particularly. Over 20,000 people died of starvation before the Allies could liberate the western Netherlands in May 1945.

1964

Tokaido Railway

Country: Japan

Type: Passenger

Length: 320 miles (515 km)

I n the latter part of the twentieth century photos started to appear of a white, streamlined train passing by snow-capped Mount Fuji. It was Japan's *Shinkansen* and it heralded the most important breakthrough in public transport since the birth of the diesel train.

✦ SOCIAL

✦ COMMERCIAL

✦ POLITICAL

✦ *ENGINEERING*

✦ MILITARY

INNOVATIVE ENGINEERING

Shortly before Tokyo's Olympic Games opened in 1964 a new train glided into Tokyo Station. Sleek, streamlined and the fastest machine on steel wheels, it was nicknamed the Bullet. Its proper name was *Shinkansen*, meaning "new trunk line," and it could carry 6,000 passengers at an average speed of 100 mph (161 kph). Japan had been on its knees when World War II ended. The *Shinkansen* was born out of the nation's phenomenal postwar economic boom.

The world had witnessed Japanese engineering expertise before. In 1905, after the Russo-Japanese war, the 521-mile (838 km) South Manchurian railroad from Port Arthur (Lüshun, close to the seaport of Dalian) on the coast to Changchun, south of Harbin, fell into Japanese hands. Their engineers rapidly repaired the line, sabotaged by the retreating Russians, and added an extra 180 miles (230 km) between Mukden and Antung. Creating a free port at Dalian, they began serving the line with American-built locomotives. They dealt with the narcotics problem (opium was having a deleterious effect on local workers) and encouraged Japanese settlers to move in to work at a new carriage and locomotive factory at Shakako near Dalian.

The Japanese expansion saw the takeover of former Chinese railroads and by 1934 one of the world's first streamlined trains, the *Asia*, was steaming along the 434-mile (698 km) line between Dalian and Changchung (now rebranded as Hsinking)

VISIONARY JAPAN
Launched to coincide with the Olympic Games in Tokyo, the *Shinkansen* revolutionized rail travel. It was so fast it was nicknamed the Bullet.

at up to 87 mph (140 kph). At one point 2,000 workers took just three hours to re-gauge 149 miles (240 km) of the former Chinese Eastern Railroad. This allowed the *Asia* to run all the way from Dalian to Harbin, 548 miles (882 km), in 13.5 hours. It also meant that the intrepid railroad traveler could board a train in Paris and arrive in Dalian eleven days later.

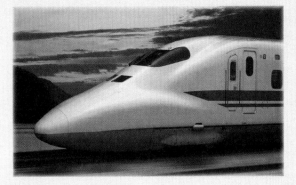

RISING SUN
Japan began work on one of the world's fastest trains just thirteen years after its defeat in World War II.

Japan's dizzy expansion of the South Manchuria Railroads ended with its defeat in World War II. Thirteen years later work started on the *Shinkansen*. The new line was to run through the Tokaido belt, the most densely populated part of the country between Tokyo and Osaka. With three quarters of the country's industry concentrated here, the railroads were struggling to cope with transporting almost a quarter of all Japan's freight and passengers.

The *Shinkansen* was an immediate success, although the train's speed caused some initial problems. Entering a tunnel at speed triggered a sudden change in air pressure, hurting passengers' ears and forcing onboard toilets to disgorge their contents. The difficulty was solved with compressed-air devices that automatically forced the doors hard against the frames as the train entered a tunnel.

Japan was soon extending the lines, in 1975 to Hakata from Tokyo (it involved building what was then the world's second-longest tunnel after the Simplon, 11.6 miles (18.6 km) under the Kanmon Straits). In May 1975 the *Shinkansen* lines topped a million passengers in a single day.

But there were difficulties. The 1973 oil crisis caused severe inflation, competition from trucks and airlines intensified and there was a concerted campaign for the railroad to deal with noise, not so much from passing trains as from regular mainte-nance work on the line. Nevertheless the *Shinkansen* network continued to expand, to break records and, just as the first railroads had done more than 150 years earlier, breathe new life into old communities.

"I see no reason to suppose that these machines will ever force themselves into general use."

Duke of Wellington, 1830

SOUTH MANCHURIAN RAILROAD

♦

In August 1945 Russians invaded South Manchuria and stripped the railroad, taking it away as war booty. The region then became a battleground between the Chinese Nationalists and Mao Tse-Tung's Communist forces before finally falling to the Communists. The South Manchurian Railway's managers, acknowledged experts in railroad engineering, would later help Dalian become the birthplace for China's diesel locomotive manufacturing.

1972

Bay Area Rapid Transit

Country: U.S.A.

Type: Passenger

Length: 71.5 miles (115 km)

+ **SOCIAL**
+ **COMMERCIAL**
+ **POLITICAL**
+ **ENGINEERING**
+ **MILITARY**

San Francisco's Bay Area Rapid Transit (BART) opened almost a quarter of a century after America's powerful automobile lobby contributed to the closure of its predecessor. Many doubted that BART could succeed.

SYMBOL OF SUCCESS

Curious Californians, enjoying the novel New Zealand craze for slow running or jogging, had a new route to explore in the late 1960s—San Francisco's 3.7-mile (6 km) Transbay Tube. In the months before contractors closed it for the installation of its train tracks, the Oakland subway, composed of 57 giant sections that had been floated out into the bay and sunk on the sea floor, was opened briefly to joggers, walkers and cyclists. The tube seemed to them like the first visible symbol of success for the troubled Bay Area Rapid Transit system, BART.

First proposed in the late 1940s in response to the growing problem of "King Car," BART had been struggling against record levels of inflation, the changing demands of the public and painfully escalating

CALIFORNIA DREAM
Many cities have built, or are building, their own rapid transit rail systems. San Francisco chose to do so twice.

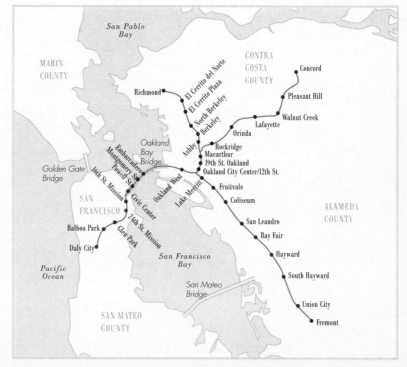

costs. The largest single public works project ever undertaken by local governments in the U.S. was having a troubled ride.

Initially five Californian counties committed to plans for 71.5 miles (115 km) of high-speed train tracks and 33 stations across the Bay Area. Then San Mateo and Marin counties pulled out, leaving the remaining three counties, Alameda, Contra Costa and San Francisco, to manage several courtroom challenges to the scheme. Litigation racked up costs and technical difficulties included securing the right type of rolling stock and overcoming the high water table during construction of a five-story-high station more than 80 feet (24 m) beneath Market Street in San Francisco. Despite all the odds BART's station staff, in their spanking-new blazers, ties and bell-bottomed trouser suits, welcomed the first passengers aboard in September 1972.

MOVING FORWARD

In the latter part of the twentieth century rapid transit or metro systems such as BART were seen as the best way of moving people safely, efficiently and in an environmentally friendly fashion around the world's cities. London's underground railroads had started the trend in the 1860s (see p.112), but the more recent rapid transit systems had evolved to resolve the urban chaos created by the automobile.

TRANSBAY TUBE
Construction began on the 3.6-mile (5.8 km) tunnel under San Francisco Bay in 1965. It was completed four years later.

Since the 1950s cars had given their owners class, style, status and, above all, freedom. It was the freedom to drive the family down to a little place by the sea, to borrow Dad's car and run a few risks on the highway, to hit the shops without having to heave a cart-load of groceries back home on the bus. Car owners included all but the very young, the very old and the very poor and they were free to go where they wanted, when they wanted.

However, as drivers exercised their freedom and more freight was shifted from rail to road, the social costs began to bank up. Avenues of asphalt were log jammed with traffic, palls of toxic smog collected over cities like San Francisco and accident statistics took on alarming proportions. Rail wrecks were terrible things: in 1951 *The Broker*, a Pennsylvanian passenger train, derailed in New Jersey, killing 85 passengers; in September 1958 a New York commuter train crashed through barriers and plunged into the water of Newark Bay; 48 people drowned. Yet on that same day, and for every day of that year, around 100 people died on U.S. roads.

The carnage continued. Half a century later, according to the World Health Organization, around 3,500 people were dying daily on the world's roads. Nations seemed resigned to high levels of highway deaths, and the political will to invest in alternative forms of transport only came about when traffic levels threatened to seize up the cities. Singapore opened its mass transit system in 1987: by 2011 it was moving almost 2.5 million travelers a day between 102 stations. The Shanghai metro in China grew from its opening in 1995 to become the longest network in the world, while in Tokyo, Seoul and Moscow almost 8 billion people a year were transported on the world's three most heavily used systems.

TRAVELING LIGHT
A maglev train emerges from Pudong Airport in China. Maglev is short for magnetically levitated.

IDEAS OF MONORAIL

Although most rapid transit systems used trains, planners continued to explore potential alternatives including high-speed passenger walkways, maglevs (see box) and monorails. Henry Palmer, an English engineer, had proposed a monorail in the 1820s where wagons, suspended from a single overhead rail, were hauled along by horses. It had, as he pointed out, the singular advantage of being "released from the impediments occasioned by snow."

By 1888 Ballybunion in Ireland was running its rural monorail (see p.39) and fifteen years later an Irish inventor, Louis Brennan, patented his own design for a monorail train. When a German, August Scherl, announced plans to demonstrate a monorail at Berlin's Zoological Gardens in 1909, Brennan rushed his machine to Germany for a rival demonstration. And it was in Germany that the monorail proved a long-lasting success. The Wuppertaler Schwe-

SINGLE RAIL
The simple principle of the monorail was demonstrated by its inventor, Henry Palmer. The system was put into practice at Ballybunion in Ireland.

bebahn or floating train opened between Oberbarmen and Vohwinkel in 1901. A century later it was still moving 25 million passengers a year.

New monorails continued to develop through the twentieth century. In the 1950s the futuristic-looking Skyway monorail opened at Fair Park in Dallas, Texas, while at Disneyland in California tourists whizzed around the theme park aboard a special monorail train (Walt Disney was convinced that the future lay in monorail). Visitors to Seattle traveled to the Century 21 Exposition by monorail. In the 1980s Sydney opened a 2.2-mile (3.6 km) monorail through the city.

A century earlier plans had been proposed to run a 33-mile (53 km) high-speed passenger monorail between Liverpool and Manchester and another from London to Brighton, 44 miles (71 km) away. They failed to come to fruition because of opposition from the railroads. Just as the canal owners had fought to stop the railroads, the railroad companies were now anxious to protect their own interests. But in the mid-1900s opposi-

> "If we're going to talk about transport, I would say that the great city is not the one that has highways, but one where a child on a tricycle can go safely everywhere."
>
> *Enrique Peñalosa, former mayor of Bogotá*

RAIL REGENERATION

✦

Britain's first major driverless, rail-based transport system, the Docklands Light Railroad, opened in 1987. The railroad was seen as a key component of the regeneration of East London's old shipping docks and a variety of different transportation systems were considered including buses and a monorail. The planners opted for a light railroad and in just over 20 years this was carrying 70 million passengers a year over a 21-mile (34 km) network that served 40 stations.

tion to all forms of rapid transit systems including monorails came from a new quarter: the automobile lobby. Their Machiavellian maneuvering would be exposed during wrangling over the forerunner of BART, the San Francisco Key System.

KEY SYSTEM

The Key System, so named because its route map resembled a skeleton key, used trains, ferries and streetcars to transport people in the East Bay area, with services from Oakland and elsewhere into San Francisco. It had opened in 1903 with funding from an unlikely source: an American passion for clean sheets. An entrepreneur named Francis Smith, who had made a fortune from borax, the soluble mineral widely used in detergents, founded the Key as a private transportation system.

"Borax" Smith, as he was called, had discovered and mined borax in the Nevada Desert, hauling it by mule train 160 miles (260 km) to the Central Pacific Railroad railhead. By the 1880s he was running a similar operation in Death Valley, California, and building freight railroads to take over from the mules. However, he held on to his trademark product, 20 Mule Team Borax, "used by every good laundress." On their Sundays off these loyal laundresses would take Smith's trolley-bus to the end of the line and Idora Park on the banks of the Temescal Creek. Eventually the trolley park with its giddy figure-eight Sky Railroad fell out of favor and was pulled down in 1929.

By now plans were being made to link San Francisco with Oakland by the Bay Bridge. Designed to carry automobiles on a top deck and the Key's trains on the lower deck, the Bay Bridge opened six months before its famous neighbor, the Golden Gate Bridge, in 1936.

A decade later the Key came under the ownership of National City Lines and the problems began. In 1948 the new owners reluctantly scrapped the familiar old streetcars, replacing them with convoys of buses. It was, they explained, an inevitable consequence of the rising popularity of the automobile. As they presided over the unavoidable "motorization" of the Key they were compelled, with heavy hearts, to raise fares. It took a series of court cases to expose National City Lines as little more than a front for the automobile lobby.

General Motors, Firestone Tire, Standard Oil of California and Phillips Petroleum were named in legal actions and accused of pursuing a national strategy of buying up transit systems elsewhere in order to shut them down. Court cases notwithstanding, the Key closed in 1958, its passenger numbers having fallen by more than a half in just over a decade.

The Bay Area Rapid Transit system managed to succeed where the Key had failed. In 2012, despite occasional grumbles from commuters, BART celebrated forty years of service. Now serving forty-four stations, the Californian rail experiment was judged a success and in 2012, the same year that its weekday ridership topped the 400,000 mark, the air quality in the Bay Area finally fell off the American Lung Association's top 25 list of smog-polluting districts.

OVER THE BAY
Built to carry the Key System trains, automobiles and streetcars, the Oakland Bay Bridge opened in 1936. The streetcars stopped, controversially, in 1948.

TRAVEL FUTURES
Although not as large as the New York Subway, San Francisco's rapid transit system was to become one of the busiest in America.

Talyllyn Railway

Country: Wales

Type: Passenger

Length: 7.5 miles (12 km)

*I*n the late 1900s trains were running out of tracks, falling victim to the rise of the automobile. Efforts to rescue railroads gathered pace after volunteers set one little Welsh train back on the rails.

✦ **SOCIAL**

✦ **COMMERCIAL**

✦ **POLITICAL**

✦ **ENGINEERING**

✦ **MILITARY**

SLATE TRAIN

In 1976, sixteen years after the little train to Mumbles ran off the rails (see p.14), another was making its maiden journey through mid- Wales. It was the Talyllyn train; one of the world's first railroad rescues.

The Talyllyn opened in 1866, a consequence of the American Civil War that interrupted cotton supplies to Manchester's mill owners. A group of mill owners had banded together to raise the capital to invest in an alternative business to cotton cloth: roofing slate.

In the western regions of Europe—Galicia in Spain, Brittany in France, Cornwall, Cumbria, Scotland and North Wales—the local mud-stones had, many millions of years earlier, metamorphosed into great gray seams of slate. The stone was a builder's gift. Tough, waterproof and impervious to frost, it made its mark on vernacular buildings, serving as salt and water troughs, lintels, sills, steps and house walls. It paved floors and provided cheese slabs in the dairy. Around the Talyllyn district it even fenced the fields with fangs of slate wired together to form a livestock-proof wall. Above all, it made an unbeatable roofing material and in the building boom of the Victorian age it was in great demand.

The Bryn Eglwys quarry near Tal-y-Llyn employed over 300 men to sort the empresses, duchesses, countesses and wide ladies (slate sizes were named after female nobility) before they were carted down to the coast at Tywyn. The Talyllyn line was designed to transport slate faster and to carry passengers.

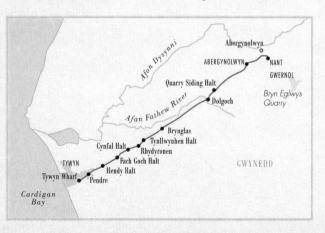

WELSH WONDER
In the 1970s the former mid-Wales slate train became the focus of one of the earliest, volunteer-led heritage railroad rescues.

The passenger plan worried the railroad inspector, Captain Henry Tyler, who considered the clearances between the train and some bridges dangerously tight. The railroad responded by bolting all doors and windows on one side of the train and Captain Tyler was forced, reluctantly, to sanction the line. The Talyllyn swung into action. Sometime in the late 1890s replacement steam locomotives and rolling stock were bought in, but squeezing an income out of Bryn Eglwys remained as hard as the stone itself. Although the owners continued using the same rolling stock until 1951, the quarry and its railroad eventually closed.

MOUNTAIN LEADER
Railroad enthusiasts showed others the way when they successfully saved the Talyllyn Railway from closure.

In the twenty-first century rescued railroads provided plenty of pleasure but rarely made headlines. There were so many: America, in 2012, possessed over 250 lines and rail centers, Britain 150 and Australia and New Zealand another 100 or so. But the press was out in force for the reopening of the first heritage line in 1976, the Talyllyn line from Abergynolwyn to Nant Gwernol. The ceremonial ribbon was snipped by a Welsh broadcaster and journalist, Wynford Vaughan-Thomas, who, declared the real hero of the hour to be a fellow writer and journalist, Tom Rolt.

In the 1950s Tom Rolt, who had written the biographies of many of the railroad greats including Telford, Brunel and the Stephensons, called a meeting in Birmingham to rescue the Welsh railroad. Ten years later, thanks to a timely exercise in bridge building and track laying by the Territorial Army, the Talyllyn Railway was back in business, powered by railroad enthusiasts. It was the beginning of a boom for the world's heritage railroads.

WILBERT AWDRY

✦

Reverend Wilbert Awdry, as the creator of Thomas the Tank Engine, was passionate about the railways. When in 1951 Awdry was sent a newspaper clipping about the rescued Talyllyn Railway he elected to join the volunteers. The author of the Railway Series, Wilbert Awdry liked to weave tales of the Talyllyn into his own stories. After his death in 1997 the study where he had composed the tales was transplanted to the Talyllyn museum along with his model train set of the Ffarquhar Railway, the fictional line that featured in so many of his stories.

"The only way of catching a train I have ever discovered is to miss the train before."

G.K. Chesterton

1981

Paris to Lyon Railway

Country: France

Type: Passenger

Length: 266 miles (425 km)

+ **SOCIAL**
+ **COMMERCIAL**
+ **POLITICAL**
+ **ENGINEERING**
+ **MILITARY**

The Paris to Lyon Railway carried a host of famous figures to the South of France, from Vincent Van Gogh and Paul Gauguin to Ernest Hemingway and F. Scott Fitzgerald. But in the 1980s it was the train, not the passengers, that made history.

APPROACHING RECORD SPEED

When the early movie makers, Auguste and Louis Lumière, showed their film *L'Arrivé d'un train en gare de la Ciotat* (*The Arrival of a Train at La Ciotat Station*) in the 1890s, the audience fled in panic. The brothers had positioned their *cinématographe* camera so close to the tracks it looked as if the locomotive was rushing into the cinema itself.

The story may be apocryphal (although the brothers' later 3D version really did scare audiences). There was no faking it, however, in a film posted on YouTube in 2007 that showed a group of people on board a speed record-breaking train. Three slightly tense men sat or stood, in their clean sweatshirts, in the cab of a French TGV (Train à Grande Vitesse). In the carriage behind, a row of designers and engineers studied their computers. When the digital display hit 356 mph (574 kph) it prompted a muted cheer from the staff.

Both films were a testimony to the genius of Auguste and Louis, serious Lyonnais men, born and bred in France's second metropolis, a city founded on the entrepreneurial skills of silk weavers and now famous for its early cinema. In the 1890s the brothers departed by train from Lyon Station to demonstrate their cinématographe to audiences in Paris, London, New York and

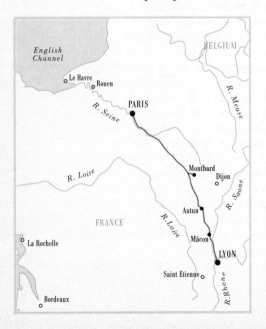

FRENCH INNOVATION
The Train à Grande Vitesse or TGV lived up to its name when it set a world speed record in 2007.

Montreal. The train journey to Paris was long and tedious, although it was an improvement on the 25-hour journey times of the 1880s.

Even in the 1960s the dogleg, 320-mile (512 km) line occupied well over four hours of passengers' time unless the traveler managed to catch the electric-powered *Mistral* which made the trip in just under four hours. (In 1967 a *Mistral* broke the 124 mph [200 kph] threshold.) After the arrival of the *Shinkansen*, France announced plans for its own high-speed train, promising to design, build and run a people's train. "*Le progress ne vaut que s'il est partagé par tous*" ("Progress means nothing unless it is shared by all"), as one national railroad slogan put it.

The express to beat all other expresses, a *grande vitesse* of a train, was to run on the Lumière brothers' old route between Paris and Lyon. The track would combine new high-speed rail and existing city track to keep costs down, and around a million people a year were expected to use the line. (The passenger forecast proved an underestimate.) The construction costs, however, were high and the government stepped in to fund the development of prototypes *Patrick* and *Sophie* and their gas-turbine drives.

> "Bang! We have let another Station off, and fly away regardless. Everything is flying."
>
> *Charles Dickens on a journey to Paris,* Household Words, *1851.*

Then, in 1973, the West was confronted with a Middle Eastern problem. A dispute between the oil-producing countries led to an oil embargo. Reserves ran low and the British government panicked its drivers with gasoline coupons. Motorists were quick to forget the oil shock. Motorways continued to be built along with suburban hypermarkets and housing developments dependent upon automobile ownership. Manufacturers, meanwhile, went on selling cars on the basis of how fast they could accelerate to 60 mph (96 kph) rather than on how slowly they depleted finite oil supplies. The TGV planners, however, took a long, cool look into the oil-based future and found it wanting. They switched from their gas turbines to trains that could be powered by electricity from France's nuclear power plants.

WORLD'S FASTEST TRAIN ARRIVES

In 1981 a trial TGV reached a record 236 mph (380 kph). Later that year, as *Patrick* and *Sophie* were scrapped, the new TGV made its maiden run from Paris to Lyon at a modest 168 mph (270 kph). The travel time had been almost halved. The world's fastest train had arrived.

Railroad men had raced each other for 170 years. In 1829 the directors of the Liverpool and Manchester Railway had arranged a locomotive race at Rainhill outside Liverpool to help them decide whether steam locomotives were up to the job. (They had been considering using fixed steam engines to haul the trains.) *Cycloped*, *Novelty*, *Perseverance*, *Sans Pareil* and Stephenson's *Rocket* met to do battle, *Novelty* clocking an impressive 28 mph (45 kph). Only *Rocket*, hauling 13 tons at a top speed of 30 mph (48 kph), survived the course.

Steam locomotives were battling it out again in the 1880s, competing for the lucrative London to Portsmouth and London to Scotland markets. In the south the railroad companies hired workers to protect their trains from sabotage. It did not prevent one railroad company from stealing a rival's locomotive and driving it away. The battle for the London to Scotland route left passengers red-faced on the platforms as the

ETTORE BUGATTI
A petrol-driven train, the Royale, designed by the racing-car maker Bugatti, sped from Paris to Lyon between the wars, but the TGV (right) would break all previous records.

railroad companies ignored the timetables and raced to reach Kinnaber, south of Aberdeen. Here the signalmen, reputed to be bribable, were often asked to judge the winner. A decade later there were similar scenes in southern England as rival companies vied with one another to provide the fastest train services between London, Paris and Brussels.

For the flamboyant American cowboy Walter Scott it was more a matter of setting a record than beating another train. In 1905 he persuaded the Los Angeles office of the Atchison, Topeka and Santa Fe Railroad with $5,500 in cash to run him over to Dearborn Station in Chicago. It was 2,267 miles (3,627 km) away. It took nineteen crews and locomotives, including nine Atlantics, four Prairies and three Pacifics to cover the distance in a record 44 hours and 54 minutes, and it established the Santa Fe as the high-speed winner on the Midwest to California railroad.

While the Germans and Italians set records of their own in the 1930s, the world's largest steam locomotives, the American Big Boys, designed to haul freight fast, were managing 80 mph (129 kph). The world record for the fastest steam locomotive, however, was left to a proud Englishman, Nigel Gresley, and his *Mallard* in 1938 (see box).

World War II temporarily halted rail racing and left the railroad networks less concerned with world records than staying on track. France itself abandoned around 12,500 miles (20,000 km) of railroad line while Britain's railroads were painfully pruned back after the Beeching affair (see box on p.143).

Even after electrification and the introduction of cleaner diesel locomotives, the railroads were seen as old-fashioned, inconvenient and expensive. As road death tolls crept ever higher, any wreck on the railroads made momentous headlines.

Then the TGV arrived. The French experiment would shortly be followed by other high-speed railroad networks, but for the moment it represented a bright step into the future.

FAST STEAM
✦

In 1938 the streamlined *Mallard* swept down South Bank on England's East-Coast Line to set a new steam-engine speed record. It just topped a record set two years earlier by a Deutsche Reichsbahn steam locomotive that had touched 125 mph (200.4 kph). *Mallard* was a credit to Nigel Gresley, the English public school boy who loved locomotives and became one of the foremost steam locomotive designers of the interwar years. His locomotive, however, was no match for German's *Schienenzeppelin*, a propeller-powered, BMW-engined machine that had touched 143 mph (230 kph) back in 1931.

Channel Tunnel Rail Link

Country: Great Britain

Type: Passenger, Freight

Length: 67 miles (108 km)

+ **SOCIAL**
+ **COMMERCIAL**
+ **POLITICAL**
+ **ENGINEERING**
+ **MILITARY**

A century late in arriving, the Chunnel represented one of the world's longest railroad delays. Once in operation, however, it opened up the opportunity for a new era in high-speed rail travel.

INDEPENDENT OF THE SEA

Two hundred years after the first passenger train chugged along the Welsh coast, a cloud of travelers emerged from a streamlined train parked in the Victorian splendor of St. Pancras Station, London. They were guinea-pig passengers, testing a new, fast train to Europe, the High Speed 1. The operator, Eurostar, promised that it was going to radically change rail travel.

The gothic confection of St. Pancras Station was created in the 1870s to present an elegant face to the London streets. Some rather more mercantile functions lurked behind the grand façade. The station was the receptacle for all East Midland trains including the ever-frequent Burton-on-Trent beer trains: the bricklayers who built St. Pancras even measured out the freight hall in beer by the barrel.

The beer barrels were tucked out of sight when, in 1873, Queen Victoria arrived to open the station hotel, the Midland Grand. A century or so later her great-great-granddaughter, Elizabeth II, arrived at a renovated St. Pancras (like New York's Grand Central, St. Pancras had narrowly dodged the demolition ball) for the inaugural run of a fast train to Brussels. Her High Speed 1 sped through the Kent countryside on its 1-hour, 51-minute journey, dipping beneath La Manche (as the French call the English Channel) at "*Le Chunnel.*"

Linking England and France and opened in 1994 after the U.K.'s Prime minister Margaret Thatcher and France's president François Mitterrand finally reached an accord, the tunnel was a long

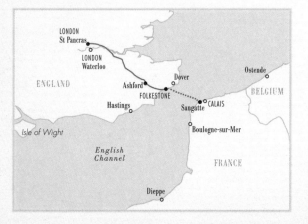

LE CHUNNEL
Alexandre Lavalley in France and Edward Watkins in England began tunneling in 1881. The present tunnel was not completed until 1994.

time coming. "Dr. J.M.A. Lacomme, of Paris, proposes to use a submarine carriage for crossing the Channel," ran one ill-fated prediction in 1875, while *Cassell's Family Magazine* announced the same year: "At last we are going to be independent of the sea, and get to the Continent by land." The magazine explained: "On completion of the tunnel, whenever that may be, a double line of rails will be laid down in it." The Tunnel was to be shelved once again.

The Tunnel was still under discussion when Germany's Deutsche Bundesbahn initiated its ICE trains in 1985. ICE stood for InterCity Express, and while one ICE train broke a world speed record (253 mph / 406.9 kph) in 1988, its primary aim was to establish an efficient system of high-speed trains in Germany and surrounding countries including Switzerland, Belgium, the Netherlands, Denmark and, with the TGV (see p.212), France. Unlike the TGV and *Shinkansen*, ICE was to be integrated into the existing railroad network. It was, argued "the Man in Seat 61," "the most comfortable, civilised and impressive high speed train in Europe." The author was former railroad man Mark Smith, whose website aimed to offer travelers "a more rewarding, low stress alternative to flying" and reduce their contribution to global warming. Seat 61? It was, he claimed, the best seat on the High Speed 1.

> **"A tunnel under the Channel has long been spoken of, and . . . shortly it will, so it is said, be an accomplished fact."**
>
> Cassell's Family Magazine, *1875*

Further Reading

Ackroyd, Peter, *London Under*, Chatto & Windus, London, 2011

Allen, Geoffrey F., *Railways Past, Present and Future*, Orbis, London, 1982

Barnett, Ruth, *Person of No Nationality*, David Paul, London, 2010

Brown, David J., *Bridges: Three Thousand Years of Defying Nature*, Mitchell Beazley, London, 2005

Burton, Anthony, *The Orient Express; The History of the Orient Express from 1883 to 1950*, David & Charles, Newton Abbott, 2001

Chant, Christopher, *The World's Greatest Railways*, Hermes House, London, 2011

Dorsey, Edward, *English and American Railroads Compared*, John Wiley, New York, 1887

Faith, Nicholas, *Locomotion: The Railway Revolution*, BCA, London, 1993

Garratt, Colin, *The World Encyclopaedia of Locomotives*, Lorenz, London, 1997

Garratt, Colin, *The History of Trains*, Hamlyn, London, 1998

Hollingsworth, Brian, and Cook, Arthur, *The Great Book of Trains*, Salamander, London, 1987

Kerr, Ian J., *Engines of Change: The Railroads that made India*, Praeger, Westport CT, 2007

Latrobe, John H. B., *The Baltimore and Ohio Railroad: Personal Recollections (1868)*, reprinted in Hart, Albert B. (ed.), *American History Told by Contemporaries*, vol. 3, 1927

Loxton, Howard, *Railways*, Hamlyn, London, 1972

Lyman, Ian P., *Railway Clocks*, Mayfield, Ashbourne, 2004

Metcalfe, Charles, "The British Sphere of Influence in South Africa," *Fortnightly Review Magazine*, March 1889

Mierzejewski, Alfred C., *Hitler's trains: The German National Railway and the Third Reich*, Tempus, Stroud, 2005

Nock, O. S., *Railways of Australia*, A. C. Black, London, 1971

Parissien, Steven, *Station to Station*, Phaidon, London, 1997

Pick, Alison, *Far To Go*, House of Anansi, Toronto, 2010

Riley, C. J., *The Encyclopaedia of Trains and Locomotives*, Metro, New York, 1995

Ross, David, *British Steam Railways*, Paragon, Bath, 2002

Ruskin, John, "Imperial Duty, 1870," *Public lectures on Art*, 1894

Smiles, Samuel, *The Life of Thomas Telford*, Civil Engineer, 1867

Smiles, Samuel, *The Life of George Stephenson and his son Robert Stephenson*, Harper and Brothers, New York, 1868

Sahni, J. N., *Indian Railways 1853—1952*, Ministry of Railways, Government of India, New Delhi, 1953

Theroux, Paul, *The Old Patagonian Express*, Penguin Classics, London, 2008

Tolstoy, Leo, *Anna Karenina*, Penguin Classics, London, 2003

Trollope, Anthony, *The Prime Minister*, Chapman and Hall, London, 1876

Whitehouse, Patrick B., *Classic Steam*, Bison, London, 1980

Wolmar, Christian, *Fire & Steam*, Atlantic Books, London, 2007

Wolmar, Christian, *Blood, Iron & Gold*, Atlantic, London, 2009

WEBSITES:

America's First Steam Locomotive
www.eyewitnesstohistory.com/tomthumb.htm

Australian Railway History
www.arhsnsw.com.au

Australian transport history
www.environment.gov.au/heritage

Best Friend of Charleston Railway Museum
www.bestfriendofcharleston.org

Cape to Cairo Railway
www.tothevictoriafalls.com

Cité du Train—European Railway Museum
www.citedutrain.com

Darlington Railway Preservation Society
www.drps.org.uk

Grand Central Terminal
www.grandcentralterminal.com

Great Western Railway
www.didcotrailwaycentre.org.uk

Imperial War Museum, U.K.
www.iwm.org.uk

London Underground at London
Transport Museum
www.ltmuseum.co.uk

Music and Railways
www.philpacey.pwp.blueyonder.co.uk

National Railroad Museum, U.S.A.
www.nationalrrmuseum.org

National Railway Museum, U.K.
www.nrm.org.uk

Otis Elevating Railway
www.catskillarchive.com/ otis

Richard Trevithick
www.trevithick-society.org.uk

Samuel Smiles' Lives of George Stephenson
and Thomas Telford
www.gutenberg.org

San Francisco Bay Area Rapid Transit
www.bart.gov

Swansea and Mumbles Railway
*www.welshwales.co.uk/mumbles_railway_
swansea.htm*

Talyllyn Railway Preservation Society
www.talyllyn.co.uk

The Man in Seat Sixty-One
www.seat61.com

U.S. Railway and Locomotive
Historical Society
www.rlhs.org

Volk's Electric Railway
www.volkselectricrailway.co.uk

ACKNOWLEDGMENTS:

Staff at the National Railway Museum, York, the British Library and the Imperial War Museum (IWM Sound Archive, Caroline Rennles, 566/7 reels), Tristan Petts for assistance on China's railroads, Ruth Barnett for permission to quote from *Persons of No Nationality* (David Paul, London, 2010), former evacuees Pamela Double and Mavis Owen (www.herefordshirelore.org.uk), Louise Chapman, and Chelsey Fox of Fox & Howard.

Index

A

Ackroyd-Stuart, Herbert 184
Afghan Express 175
Allen, Horatio 35
Allied Supply Lines, WWI
    168–73
American Civil War 96–7
Ames, Oakes 59
Arnold, Dr. Thomas 51
art 77–8, 81
Aspdin, Joseph 62
Aspinwall, William 92, 93
Auden, W.H. 110–11
Auschwitz Spur 194–5
Awdry, Wilbert 211

B

Baader, Joseph von 43
Baden Powell, Robert 98–9
Baltimore and Ohio Railroad
    28–31, 146
Bay Area Rapid Transit (BART)
    204–9
Beach, Alfred 114
Beaumont, Huntingdon 9
Beck, Harry 115
Beira Line 152
Berkeley, James 85–6, 87, 88
Berlin to Hamburg Railroad
    182–5
Betts, Edward 95, 99
Biada, Miquel 54, 55
Bienvenüe, Fulgence 115
Birkinshaw, John 20
Blackett, Christopher 12
Blake, William 41
Boer Wars 98–9
Booth, Henry 23, 24
Bouch, Thomas 181
Boulton, Matthew 8, 10

Brade, W.C. 41
Bradfield, John 179
Bradshaw, George 79
Bragge, William 83
Branson, Richard 163
Brassey, Thomas 46, 65, 95
Brennan, Louis 207
bridges 176–81
Brief Encounter 159
Brogden, James 91
Brown, George 29–30
Brown, Samuel 178
Brunel, Isambard Kingdom
    60–5, 179, 180
Brussels to Mechelen
    Railroad 40–1
Buhlan, Billy 193
Burma to Siam Railway
    89, 196–7

C

Callum, D.C. 97
Canadian Pacific Railway 128–35
Canteloube, Marie-Joseph 191
Cape to Cairo Railway 148–53
Carrier, Nathaniel 79
Cartier-Bresson, Henri 81
Catch-Me-Who-Can 12
Catherwood, Frederick 82
Central Pacific Railroad 118–25
Chadwick, Edwin 73, 75, 113
Channel Tunnel Rail Link 216–17
Chicago–St. Louis Railroad 100–5
child refugees, WWII 186–9
Chinese labor 92, 124, 131
clocks 160
Coleman, Vince 170
Collas, Bernard 137
Colman, Jeremiah 140
Cook, John 67–8
Cook, Thomas 66–8, 71
Cooper, Peter 28–9
Cooper, Theodore 180–1
Crimean War 94–5

Crocker, Charles 124
Cugnot, Nicolas-Joseph 8
Cuneo, Terence 79

D

Dalhousie, Lord 84–5
Darby, Abraham 10, 18
Dargan, William 36–7
Darrell, Nicholas W. 35
Daumier, Honoré: *The Third
    Class Carriage* 78
Davenport, Thomas 144
Davidson, Robert 144
Davis, William A. 108
De Mille, Cecil B. 80
Debs, Gene 200, 201
Decauville, Paul 169–70
Degnon, John 35
Denis, Paul Camille 43–4
Deutsche Reichsbahn
    194–5
Dickens, Charles
    51, 70, 76, 160, 213
diesel 157, 182–5
Diesel, Dr. Rudolf 184–5
Doyle, Arthur Conan 76, 99
Dublin and Kingstown
    Railroad 36–9
Durant, Thomas 119, 120

E

Eads, James 178–9
Eastern Counties Railroad 59
Ellis, Vivian: *Coronation Scott*
    192
Emett, Rowland 79
Engerth, Wilhelm von 90
Evans, Oliver 32–3, 135

F

Fabergé, Peter 165
Fell, John Barraclough 91
Ferrocarril de Camagüey a
    Nuevitas 54–5

films 80–1, 212–13
Finney, James 177
Fleming, Sandford 130–1, 132
Fliegender Hamburger 184, 185
Flying Dutchman 63
Flying Scotsman 163
food and drink trade 138–43
Ford, John 80–1
Fougasse (C. K. Bird) 79
Franco-Prussian War 98
Freeman, Ralph 179
Frith, William: *The Railway Station* 78

G

Galvani 144–5
Gast, John: *Manifest Destiny* 123
Georgetown and Plaisance Railroad 82–3
Gerstner, Franz Anton von 52–3
Ghega, Carl von 90
Girouard, Edouard 152
Gladstone, William 63, 69, 114
Gooch, Daniel 64–5
Gordon, General Charles 152
Gordon, Mack 193
Göring, Hermann 44, 187
Grand Central Terminal, New York 158–63
Grand Crimean Central Railroad 94–9
Grand Junction Railway 48–51
Grand Trunk Railroad 127, 133–5, 180–1
Great Indian Peninsula Railroad 84–9
Great Western Railway 6, 60–5, 110, 160
Grenfell, Mary 16
Gresley, Nigel 215
Guimard, Hector 116
Gully, James 70

H

Hackworth, Timothy 13
Hamer, Bent 81
Hanford, Peter 190
Hannibal to St. Joseph Railroad 106–11, 178
Hardy, Thomas 158–9
Hassall, John 80
Haupt, Herman 97
Hawkshaw, John 45
Hays, Charles Melville 134
Head, Francis 160
Hedley, William 13
Helleu, Paul 162
Herzl, Theodore 137
high-speed rail 137, 154–5, 202–3, 212–15, 217
Highland Railway 138–43
Hill, James J. 130
Himmler, Heinrich 194, 195
Homfray, Samuel 11
Honegger, Arthur 191
Hopkins, Mark 124
Hudson, George 56–9
Hughes, Colonel George 93
Hughes, Henry 15, 16
Huntington, Collis 124

I

ICE trains 217
Irish standard gauge 38
Ives, James 79

J

James, William 22, 24, 25, 26
Jerusalem to Jaffa Railroad 136–7
Jervis, John B. 31
Jingzhang Railway 154–7
Jones, Casey 190, 191
Judah, Theodore 124
Jullien, Adolphe 77

K

Kalgoorlie to Port Augusta Railway 174–5
Kandó, Kálmán 146
Karstadt, George 109
Kawalerowicz, Jerzy 81
Keate, John 62–3
Kemble, Fanny 6, 19, 25
Kennedy, John 23–4
Key System, San Francisco 208–9
Kinder, Claude 155–6
Kindertransportees 188–9
Kitchener, Lord Herbert 152, 171

L

Lacomme, Dr. J. M. A. 216
Lafayette 31
Lartigue, Charles 39
Latrobe, Benjamin Henry, II 31
Le Strange, Henry 70
Lean, David 159, 196
Lecount, Peter 50
Leech, John 70
Legrand, Louis 47
Leicester and Loughborough Railway 66–71
Leipzig to Dresden railroad 45
Lenin, Vladimir 164, 165, 167
Leopold I of Belgium 40
Leopold II of Belgium 104
Lesseps, Ferdinand de 93, 137
Lincoln, Abraham 97, 100, 101, 178
Lincoln, Robert Todd 101
literature 76–7, 88
Liverpool and Manchester Railway 22–7, 109, 214

Lloyd George, David 171–2
Locke, Joseph 46, 50,
  74, 179, 180
London to Birmingham
  Railroad 48–51
London to Greenwich
  Railroad 49
Ludendorff, Erich 169, 172
Ludwig I of Bavaria 42–3
Lumière, Auguste and Louis
  212–13
Lusitania 173

M

Macdonald, John A. 59, 129–30,
  131, 133, 135
Mackenzie, William 46, 133
maglevs 206, 207
mail services 27, 106–11
Mallard 215
Mann, Donald 133
Mann, William D'Alton 103–5
Mannl, Walter 195
Matthews, Edward 141
Melnikov, Pavel Petrovich 52, 53
Menzel, Jiří 81
Merthyr Tydfil Railway 8–13
Metcalfe, Charles 150
Metropolitan Railway 112–17
Michaelis, Ruthehen 188–9
milk trains 140–1
Mill, John Stuart 73, 75
Miller, Ezra L. 35
Miller, Glen 193
Moltke, Field Marshall
  Helmuth von 168, 169
Monet, Claude 77–8, 80
Monier, Joseph 181
monorails 39, 207–8
Montefiore, Moses 136
Mouron, Adolphe 79
Murdoch, William 8, 10
music 190–4
Mussolini, Benito 147

N

Nagelmackers, Georges
  103–5
Nash, Paul 79
Navon, Joseph 136–7
Nesbit, Edith 186
Newcomen, Thomas 10
Nicholas I, Tsar 52–3
Nicholas II, Tsar 165
Nishikori, Yoshinari 81
Norris, William 31
Nuremberg and Fűrth
  Railroad 42–5

O

O' Gorman, Mervyn 159
Operation Market Garden
  198–9, 200
Orient Express 105
Osborne, Jeremiah 63

P

Pagano, Giuseppe 147
Paine, Thomas 177
Palmer, Harry 207
Panama Railroad 92–3
Paris to Lyon Railway 212–15
Paris to Le Havre Railway 76–81
Paris to Le Pecq Railway 46–7
Pauling, George 150–3
Pawer, Georg 9
Pearson, Charles 113
Pease, Edward 18–19, 67
Pease, Joseph 18, 21
Pennsylvania Railroads
  174, 192, 199–201
Péreire, Émile 47
Péron, Juan 83
Perronet, Jean-Rodolphe 176
Peto, Samuel 83, 94–5, 99
Pick, Frank 79
Pioneer Zephyr 182–3, 184
Platner, George 43–4
Pony Express 107–8

Port Chalmers Railway
  126–7
Porter, Edwin 80
Prague to Liverpool Street
  Station, London 186–9
Pullman, George 8,
  100–3, 105, 200
Purdon, Wellington 73

R

Raderman, Harry 192
Rainhill Trials 26–7, 35, 214
Ramsey, John 109
Rankine, William 47
Rastrick, John 22
Ray, Man 79
Reich, Steve 193
Rennie, George 26
Rennie, John 26, 179
Rennies, Caroline 172–3
Rhodes, Cecil 148–50,
  151, 152, 153
Robinson, W. Heath 79
Rocket 26, 27, 214
Roebling, John 178
Rogers, Major A.B. 130–1
Roscoe, William 25
Rossini, Gioacchino 191
Rothman, Benny 71
Ruskin, John 71, 148
Russell, William H. 107

S

Sadleir, John 59
St. Leger 68
Sandars, Joseph 23, 24
Scharrer, Johannes 43–4
Scherl, August 207
Schlieffen Plan 169
Schnell, Paul 195
Scott, Walter 215
Semmering Railroad 90–1
Sheffield, Ashton under Lyme and
  Manchester Railroad 72–5

Shields, Francis 38

Shinkansen 202–3

Siemans, Werner von 145, 147

signaling 27

Sinclair, Upton 127

Smiles, Samuel 7, 19, 24, 25,
27, 51, 58, 177

Smith, Donald 130, 132

Smith, Francis 208

Smith, Mark 217

Sommeiller, Germain 91

South Carolina Canal and Rail
Road Company 32–5

South Manchurian Railroad 203

Spence, Elisabeth Isabella
15, 17

Stanford, Leland 119,
120, 124, 125

stations 158–63

steam engines 10

Steels, Thomas 201

Stephen, George 130, 132, 135

Stephens, John Lloyd 82

Stephenson, George 13, 19–20,
25–6, 27, 35, 41, 44, 50, 57

Stephenson, Robert 25, 49, 50,
61, 85, 146, 152, 179–80

Stephenson's Gauge 37–9, 64

Stevens, John 93

Stockton, Richard 28, 29

Stockton and Darlington Railway
18–21, 67, 178

Stokes, William B. 28, 29

Strauss, Johann,
the Younger 191

streamlining 112, 184

strikes 198–201

Strobridge, James 124

Sun Yat-Sen 156, 157

Sutherland, Graham 79

Swansea and Mumbles
Railroad 14–17

Swift, Gustavus Franklin 127

Sydney City Railway 176–81

T

Taff Valley Railroad 201

Talyllyn Railway 210–11

Tayleur, Charles 41

Telford, Thomas 36, 37, 179

TGV 212–14, 215, 217

Thayer, John 134

Thomas, Dylan 14, 17

Thomas, Edward 168, 173

Thomas, Philip E. 29–30

Thomas Viaduct 31

tickets 162

Tokaido Railway 202–3

Tolstoy, Leo: *Anna Karenina*
77

Tom Thumb 28, 29, 35

Tong King-Sing 156

tourism 67–71

Le Train Bleu 105

trams 15, 17

Trans-Siberian Railway
164–7, 174

Tredwell, Solomon and
Alice 86

Trevithick, Francis 13

Trevithick, Richard 8,
10–12, 32, 33

La Trochita 83

Trollope, Anthony 160

Trotsky, Leon 164

truck system 75

Tsarskoye Selo Railway 52–3

Turin, Viktor 111

Turnbull, George 86

Turner, J. M. W.: *Rain Steam
and Speed* 64, 65

Twain, Mark 68, 102–3, 106,
110, 178

Tyler, Captain Henry 211

U

underground railroads 112–17

Union Pacific Railroad
123, 124, 125, 182

V

Valtellina Railroad 144–7

Van Horne, William Cornelius
130, 132, 135

Vanderbilt, Cornelius
161–2

Verne, Jules 88

Victoria, Queen 6, 40,
56, 58, 70, 216

Vignoles, Charles 26, 74

Villa-Lobos, Heitor 191–2

Vogel, Julius 126

Volk, Magnus 145, 147

W

Wagons-Lits 68, 103–5

Walker, James 45

Wallace, James 39

Warren, Harry 193

Waters, Muddy 192–3

Watt, James 8, 10, 48

Watt, James (son) 48

Wellington, Duke of
6, 20, 27, 203

Westinghouse, George 91

Whitney, Asa 121–2

Whyte, Fred 167

Williams, Robert 153

Wilson, James 70

Winton, Nicholas 188, 189

Wood, Ralph 177

Woodhead Tunnel
scandal 72–5

World War I, Allied Supply
Lines 168–73

Y

York and North Midland
Railroad 56–9

Z

Zhan Tianyou 155, 156

Zola, Émile: *La Bête
Humaine* 76–7, 81

IMAGE CREDITS